EXPERIENCING ETHNOMUSICOLOGY

For David

Experiencing Ethnomusicology
Teaching and Learning in European Universities

SIMONE KRÜGER
Liverpool John Moores University, UK

ASHGATE

Published by
Ashgate Publishing Limited
Wey Court East
Union Road
Farnham
Surrey, GU9 7PT
England

Ashgate Publishing Company
Suite 420
101 Cherry Street
Burlington
VT 05401-4405
USA

www.ashgate.com

British Library Cataloguing in Publication Data
Krüger, Simone.
   Experiencing ethnomusicology: teaching and learning in European universities.
   1. Ethnomusicology – Study and teaching (Higher) – Europe.
   I. Title
   780.8'9'0711'4–dc22

Library of Congress Cataloging-in-Publication Data
Krüger, Simone.
   Experiencing ethnomusicology: teaching and learning in European universities / Simone Krüger.
      p. cm.
   Includes bibliographical references and index.
   ISBN 978-0-7546-6778-0 (hardcover: alk. paper) 1. Ethnomusicology. 2. Ethnomusicology – Study and teaching – Europe. I. Title.
   ML3798.K78 2009
   780.89–dc22

2009016838

ISBN   9780754667780 (hbk)

Mixed Sources
Product group from well-managed forests and other controlled sources
www.fsc.org Cert no. SA-COC-1565
© 1996 Forest Stewardship Council
FSC

Printed and bound in Great Britain by
MPG Books Group, UK

Contents

List of Figures and Music Examples

Figures

Music Examples

Acknowledgements

The book provides a rich account of what university students experience when they listen to, watch, learn to perform and transcribe music, research and write about a music culture and make ethnographic films. The book thus depended on a considerable number of students from different universities who have participated in my research, and to whom I am greatly indebted.[1] From the University of Sheffield, I am grateful to Graeme, Jessica, Angela, Oli, Sarah, Melinda, Chris, Rachel, Celia and Stephan, as well as Carla, Lindsay and Richard. I express my sincere thanks to Carolan, Matt, Barbara, Laura and Alison from the University of Wales, Bangor. Here, I am also grateful to Samantha, Kevin, Delyth, Jennifer, Barbara, Leeroy, Laura, Charlotte, Hannah, Ruth, Victoria and Tim with whom I worked in 2005/2006 in my role as lecturer in ethnomusicology. From Goldsmiths College London, I am specifically indebted to Argibel and Fiorella, as well as Amaryllis, Stella, Tinoosh, Sheng Shi, James, Natalie, Val, Tom and Patrick. I am very thankful to Emily (SOAS) as well as Terrie, Sally and Gordon (QUB). I express sincere thanks to Emily and Alex (University of Durham) and Jo and Sophie (University of York). I am also grateful to Leah-Beth and Jennifer (University of Newcastle) as well as Debby, and a range of my own students at the universities of Liverpool, Manchester and LJMU, including Craig, Jonathan, Liz and Thomas. I am grateful to all German students whom I met at the University of Köln and the Hochschule für Musik und Theater Rostock, including Jana and Constanze, as well as Florian and Martin (Hochschule für Musik und Theater Hannover). I am also very grateful to Jess, Holly and Emma (University of Manchester), Jane, Joseph, Rachel and Miku (Royal Holloway, University of London), as well as Gabby and Luke (City University London).

The book also illustrates what is important to ethnomusicologists and music scholars in their roles as primary transmitters of ethnomusicological knowledge. I am very grateful to all ethnomusicologists, music ethnologists and tutors who have generously supported this project by giving their time and allowing me to reproduce their voices in my book. I express my sincere thanks to Jonathan P. J. Stock, Stephanie E. Pitts and Andrew Killick (University of Sheffield). To Jonathan, in particular, I am grateful for modelling the ethnomusicological ways in which I learnt to read, think and write, and to Stephanie E. Pitts for reminding me not to lose the 'other' perspective. I also wish to thank my examiners Vic Gammon and Jane Davidson who provided invaluable feedback and encouragement for

---

[1] Note that students have been acknowledged by their real names. In the book, however, I have used pseudonym names so as to protect students' identity, except in instances when I received explicit permission from students to use their real names.

this book publication. I am greatly indebted to John Baily (Goldsmiths College London) for his enduring and generous support. I also express my sincere thanks to Caroline Bithell (University of Wales, Bangor; now University of Manchester) for her continued help with research for the book. I am also very grateful to Hae-kyung Um (Queen's University of Belfast; now University of Liverpool) and Neil Sorrell (University of York) for generously giving their time and sharing their opinions. I am very grateful to Britta Sweers (now Universität Bern, Switzerland), Hartmut Möller and Wolfgang Schmiedt (Hochschule für Musik und Theater Rostock). I also wish to thank David Hughes and Richard Widdess (SOAS) for sharing their perceptions. I am grateful to Laudan Nooshin (City University London) and Henry Stobart (Royal Holloway, University of London) for their support during the latter stages of research for the book. I am also very thankful to Reem Kelani, Inok Paek, Kay Milton, Seikou Susso, Koong Paphutsorn Wongratanapitak and Chou Chiener for their help.

This project has been generously supported by Rüdiger Schumacher (Universität zu Köln). With sadness I learnt that Rüdiger Schumacher passed away in December 2007, and I am greatly indebted to the family of Rüdiger Schumacher for giving me their support in allowing his voice to be heard in the book. Many thanks, therefore, to Jutta and Julia Schumacher.

This book has taken six years in the making, which began with research for my PhD and continued right up to the present day. It has depended on the help of many people, and I would be unable to name them all. At Ashgate, I would like to thank Heidi Bishop (*née* May) and Lianne Sherlock for their excellent support and guidance in bringing the book to completion. I am grateful to the anonymous referees whose comments and suggestions have made a significant impact on the book. I am very grateful to the AHRC, the University of Sheffield and Liverpool John Moores University who have provided financial support towards some aspects of research for this book. I have greatly enjoyed researching and writing the book. It has been a life-changing experience. To my parents, Bodo and Sabine Krüger, I am greatly indebted for their lasting love and care. My dearest gratitude is dedicated to David, whose support, understanding, enthusiasm and humour have made this book possible. You are the inspiration for my continued journey.

Prologue

This book studies the transmission of ethnomusicology. It explores the ways in which students experience and make sense of their musical and extra-musical encounters. The book is based on the idea that studying musical transmission can generate an understanding of the ways in which people make music useful and meaningful in their lives. It acknowledges that musical transmission is a reflector and generator of social and cultural meaning. A musical tradition is its transmission. This has long been recognised by ethnomusicologists who often study the transmission processes of particular musical traditions, while drawing conclusions that link aspects of the means and dynamics of musical transmission to people's shared patterns of musical concepts, beliefs, behaviours, institutions and technologies (excellent studies into the transmission of selected non-Western musics include Berliner, 1978; Blacking, 1973; Chernoff, 1979; Neuman, 1980; Rice, 1994; Stock, 2002a). Such studies seek to understand musical transmission in the context of human life and discard the idea that a musical tradition is transmitted intact and static from one generation to another. Ethnomusicologists thus often consider other kinds of processes during musical transmission that impact on and shape people's experiences and perceptions.

This is the approach adopted by the book with its specialist focus on the transmission of music at European universities, a topic thus far rarely researched amongst ethnomusicologists. Henry Kingsbury (1988) was one of the first ethnomusicologists to study the transmission of Western art music in an American conservatory, an emphasis followed later by Bruno Nettl (1995) with an ethnomusicological analysis of Western art music culture in an American school of music. Meanwhile, Stephen Cottrell (2004) applied ethnomusicological thinking to professional, classically trained musicians in London. The book complements such discourse on institutionalised musical transmission, yet focuses on the transmission of ethnomusicology in Europe seen from a perspective of cross-institutional and cross-cultural comparison. The book's major concern is ethnomusicology's role in Western higher education, a setting that is increasingly important but far less richly researched than primary, secondary or pre-school education. Specific emphasis is placed on university students during their encounters with ethnomusicology and music cultures from around the world. How do students make these musics meaningful and useful in their academic and personal lives? How does the transmission of ethnomusicology at universities impact on the way that a local and global sense of music is experienced and imagined by students? What do students learn when ethnomusicology is transmitted in the university classroom? The book illustrates students' attitudes, perceptions and experiences, and what these experiences mean to them both musically and personally.

The book is also a critique of ethnomusicology by assessing its impact on students' transformations in attitude and perspective, which is a particularly pertinent issue in educational policy in Western society (for discussions on current educational policy in the UK, see Beere *et al.*, 2005; Claxton, 2004; DfES, 2003; McGettrick, 2005; Wagner and Ramsden, 2005). It specifically illustrates the extent of students' active constructing and reconstructing of essentialist concepts of the world's (music) cultures and enables ethnomusicologists and music educators to see their own values and practices reflected. The book also proposes the first conceptual model for the transmission of ethnomusicology and world musics. Attempts to identify and establish an educational framework in this area exist (see Boyce-Tillman, 1996; Campbell, 2004; Skelton, 2004; Wade, 2004), yet none of these models has yet been fully recognised in music pedagogy nor applied widely in higher education, and none of these models or frameworks are as comprehensive as the model presented here. This is a model for ethnomusicology pedagogy that amalgamates current, actual practice as it occurred across universities with critical conceptualisations. Through transmitting a concern with meaning, experience and expression, the model proposed in this book can promote in students a globally, contemporary and democratic sense of all (music) cultures.

Methodological Notes

The research underpinning the book draws on an anthropological model of ethnography. This is both a research method for collecting data on cultural practice and experience and a way of writing that represents people's subjective experience and behaviour. Ethnography with its attendant methodology of participant-observation and informal interviewing is deemed particularly suitable for gaining a fuller understanding of the more complex interactions that occur during musical transmission. It enables us to illustrate the ways that selected participants in the higher education environment construct, operate in, experience and make sense of the transmission of ethnomusicology.

The Research Field

While ethnography about musical transmission is often locally or culturally specific (Stock, 2003c:139), the research conducted for the book involved a far greater and geographically dispersed field, encompassing fourteen UK universities and two German universities. The inclusion of various universities across the UK has been deliberate so as to ensure breadth and contrasting situations for analysis. Cross-institutional comparison with two German universities enabled a further level of contextualisation. The German perspective proved to be particularly useful in discussions on the differing historical and conceptual perspectives and helped to gain a relative view of ethnomusicological transmission at universities in the UK. The choice of universities was strongly determined by logistical considerations and the institutionalised nature of this music culture. Impacting factors included overlapping semester timetables, distance and accessibility, and financial constraints. This resulted in somewhat formal ways of gaining entry by assessing opportunities for research visits via email. While some ethnomusicologists did not reply to initial email enquiries, most ethnomusicologists were generously willing to support the research and invited me to visit their institution. The research underpinning this book was also determined by the urban environment (see also Reyes Schramm, 1979:308), resulting in more formal and frequent, rather than full-time and longitudinal research.[1] This raised concerns about the risk of gaining only a superficial insight into students' experiences and perceptions, and being unable to create a basis of common experience and mutual trust. I therefore tried, whenever possible, to socialise with the research participants outside the formal university environment, and paid heightened attention to every detail and person encountered.

Research Methods

The book has taken six years in the making, which began with research for my PhD and continued until the present. The research was thus conducted in three phases: firstly, I organised a concentrated programme of participant-observations across universities during 2003/2004 for research towards my PhD; secondly, I arranged follow-up observations and interviews, including telephone and internet interviews as well as reflexive analyses of my own teaching practices in 2005/2006 so as to gain further insights into pertinent issues that required more in-depth explorations; thirdly, I arranged an additional programme of research visits and interviews at selected universities in 2008 for the writing of Chapter 12. During the research visits, I was the primary tool for collecting data, as ethnography is a direct result from human and thus social and cultural interaction (LeCompte and Schensul, 1999a). Through direct exposure to the transmission of ethnomusicology, I conducted a programme of participant-observations of classes that included lectures, seminars, tutorials, world music workshops and performance practice. I observed in detail the settings and events, people and materials, and wrote up fieldnotes during each observed class. Instances where I actively participated, such as performance classes, were written up immediately after the event, which necessitated heightened attention to student discourse in order to understand the nature and depth of their subjective musical experiences and the meanings attached to them.

---

[1] Jonathan Stock, during his study on *Huju Traditional Opera in Modern Shanghai*, found it equally impossible to conduct full-time research. The urban space inevitably determined the arranging of meeting times for observations of performances and rehearsals, and the conducting of more formal interviews. Similarly, making use of performance as a tool for research was not practicable in Stock's research into Chinese opera (Stock, 2003b:205–27).

I also often videoed classes, workshops and performance practices, collected photographs and images of musical instruments and ensembles, and assembled a stack of course descriptions, module booklets, websites and other print materials that revealed insights into the ethnomusicology curriculum at universities. This proved particularly useful at a later stage for recalling particular situations or abstracting photographs from digital video recordings. Additional reflections on my own teaching practice as a lecturer in ethnomusicology at universities in Liverpool, Manchester and Bangor as well as Liverpool John Moores University provided further data and a level of personal experience as a primary transmitter of ethnomusicological perspectives and material. I also participated in the ethnomusicological culture in a broader sense by attending national and international conferences of the British Forum for Ethnomusicology (BFE), the Society for Ethnomusicology (SEM) and the International Council for Traditional Music (ICTM) where I encountered an interesting range of reactions: some ethnomusicologists dismissed my research as unnecessary or tangential; some conveyed a sense of unease and concern, and noted that they were usually the ones who observed others; others admitted to being fascinated by the topic and its potential results. (In one instance I was rather humorously described as an 'inspector'.) I also participated in and observed the BFE and SEM email discussions, whereby some contributions have found their way into the book.

The observational part of the data collection was complemented by formal and informal interviews with students and ethnomusicologists. At some universities, I also conducted interviews with non-ethnomusicologists, including a principal, a head of school and a popular music scholar. Interviews were held both individually and in small groups, and followed up with more recent telephone and internet interviews. Depending on the length and frequency of my research visits, interviews with ethnomusicologists were of varying frequencies and lengths, which meant that I had to be cautious in not letting particular voices dominate my analyses. For interviews with students, by contrast, I kept a fairly open mind as to how many students to include, and how often and long to interview them. At universities which were visited for shorter periods, I typically interviewed individual students just once, and only for the duration of one hour, so that I gained less a sense of the personality and characteristics of the students. I therefore relied on drawing comparisons to students' experiences at other universities where interviews could be conducted more frequently and in-depth. These interviews typically focused on students' experiences of any and all facets of activities related to the transmission of ethnomusicological knowledge. Discourse emerged from students' narrative stories and responses, which was often rich in detail and allowed students to define the research agenda. During interviews with ethnomusicologists, by comparison, I found out about scholars' concepts, beliefs and perceptions when transmitting ethnomusicology to students, and how this related to their own understanding of ethnomusicology. Whilst the interviews were broad and flexible to accommodate unforeseen and interesting responses by ethnomusicologists, a broad conceptual framework provided some direction, which included questions such as: What are the distinct characteristics and subject matters of ethnomusicology? How do you instil this into your students? How does your own research impact on what you transmit to students, and why? What, in your opinion, is the general aim of ethnomusicology education?

Writing Ethnography

The book relies less on a review of literature for direction (this merely informed the discussions and helped to find meaning in participants' expressions) and instead applies an inductive, bottom-up approach. The structure of the book emerged 'freely' (that is, without prior determining of headings and subheadings) from grounded data analysis and interpretation.[2] Both analysis and interpretation started immediately and intuitively upon entering the music culture during data collection, and were followed by more formal analytical processes that involved the transcribing, reading and coding of collected text-based data. During the writing process, I constantly re-organised data around emerging themes, followed by abstracting more theoretical conceptualisations that formed the basis of the book's structure. Forefronting certain themes over others involved a systematic process of triangulating between my own experiences, students' and ethnomusicologists' voices and relevant literature. Certain themes, although rich and significant for consideration, have been omitted or only briefly mentioned, as they were deemed tangential to a representation of participants' perspectives. It must be re-emphasised here that the book seeks to portray the views of students and what is important to them, rather than selecting themes on the basis of relevance to certain predetermined research questions. This enabled determining whether a specific situation, event or comment revealed itself to be a 'good' example to be included in the writings, whilst illustrating the experiences and perspectives of students without the focus being hampered by any predetermined hypotheses.

The writing style adopted in the book is typically ethnographic by combining descriptive and theoretical discussions, and taking a critical self-reflexive stance towards my own, personal experiences. Clearly labelling shifts of voice allowed me to present and contrast the views of participants as opposed to my own interpretation and understanding. Making the methodology explicit by describing the ways in which I learnt from participants also helped in conveying a sense of the quality of my interactions with students and ethnomusicologists, whilst explaining terms and terminology whenever necessary. The ethnographic writing

---

[2] I recognise that the idea of a freely emerging structure may be problematic, as the conceptualisations made in this book were surely modelled by my very personal and unique ways of understanding and sense-making. For this reason, the term is used here to describe my conscious efforts to distance myself from any prior determining of headings and subheadings. This is also true for the use of the widely applied tripartite model of listening, performing and constructing, which emerged as a suitable framework only during the course of my analyses.

style is also particularly useful for presenting participants' emic perspectives, which were typically varied and diverse. Their voices thus appear seemingly random throughout the book, particularly in Chapters 1 to 5, which bring together the perceptions and experiences of numerous ethnomusicologists and students under particular themes (e.g. progression, culture, identity, authenticity and democracy) to enhance cross-institutional comparisons.[3] This means that less attention is paid towards introducing the reader to individual participants in these chapters, a strategy that has instead been adopted in the subsequent Chapters 6 to 12. These chapters are less concerned with cross-institutional comparisons under an overarching umbrella theme, but instead allow a fuller picture of individual participants within the context of a specific educational topic (e.g. performance practice, musical transcription, ethnographic research and writing, ethnographic filmmaking) to emerge gradually.

The Ethics of Ethnography

Ethnography typically positions the researcher as social actor within the music culture studied. It is an approach to learning about people's musical and cultural experiences that is investigative, using the researcher as the primary tool for data collection. This in turn has significant ethical implications for the people studied. Yet whilst all research that involves human participants raises ethical concerns, ethnographers must specifically account for the impact of their fieldwork presence on people's rights, interests and experiences. Ethical considerations involved, for example, gaining formal permission to enter the research sites prior to fieldwork and to be of little disturbance to ethnomusicologists' and students' day-to-day routine during research visits at their universities. I also considered how most appropriately to leave each institution at the end of my visits whilst ensuring to maintain relationships with selected participants for follow-up visits, interviews and feedback on written drafts. Interestingly, the formal educational environment that marked the context for the research brought numerous advantages to my presence as a researcher. To ethnomusicologists and students, I often had an understandable role without the need for lengthy explanations as to why I was there and what I was doing. I also shared a similar identity with the research participants both as a postgraduate ethnomusicology student and university lecturer, which helped me quickly to establish mutual trust and friendships. I also considered reciprocity, including verbal and written acknowledgements in the form of cards, emails and acknowledgement, small gifts as well as study support. Stephanie at the University of York, for example, wrote an assignment on the use of *gamelan* in school music education, and I sent her some specialist materials that were unavailable through

---

[3]   Note that translations of participants' commentary from German into English are edited so as to convey their meanings accurately to the English readership. Meanwhile, comments by native English speakers are kept in their original.

libraries. Meanwhile, students are completely veiled by anonymity by using a pseudonym name, except in cases when I received written permission from them to use their real names in the book publication. I also sought permission for images depicting my research participants, which involved verbal permission at the time of my research, followed up with written permission requests to ethnomusicologists, music scholars and musicians. In instances where I was unable to trace participants, including students and foreign guest tutors, I omitted the images.

It was equally pivotal to ensure participants' rights by informing them about the purpose and aims of my research, and by providing information about the way in which results would be used. For example, all ethnomusicologists, scholars and tutors were involved in reading excerpts of the book, allowing them to see how I represented their voices and perspectives. I also wanted to ensure that all ethnomusicologists, music scholars and tutors were aware about the book publication, given that some of the research was conducted a few years ago in 2003/2004. For moral and ethical reasons, I found it important to assess whether ethnomusicologists and scholars objected to my use of quotes in the book. I received very varied responses, which ranged from instant permission by a range of ethnomusicologists to expressions of interests to view the relevant excerpts prior to publication. The feedback and comments I received were considered carefully in my writings. It is unfortunate to note, however, that in one instance I received outright objection from an ethnomusicologist to reproduce quotations from interviews as well as references to his/her university. Given the sensitive nature of my topic, I always considered questions of ethics and morale so as not to harm any participant, be it personally, professionally, emotionally, or otherwise. Yet this was one unfortunate instance where I was unable to maintain a trusting relationship with the ethnomusicologist, even though I always aimed at taking stock of how I was perceived by my research participants. At one institution, for instance, I discontinued research altogether as the scholar clearly felt uncomfortable with my researcher presence.

With such moral and ethical issues in mind, I aimed at representing the experiences of my research participants fully, honestly and realistically without altering the findings to suit a particular agenda. My ethnographic encounters were guided by honesty, integrity and openness, considerations that arose specifically from my work with 'real' people. This also involved questions of ownership, exploitation and representation, and the etiquette of reciprocity. The ethics of my ethnography was generally guided by questions of standpoint and attitude towards the people studied.

Book Structure

The book focuses on the transmission of ethnomusicology in UK and German universities and explores the ways in which students experience and make sense of their musical and extra-musical encounters. It aims to illustrate musical transmission as a reflector of social and cultural meaning, asking questions as to what (musically, personally, culturally) students learn about and through world musics so as better to understand ethnomusicology's impact on students' transformations and changes in attitude and perspective towards self and others. The book also advances discourse on ethnomusicology learning and teaching while proposing a model for ethnomusicology pedagogy that promotes in students a globally, contemporary and democratically informed sense of all musics. The book is divided into four larger parts containing 12 chapters, which are proceeded by an epilogue as follows.

Part I. Disciplining Ethnomusicology

Introducing the contexts and broader organisational structure of higher education is at the heart of Part I, which contains two chapters. Drawing on the voices of ethnomusicologists, the chapters illustrate the ideological and social practices that inform the disciplining of ethnomusicology and its transmission to students at universities. Asking questions such as 'How is the transmission of ethnomusicological knowledge constructed and negotiated by its scholars?', the chapters illuminate the ideologies, intentions and musical imaginations of ethnomusicologists, and introduce the formal structures of ethnomusicology courses at universities so as better to understand the nature of their formal transmissions. Inductive analysis of the contexts and organisational structure of higher education revealed notions of 'progression' both at micro and macro levels of learning. Under this overarching theme, Chapter 1 introduces the frameworks of study in the areas of world musics and ethnomusicology at universities in the UK and Germany, followed by a classification of courses in world musics and ethnomusicology at undergraduate and postgraduate level. The latter involved critical reflections on the suitability of world music survey courses, regional and area studies, themed courses and ethnomusicology courses. The chapter then closes with discussions on the use of textbooks in ethnomusicology.

A second theme concerns ethnomusicology's anthropological orientation and the study of 'music in and as culture', which will be explored in the second chapter. Due contextualisation will be made by illustrating historical perspectives seen from the standpoint of American ethnomusicology as compared to European ethnomusicology. The shift towards an inclusive, eclectic stance in terms of the subject matters for ethnomusicological study is discussed, yet noting that current ethnomusicology pedagogy may acknowledge more strongly the transmission of hybrid musical forms and Western musics. Following this, the ethnomusicological concern with an approach to the study of all musics is introduced, from which a tripartite model to the transmission of ethnomusicology through listening, performing and constructing is derived to provide a framework for the three parts to follow. The chapters in these subsequent parts contrast significantly to Part I, as their focus is on how students make music meaningful and useful in their academic and personal lives, and what and how they learn when ethnomusicology is transmitted in the university classroom.

Part II. Listening to Ethnomusicology

The chapters in the second part of the book will listen to students' voices during their listening to world musics and ethnomusicologists, illustrating their often complex and entwined listening-based experiences within the broader social and cultural contexts in which they are embedded as students try to make sense of particular educational encounters. This includes discussions on students' constructing and articulating of identity in Chapter 3, which examines the relationship between students' experiences of listening to the world's musics and the impact of these experiences on students' sociocultural identities, reflected by students' expressions of musical taste. Notions of taste as a 'natural' concept and as a result of familiarity will be explored, followed by discussions of the correlation between musical preference and social identity. Shaping factors, such as social class/status and age/ life experience will be considered so as to bring a more nuanced understanding to the preferences that students evinced in response to listening experiences. A second theme is concerned with the role played by ideas of authenticity in directing students' listening experiences of the world's musics, which is the focus of Chapter 4. Initial discussions will illuminate how ethnomusicology's concern with older, traditional repertoires shapes the content and ways in which the world's musics are being transmitted, yet arguing that formal musical transmission in Western institutions necessitates some degree of Westernisation. Subsequent discussions will thus show (by providing numerous examples) how students' concept of authenticity is socioculturally constructed through the physical, material, literate and sonic spaces, as well as ethnicity of the ethnomusicologist. The final chapter in this part (Chapter 5) will consider the impact of listening on musical experiencing of moves away from canonising – the institutionalisation of certain music cultures for study over others – and towards expressing a form of global democracy, a belief in equality between all people and their musics. Students' desire of mapping and canonising world musics versus ethnomusicologists' eclectic and inclusive approach (referred to as 'eclecticising') will be discussed first, yet noting that students' eclectic musical experiences may not fully explain their expressing of democratic social and musical concepts. Subsequently, it will be argued that students' democratic desires resulted from ethnomusicology's anthropological emphases (music in and as culture) by presenting a range of relevant examples that assess ethnomusicology's impact on students' awareness, tolerance, understanding and acceptance of the world's different cultures, its peoples and their music.

Part III. Performing Ethnomusicology

Musical performance often occupies a crucial position not only in ethnomusicological scholarship but also in the transmission of ethnomusicological knowledge at universities, yet little has been written about the ways in which students access the musical other through performance. The chapters in this part will address this obvious gap in the literature. Initial discussions will bring forward the various rationales for using performance in ethnomusicological research and learning as voiced by ethnomusicologists themselves. Specific emphasis will then be placed on student experiences to better assess the ways in which performing ethnomusicology at universities led students towards changes of attitude and perspective. The discussions will usefully be located along a continuum that includes students' discovering of (a) world musics' material culture, (b) musical expression and form, and (c) cultural values. Further considered will be students' expressing of emotional responses in the form of enjoyment and anxiety, which, whilst sharing a dichotomous interrelationship with one another, will be illustrated as being socially and culturally constructed. This part of the book will show overall how students' attitudes and perspectives changed along the performance continuum: from *animation* and enjoyment towards deeper insights into music-as-music combined with performance anxiety, finally reaching deeper understandings of music-as-culture.

Chapter 6 will discuss students' deeper engagement (at physical and cognitive level) with the material culture. Simple musical imitations (seeing-hearing-trying of musical instruments) will be illustrated first, showing that students' experiences became more complete and meaningful, and often led towards excitement and further interest in the music culture. Discussions will move on to students' experiences whilst participating in occasional world musics workshops. A differentiation will be made between (a) workshops that imitated the music's material culture in the form of sing-along and play-along participation and (b) workshops that utilised real musical instruments. Overall the use of vignettes and students' voices will convey how such workshops were musically, culturally and personally more meaningful. It will also be concluded that this form of performing ethnomusicology led towards highly enjoyable experiences among many students. The following Chapter 7 will be concerned with students' longer-term ensemble participation and learning to perform a musical instrument, during which they discovered musical expression and form. Specifically, performance transmission in the form of 'learning to perform' as an ethnomusicological research technique will be discussed by illustrating students' experiences in general as well as the experiences of one particular student. It will be shown that whilst students experienced deeper-level understandings of music-as-music, they also expressed considerable performance anxiety. Questions will be raised about the extent of students' appropriation of Western methods into performing ethnomusicology, while arguing that the problematic issue of reinforcing eurocentrism requires further consideration by ethnomusicologists in the transmission of ethnomusicological knowledge to students at universities.

Chapter 8 will build upon and illustrate students' experiencing of emotions, such as enjoyment (Chapter 6) and anxiety (Chapter 7). The view that emotions are sociocultural constructs will be adopted here, while illuminating three pivotal factors: students' perceptions of simplicity versus difficulty in acquiring performance skills; students' unfamiliarity versus familiarity with the musics; and students' experiences of performance as a social versus individual event. A cross-institutional comparison will help here in examining these factors as they impacted on students' emotional experiences. The final chapter in this part of the book (Chapter 9) will discuss the ways in which performance concerned a more socially engaged, experiential ethnomusicology through music. The experiences of two students will be examined during their engagement in performance ethnography. It will be shown how ethnography involved their participation in actual performance as a privileged means of access to embodied knowledge and fellow feeling. Performance ethnography can sensitise the performer-researcher to aspects directly or indirectly related to a creative work and precipitate a sense of the style and aesthetics of a piece of music. It will be illustrated how these students gained insights into music-as-culture in order to understand the values, people and societies hold about and express through their own music. Part III will be closed with discussions on the extent to which performing ethnomusicology led students towards changes of attitude and perceptive.

Part IV. Constructing Ethnomusicology

The final part will open the discussions on musical creativity and pre-empt that musical composition in a non-Western style is largely absent in higher education. However, it will be argued here that students may also achieve creativity through musical activities other than musical composition alone, for example creative transcription, ethnographic writing and ethnographic filmmaking. The chapters contained in this part will thus focus on students' experiences during the constructing of a musical transcription, the creative composing of ethnomusicological texts, and ethnomusicological uses of film and video. Chapter 10 will illustrate the ways in which students approached and experienced the composing of musical transcription. The opening discussions will be concerned with ethnomusicologists' perceptions of using musical transcription. Their aspirations of reflecting the emic musical perspective will be emphasised here, and the consequences of this viewpoint on the formal transmission to students at universities. Yet students' actual constructing of a transcription often represented eurocentric (thus etic) perspectives, and this will be shown in the following four sub-sections: returning to familiarity; applying top-down approaches; adapting musical literacy; and utilising tools for constructing a musical transcription. It will generally be argued that ethnomusicologists should also involve students in critical reflection and interrogation so as to develop non-canonic, non-essentialist perspectives towards non-Western musics and their makers.

Students' experiences of constructing ethnographic texts will be at the centre of Chapter 11. The opening discussions will describe ethnography, and the ways in which it is transmitted and utilised in university education. This will be followed by more specific discussions on the experiences of three undergraduate and two postgraduate students engaged in the constructing of ethnography. (Further comparisons and contrasts will be drawn from the experiences of numerous other students throughout this section.) The discussions will then focus on the strategies employed by students to analyse and interpret data and show that whilst many were able to form perspectives about their chosen music culture, only few students reached more thorough, deeper understandings. Subsequent discussions will illustrate four factors impacting on students' composing of ethnography, namely ethnomusicological discourse, ethical considerations, supervisor's feedback and formal examinations. The chapter will close with discussions on the extent to which the ethnographic experience impacted on and transformed students' attitudes and perspectives towards self and others. Meanwhile, Chapter 12 will be concerned with the mediation of fieldwork experience through ethnomusicological uses of film and video in formal ethnomusicology education. It will open with discussions on the use of film and video in the university classroom, including the kinds of film and video utilised in formal classes and the pedagogical strategies employed by ethnomusicologists. A brief section will show how and to what extent film and video has the capacity to mediate fieldwork experiences. The second part will then focus on ethnomusicological filmmaking, opening with discussions on the ways in which ethnomusicological filmmaking is formalised in the ethnomusicology curriculum at one institution. Subsequent discussions will illustrate the experiences of one student in constructing an ethnomusicological film. The chapter will close with an assessment of the value of ethnomusicological uses of film and video for ethnomusicology education. A brief summary on the problems surrounding processes of appropriation and representation of world musics in the constructing of ethnomusicology will bring this part to a close.

Epilogue

The epilogue will open with the argument that musical transmission should develop in students' universalist and democratic attitudes towards all musics and their makers. A model for ethnomusicology pedagogy will be proposed that promotes in students a globally, contemporary and democratic sense of world musics, and is concerned with meaning, experience and expression. The model draws on the discussions presented throughout the book, whilst reflecting two overarching concerns: an emphasis on an approach towards studying and understanding musics, and a focus on effective musical learning. Using the model as a starting point and drawing on current practice in the transmission of ethnomusicology, the epilogue will then propose new directions for ethnomusicology pedagogy, arguing that ethnomusicologists ought to consider certain key issues in their transmission of ethnomusicology so as to promote in students culturally, socially and musically inclusive and eclectic attitudes and perspectives towards self and others.

PART I
Disciplining Ethnomusicology

Disciplining ethnomusicology refers to the ideological and social practices of ethnomusicologists and the ways in which they govern their behaviours and ideologies within the discipline of ethnomusicology (see also Bergeron and Bohlman, 1992; Nettl, 1999). Since the emergence of ethnomusicology, its scholars have represented both a conservative stance towards ethnomusicology's history, concepts and methods, and at the same time more liberal perspectives in opening up the subject matters for study (see also Everist, 1999). During the discipline's development, ethnomusicologists have challenged the very processes of canonising the *what* as the acceptable object for study. They also rejected a eurocentric methodology that focuses on an analysis of musics in other cultures as normative Western texts. Perhaps most importantly, ethnomusicology discarded a system of musical values (Bergeron, 1992). Ethnomusicology is thus disciplined by its ethnographic writings that have resulted from a methodological focus on reflexive participant-observation during fieldwork. Ethnomusicology's canons are the very concepts, methods and values inherent within the discipline.

The particular ways in which ethnomusicology is disciplined by its scholars surely impacts on and reflects the transmission of ethnomusicological knowledge in higher education. This is the main concern of this first part, which aims to illustrate the ideological and social practices that inform the transmission of ethnomusicology to students at universities. The discussions are based on two pivotal themes that emerged during the research, namely notions of progression (Chapter 1) and concepts of culture (Chapter 2). The first idea of progression usefully describes the ways in which ethnomusicologists organise the 'progressive' transmission of ethnomusicology, an idea that also reflects more Western-centric ideas, including the operationalisation of the Western education system. By comparison, the latter concern with culture is deeply anchored within the specific disciplining of ethnomusicology with its focus on the study of music within the context of human life. Keeping in mind the emphasis on ethnomusicology's very essence as an approach to the study of all musics, this part of the book will illuminate the ways in which ethnomusicologists negotiate and renegotiate means of transmitting ethnomusicological knowledge to students in higher education, while placing particular emphasis on the voices of ethnomusicologists to make sense of their concepts, beliefs and ideas.

Chapter 1

Transmitting Ethnomusicology, Expressing Progression

The transmission of ethnomusicology at macro and micro level is often steeped in ideas of progression, so that teaching and learning becomes separatist and specialist. This was frequently reflected in the division between undergraduate and postgraduate studies, which progressed from simple to complex and covered somewhat distinct, specialist subject matters and methods. Progressive learning also exists within the content of individual courses, both at undergraduate and postgraduate levels. Both issues will be discussed in this chapter, followed by ethnomusicologists' use of textbooks, which equally resonated with the concept of progression in the transmission of ethnomusicology. Beforehand, however, I will introduce some of the overarching key characteristics of musical transmission at universities in the UK and Germany, noting the frameworks of study available there in the areas of world musics and ethnomusicology. The subsequent section will categorise, classify and critique world musics and ethnomusicology courses both at undergraduate and postgraduate level, while drawing on relevant ethnomusicological and educational discourses.[1] Throughout the chapter, the voices of ethnomusicologists will be included so as to illuminate their curricular choices.

Ethnomusicology in Higher Education in the UK and Germany

Over the past decade, I noticed a constant growth of study programmes in ethnomusicology and world musics at universities in the UK and Germany. These are most frequently situated within music departments or anthropology departments, whilst self-contained ethnomusicology departments are rare. In the UK, the higher education system differentiates between undergraduate and postgraduate level of study, and accordingly students can select from a range of different courses. At undergraduate level, music students study towards a BA (Bachelor of Arts) or BMus (Bachelor of Music), which exist in numerous permutations. An

---

[1] The terms 'course' and 'module' are used here interchangeably to refer to a 15-week, subject-specific set of classes that form one aspect of students' undergraduate or postgraduate studies. By contrast, the terms 'course of study' and 'study programme' refer to the whole degree programme either at undergraduate and postgraduate level, leading towards the qualification of, for instance, BA, MA or PhD.

undergraduate course of study usually takes three academic years or levels, each of which is generally divided into two semesters with level 1 (year 1) constituting a foundation for subsequent study and levels 2 and 3 requiring higher conceptual and critical thinking in students. Each semester contains certain compulsory courses in addition to optional courses, and the range offered depends on staff specialisms or departmental agendas, which can vary significantly between universities. Upon successful completion of individual modules students gain credits, which vary usually between 15 credits (for 15-week courses) and 30 credits (for courses or projects lasting two semesters, such as dissertations).[2] The modular system also requires students to undertake a significant amount of independent study, which can range from set weekly readings and ongoing portfolio tasks to conducting fieldwork, essay writing and exam preparation. A final-year dissertation of 10,000 words is often an optional course. Upon accumulating 360 credits in total, students qualify for the award of their degree.

At postgraduate level, students typically study towards an MA (Masters of Arts) or MMus (Masters of Music), which also exist in various permutations. An MA in Ethnomusicology often focuses on the transmission of concepts and ideas related to the discipline of ethnomusicology, while the MMus enables students more directly to engage with the world's musics, generally through extended performance, composition or dissertation writing. At SOAS, for example, where I observed and participated in classes and ensembles, and interviewed Richard Widdess and David Hughes, I found that the MA 'tends to be related to a specific geographic area ... or a theoretical issue related to an area' (David Hughes, SOAS, 11 November 2003). These courses of study are typically modular in structure, and require students to accumulate a total of 180 credits during one year (full-time). More advanced students may study towards an MPhil (Masters of Philosophy), which is gained through independent research. The highest qualification is the PhD (Doctor of Philosophy), a qualification gained by undertaking research over three to four years (full-time) and writing a dissertation of around 90,000 words. Many institutions require students to attend formal research training sessions as well as completing the dissertation, and some allow the inclusion of composition or performance in the final assessment. Students undertaking research and preparing a thesis, performance and (more rarely) composition receive supervision from an ethnomusicologist. Postdoctoral pathways are available in form of (competitively funded) national Research Fellowship schemes, yet this depends on the success of research grant applications by individual scholars. Other academic pathways lead via Lectureship and Senior Lectureship towards Readership and Professorship, which can be achieved through internal promotions, or, in the case of vacancies, the university's official job application process.

At universities in Germany where I arranged research visits with Rüdiger Schumacher (University of Köln) and Britta Sweers (Hochschule für Musik

---

[2]   Note that the credit number may differ across universities, and it was not uncommon for courses to have 12 and 24, or 20 and 40 credits.

und Theater Rostock), the discipline is often called *Ethnomusikologie* and *Musikethnologie* (music-ethnology), whereby some programmes are also dedicated to the study of *Vergleichende Musikwissenschaft* (comparative musicology). These programmes of study are typically situated within musicology departments. The German higher education system differs significantly from that of the UK as universities are tightly governed by a *Ministerium* (ministry for education; there is one in each *Bundesland* or state). German higher education is 'a purely governmental matter' (Rüdiger Schumacher, Köln, 22 July 2004) with ministries deciding about the *Studienordnung* (study rules) and determining the ways in which universities implement the curriculum.[3] An undergraduate course of study is called *Magisterstudium* (Masters study) and leads to the so-called *Magisterprüfung* (a final examination in order to gain a Masters degree; at a German university, this is the first degree) and the preparation of a *Magisterarbeit* (Masters thesis). A *Magisterstudium* consists of a *Hauptfach* (a main/primary subject) and a *Nebenfach* (a secondary subject), together with *Zusatzfächer* (additional subjects) and typically lasts nine or more semesters, yet students commonly prolong the total study time beyond this. The course of study is structured into *Grundstudium* (foundation study) during the first two years completed by a *Zwischenprüfung* (intermediate examination) and *Hauptstudium* (main study) during the remaining years completed by the aforementioned *Magisterprüfung*. The *Magisterprüfung* can (if taken in the *Hauptfach*, such as music-ethnology) consist of a final dissertation of sixty pages in length and a four hour examination followed by a 45-minutes oral examination. While courses in the *Grundstudium* are often fixed and the same for all subjects, thus providing a solid foundation in musical studies, courses in the *Hauptstudium* depend on students' choices, whereby they may specialise in different areas, selecting main, secondary and additional subjects as they progress. Contact hours, time for independent study and assessment requirements can differ significantly between courses. Certain compulsory courses qualify students for a *Leistungsnachweis* (evidence of achievement), and involve more commitment to study and formal assessment often in the form of an oral examination of 45 minutes, together with a written report. Students may also study on courses that qualify them for a *Teilnahmeschein* (certificate of attendance), which often include less contact time and no formal assessment.

At higher level, which may be compared to postgraduate studies in the UK, those students who work on the *Magisterarbeit* (Masters thesis) or undertake doctoral research can attend *Kolloquien* (colloquia, best described as seminars), yet there is no explicit requirement for students to attend lectures and classes which instead often focus on undertaking research and writing the thesis. Students' progress of research and writing is supervised individually by the ethnomusicologist. After successful completion of their *Magisterarbeit*, students can similarly

---

[3]   Diese auf privates Engagement basierende Universitätsstruktur, die fehlt uns ja völlig. Das ist ja bei uns eine rein staatliche Angelegenheit (Rüdiger Schumacher, Köln, 22 July 2004).

undertake doctoral research (called *promovieren*), often lasting several years and leading towards the *Promotion* (doctorate; PhD). During the doctoral process, the *Promovanten* (graduates) must write a substantial thesis and pass a formal *Examen* (examination), after which they may embark on a position as academic assistant (*Assistentenstelle*) for six years during which it is usual to write a larger habilitation treatise (*Habilitationsschrift*) that is defended in front of faculty members. This postdoctoral *Habilitationssystem* (habilitation system) determines whether an assistant can gain the status of professor, yet will, according to Rüdiger Schumacher, gradually disappear in many *Bundesländer* during forthcoming years. The changes are currently already evident at some universities in the introduction of the *Juniorprofessur* (junior professorship) that enables young academics with an excellent *Promotion* (PhD) to become *independent* researchers and lecturers (usually for the duration of up to six years), which in turn qualifies them for a *Lebenszeitprofessur* (professorship for life).

Comparing the higher education systems in the UK and Germany to one another, it appears that the (modular) system in the UK seems to be less rigorous than the (traditional, non-modular) German system. Yet at the same time, universities in the UK seem more self-regulated, while the German system is *Bundesland*-specific ministry-regulated, which means that structures across and within German universities are less standardised. Postgraduate students in Germany appear less supported as compared to universities in the UK. Britta Sweers agrees to this claim:

> The difficulty in Germany is, if you really want to become good, that you have to do much by yourself; you have to develop some kind of self discipline and develop your own concept. That means you also have to challenge yourself much more, and cope with your strengths and weaknesses. I think that this is the strength of our system: who gets through here, is usually very good! (Britta Sweers, Rostock, 25 November 2003)[4]

Another difference between both systems occurs in the area of performance practice. In Germany, there exists an underlying separation between the academic (*wissenschaftliche;* theoretical) study of music and performance training. At the University of Köln, for example, participation in ensembles is merely desirable,[5] whereas the curriculum at the Hochschule für Musik und Theater Rostock more

---

[4]   Und das Harte hier in Deutschland ist, wenn Du wirklich gut werden willst, musst Du selber sehr viel machen; Du musst eine Art Selbstdisziplin entwickeln, und für Dich ein eigenes Konzept entwickeln, d.h. Du musst Dich auch sehr viel stärker mit Dir selber auseinandersetzen, mit Deinen Stärken und Schwächen. Und ich bin der Meinung, das ist die Stärke unseres Systems. Wer hier durchkommt, ist eigentlich auch ziemlich gut (Britta Sweers, Rostock, 25 November 2003).

[5]   'Teilnahme am Collegium musicum vocale et instrumentale wird dringend empfohlen.' Studienordnung der Philosophischen Fakultät der Universität zu Köln für das

typically centres on performance studies. According to Rüdiger Schumacher, performance studies has until recently never played a substantial role at universities as 'praxis is – within the academic study of music – also still a little scorned because it is said that this is the responsibility of music colleges, but not of … universities' (Köln, 22 July 2004).[6] According to the principal (*Rektor*) at the Hochschule für Musik und Theater Rostock, 'it is not typical that there are ethnomusicologists at music colleges [which] in Germany are always more practice-focused. Academics are the minority [and] are only among music pedagogues' (Hartmut Möller, Rostock, 25 November 2003).[7] In the UK, by contrast, music performance is not just the domain of conservatories, yet also strongly features in universities, as Jonathan Stock explained (Figure 1.1):

> We've done this (MMus, MPhil and PhD levels with 50% performance) for quite some years already. In fact, there are now only a few UK Universities without performance options in among their higher degrees …. It is similar at undergraduate level in Britain too, where students may select probably somewhere around a third of their modules from musical performance options, sometimes more than that in the final year. Since these are options – performance is normally required at a lower level than 1/3 – not so many of the degrees have the word 'performance' in their names, but that's because it is standard practice in music degrees in this country. (Jonathan Stock, email to SEM-List, 13 October 2005)

It is also interesting to note that, while conservatories in the UK focus predominantly on students' musical training, the Hochschule für Musik und Theater Rostock also provides (besides offering performance courses) professional pathways in music teacher training. Principal Hartmut Möller commented on a general teacher shortage in schools in Mecklenburg (a *Bundesland* in Northeast Germany in which Rostock is situated) and across the country, and thus strongly advocated broad musical training (including popular and world musics) for music pedagogy students in order to enhance their employment prospects. Thus compared to universities and conservatories in the UK, *Musikpädagogik* (music pedagogy) seems to be more

---

Fach Musikwissenschaft (Haupt- und Nebenfach) mit dem Abschluß Magisterprüfung vom 10. Juli 2003, 29/2003.

   [6]   Praktizieren ist keine Priorität, nein, das ist auch erst in den letzten Jahren …. Bis dahin hat sich ja gerade die deutsche Musikethnologie mit der musikalischen Praxis sehr schwer getan …. Praxis ist auch immer im Rahmen der Musikwissenschaft eigentlich immer noch ein bisschen verpönt, weil man sagt, das ist die Aufgabe der Musikhochschulen, aber nicht … der Universitäten (Rüdiger Schumacher, Köln, 22 July 2004).

   [7]   An deutschen Musikhochschulen ist das gar nicht typisch, dass es Ethnomusikologen gibt …. Eine Musikhochschule in Deutschland ist immer mehr praktisch ausgerichtet. Die Wissenschaftler sind in der Minderzahl und die gibt's auch nur am Institut für Musikwissenschaft und Musikpädagogik (Hartmut Möller, Rostock, 25 November 2003).

important in Germany. This field of study 'is certainly an important area; to be able to expect music teachers' music-ethnological skills and knowledge at schools' (Rüdiger Schumacher, Köln, 22 July 2004).[8] By comparison, the specialised field of music pedagogy or ethnomusicology pedagogy appears to be of little significance at universities in the UK.

Figure 1.1   Jonathan Stock tuning the *erhu*; University of Sheffield; 22 January 2009

Progression from Undergraduate towards Postgraduate Studies

One common characteristic between the higher education systems in the UK and Germany can be found in the concept of progression from undergraduate towards postgraduate studies, particularly in the separatist approaches towards transmitting ethnomusicology's subject matters. This may be explained by the fact that since ethnomusicology's first appearance in the 1950s in American academia, ethnomusicology and world music were treated as divergent emphases for academic study. This in turn shaped the curricular content of newly emerging courses, which

---

[8]   Musiklehrerausbildung in Musikethnologie … in Hannover wird das gemacht … [und] ist mit Sicherheit auch ein wichtiger Bereich; musikethnologische Fähigkeiten und Kenntnisse von den Musiklehrern an den Schulen erwarten zu können (Rüdiger Schumacher, Köln, 22 July 2004).

either focused on theoretical and methodological discourse on ethnomusicology as a discipline or on world musics performance, which later also led to the emergence of more theoretical world musics courses. A similar bipartite separation is evident in universities in the UK and Germany, whereby world musics as a subject matter usually dominate the ethnomusicological share of the undergraduate curriculum.

Considering world musics courses, it is interesting to note that at European universities these do not embrace the study of musical elements or concepts, which is instead taught in school education before entering the higher education system. School pupils learn to approach the world's musics through studying musical elements or concepts, which also resembles the ways in which the Western classical tradition is transmitted (Reck, 1977; Wade, 2004). Based on the concept of progression, musical elements (rhythm, melody, harmony, tonality, structure and form) are treated separately and transmitted in a top down approach (Boyce-Tillman, 1996:55). While the transmission of musical concepts may be deemed more music-focused, intrinsically musical and musically inclusive, such courses also reinforce an ethnocentric perspective on the world's music cultures. For this reason (and other factors that will be discussed below), higher education courses in world musics do not deal with musical concepts or elements. Ethnomusicologists instead take a more critical approach, whilst embracing world musics with their various natures and functions (see also Floyd, 1996b:2). Moreover, ethnomusicologists both in the UK and Germany have a strong anthropological orientation, thereby having recognised, often through first-hand experience in the music culture they wish to understand, that not all cultures classify music and its components in the same way (if at all). The music concepts approach is thus less desirable for many ethnomusicologists in the UK and Germany. Interestingly, this differs to undergraduate world musics curricula in the United States where it is common to introduce large student populations to musical concepts. Contrary to UK and German music students who already often possess high levels of musical competence, American students may bring less musicological knowledge to these world music courses, which can be taken by non-majors in music. This also explains the focus on musical concepts in introductory world music textbooks written by American scholars, for example Miller and Shahriari, 2006; Titon, 2002; Wade and Campbell, 2003.

As mentioned earlier, world music courses in the UK and Germany typically dominate the undergraduate curriculum, and these started with more basic and general introductions to the world's musics at entrance level and moved towards more specialist regional area or themed courses in subsequent years. Such world music courses were independent, self-standing modules embedded within a music degree programme. Rarely do universities in the UK and Germany offer independent courses of study in world music/ethnomusicology at undergraduate level, such as a BA in World Musics or BA in Ethnomusicology. This may be explained by the fact that ethnomusicology has not yet been established as a self-contained department at most UK and German universities, yet there are three noteworthy exceptions. At the School of Oriental and African Studies (SOAS) there is a strong focus on area studies, including the study of language and other non-musical aspects of Asian (West Asia, Central Asia, South Asia, Southeast Asia, and East Asia) and African cultures. This specialist university apparently offers 'the most extensive ethnomusicology provision for single- and two-subject undergraduate degrees in the UK' (David Hughes, SOAS, 11 November 2003). Meanwhile, at Queen's University Belfast (QUB) where I visited Hae-kyung Um and interviewed Kay Milton (who was at the time of my research the Head of School of Anthropology), students can select exclusively world music courses towards an undergraduate BA in Ethnomusicology or BA in Anthropology. Another extensive provision in ethnomusicology occurred at the University of Köln where students can opt to devote their total study time to world music/ethnomusicology by selecting modules (*Basiseinheiten*, basic units) in *Musikethnologie* (music-ethnology). Such an extensive provision is apparently exceptional in Germany:

> We [the University of Köln] are the only university in the country, which offers this course of study to this extent .... For the western part of Germany this will, as ever, remain the central point, also for the education of research students. (Rüdiger Schumacher, Köln, 22 July 2004)[9]

While world music was the predominant subject matter at undergraduate level, ethnomusicology as a subject for study featured mostly at postgraduate level, yet not exclusively. In such rare instances where ethnomusicology was taught at undergraduate level, it was usually offered at upper levels due to its challenging theoretical concepts that required from students higher thinking skills. At postgraduate level, ethnomusicology was transmitted via independent, fully-fledged courses of study entitled MA or MMus in Ethnomusicology. Such courses usually centred on learning about the discipline's history, scope and subject matter, fieldwork and participant-observation, emic/etic perspectives, ethnography and other theoretical concepts. One such course was offered at Goldsmiths College London where I conducted participant-observation in postgraduate classes led by John Baily who explained that 'at postgraduate level, the emphasis is more on theory and method here .... This MMus is conceived as a foundation for doctoral work' (Goldsmiths, 13 February 2004). Taught Masters courses in ethnomusicology were thus theory-driven and provided a foundation for those students who wished to progress into doctoral studies in ethnomusicology. There was one exception at the University of Sheffield, which offered an independent course of study entitled MA in World Music Studies (Distance Learning). This course aimed at broadening students' horizons through exposure to a range of world musics and an in-depth look at one or more selected traditions, while also providing students with an

---

9   Und wir sind die einzige Universität im Lande, die diesen Studiengang in dem Umfang auch anbietet .... Für den westdeutschen Bereich wird das nach wie vor die Zentrale sein, auch für die Ausbildung des wissenschaftlichen Nachwuchses (Rüdiger Schumacher, Köln, 22 July 2004).

understanding and application of ethnomusicological research methods, thereby blending studies in world music and ethnomusicology.

Progression at Undergraduate Level

The discussions have shown so far that world music and ethnomusicology were treated as alternative subjects for academic study, and that world music courses occurred most typically at undergraduate level. Such courses usually moved from general, introductory world music (geographic) surveys at level 1 towards more specialised courses, such as regional area, themed and (occasionally) ethnomusicology courses at subsequent levels 2 and 3. At the University of Wales in Bangor, which I visited repeatedly and over a longer period of time, Caroline Bithell similarly emphasised this idea of progression from simpler to more complex courses in the study of world musics, whereby the thematic approach played a greater role in subsequent years of undergraduate study:

> ... in choosing a topic, history is very important, present social reality is quite important, and politics.... So I think there is a place for thematic teaching, but only *after* having already got to grips with some of the whole-culture stuff, maybe to look at the thematic stuff a bit later. It depends ... on the focus of the course, whether you are aiming to look at music, or music in people's lives. (Caroline Bithell, Bangor, 8 October 2003)

The concept of progression was also often reflected in ethnomusicologists' educational methods, which often started with more formal instruction at entrance level and led towards more active and student-centred learning in subsequent years. Hae-kyung Um explained that 'students in the first year probably ... need more of the direction of what is there and what this whole thing is about; and in the 2nd and 3rd years ... it's perhaps more complex' (Belfast, 18 November 2003). Forms of assessment similarly reflected the concept of progression, moving from smaller-scale introductory exercises in world musics to increasingly specialised, technical and critical studies, and perhaps to the completion of an original research project. The concept of progression is thus deeply anchored across the various types of undergraduate world music courses, including (a) world music surveys, which examine music less in-depth and as a worldwide phenomenon and thus taking a wide geographical focus or perhaps discuss 'big cultures' chosen for their musical significance; (b) regional or area studies, which centre in-depth on one music culture; and (c) themed world music courses, which are a combination of the previous types and are organised under themes, such as gender, race, politics, media or musical concepts (see also Miralis, 2002). As mentioned earlier, some universities also offered (d) ethnomusicology courses at undergraduate level, yet this occurred less frequently, which reflects the general 'disagreement over whether [an undergraduate] course should be primarily an introduction to the varieties of sounds and contexts the world over ... or whether it should be ... also an introduction to the history and methods of ethnomusicology itself' (Jeff Todd Titon, email to SEM-list, 23 September 2004). Importantly, the categorisation into four types of undergraduate world music courses was not necessarily consistent across all universities. At the University of Köln, the curriculum was rather fixed by a tripartite structure, including only regional, themed and ethnomusicology courses, which resembled 'the three pillars of individual courses', similar to a 'corset structure' (Rüdiger Schumacher, Köln, 22 July 2004),[10] although most other universities offered students the four types of world music courses for undergraduate study. Beginning with geographical survey courses, each will be considered further in the following sections.

Geographical world music survey courses
As already suggested, geographical world music surveys were frequently found at level 1 and aimed at introducing students to the wealth and breadth of selected music cultures of the world. Ethnomusicologists often suggested that such courses are particularly suitable for raising an interest among students, and that the aim of courses on Music Cultures of the World is:

> ... an insight into, experience of, enjoyment of different musics from different parts of the world; encourage them to think more broadly about our attitudes to music, and seeing music as not such a fixed category .... Many students find that quite exciting and interesting ... and hopefully carrying that across into other modules as well; encouraging the interest in people ... raise a humanitarian concern and to realise that it is real people. (Caroline Bithell, Bangor, 8 October 2003)

Without doubt, world music surveys are often fun and intriguing to students, yet these new musics may also strike them as strange and out-of-tune, and may signal otherness and even primitiveness (Killick, 2000:3). World music surveys have also been critiqued for restricting ethnomusicologists to transmit musics only superficially, rather than leading students towards a full understanding and sincere appreciation of the subtleties inherent in these musics (Campbell, 2004: xiii). In the eyes of one ethnomusicologist, world musics surveys represent 'a very broadly spread [form of] education, yet this is simply too flat. Within one semester one cannot do very much .... One has put a nose into it, but that doesn't suffice!'

---

[10]   Das sind eigentlich die drei Hauptbezugspunkte: regionalspezifische Studien, überregional-vergleichende, zu ... spezifischen Aspekten musikalischer Kultur, und ... theoriebildende, methodologische Phenomena .... Das sind die drei Pfeiler der einzelnen Module. Und dadurch haben wir uns in der Thematik auch etwas festgelegt. Da bin ich an eine bestimmte Reihenfolge gebunden, hab mich also stärker in ein festeres Korsett gebracht, aber habe ja diese Korsettstruktur beabsichtigt. (Rüdiger Schumacher, Köln, 22 July 2004).

(Rüdiger Schumacher, Köln, 22 July 2004).[11] Since ethnomusicologists often wish to stimulate in students a more genuine understanding and appreciation of these musics, some have thus chosen not to use world music surveys in their teaching:

> If it was a course for [the purpose of], let's say general academic entertainment, then it would indeed be attractive, almost in the sense of a TV show, like a soap opera .... It generates relatively little insights because if one covers Southeast Asia in one week, nothing can be remembered. One cannot really say anything substantial ... nothing that leads towards real understanding. One simply cannot manage that. And when there are far too many different [case studies], nothing gets remembered. Therefore I have from the start never done these world musics surveys. (Rüdiger Schumacher, Köln, 22 July 2004)[12]

Some ethnomusicologists also voiced that they feel inadequately equipped to teach a geographical world music survey. At the University of York, Neil Sorrell emphasised that 'I am not at home in all these different cultures' (York, 6 May 2004), which explains the absence of a world music course at this university. David Hughes had a similar view:

> World music surveys [taught by a single lecturer] ... are very common in America, but they are not common here [at SOAS] .... So doing a survey of many cultures, they were talking about traditions they have no first-hand experience of. They can't even pronounce the words .... But you know ... that was more acceptable in the 70s when there weren't so many ethnomusicologists and not so many posts .... Still, it's kind of embarrassing for me to lecture on Bali, and there are at least two people in London who know more about Bali [i.e. the music] than I do .... We are lucky here, there are seven of us [specialists], and we don't need to teach survey courses individually! So I don't need to lecture on something that I know nothing about. And yet, I still feel guilty when I lecture ... on Japanese Buddhist music ... because I don't know all of it from first-hand

---

[11] Das ist eine sehr breite, breitgefächerte Ausbildung, aber die ist einfach zu flach. Mit einem Semester kann man nicht viel machen .... Man hat mal reingeschnuppert, aber das reicht nicht! (Rüdiger Schumacher, Köln, 22 July 2004).

[12] Wenn es jetzt ein solcher Kurs wäre, sagen wir mal zur allgemeinen akademischen Unterhaltung, da wäre das durchaus reizvoll, im Sinne ja fast wie eine Fernsehsendung, so eine Serie .... Aber an Erkenntnissen bringt das relativ wenig, weil wenn man Südostasien in einer Woche behandelt, da bleibt ja nichts hängen. Man kann eigentlich über nichts Substantielles sagen. Man kann Eindrücke vielleicht, oberflächliche Eindrücke vermitteln, aber nichts was zum wirklichen Verständnis führt. Das schafft man einfach nicht. Und wenn es dann zu viel verschiedenes ist, dann bleibt auch letztendlich nichts hängen. Deswegen hab ich also von vornherein gar nicht oder nie diese World Music Kurse gemacht (Rüdiger Schumacher, Köln, 22 July 2004).

experience .... But still I think we are quite lucky here because we only teach traditions we know well. (David Hughes, SOAS, 11 November 2003)

Some ethnomusicologists in my research felt that such survey courses create cultural and musical stereotypes, whilst other scholars cautioned about the risk of confirming racist attitudes and tensions (Massey, 1996:18–19,21) or canonising music cultures for study (Campbell, 2004:xiii; Shelemay, 2001:xiv). The latter criticism requires further consideration as some UK and German ethnomusicologists felt it would be important to introduce key topics in an introductory world music course, which is also necessitated by time constraints in such courses:

> This is an introduction to world musics, thus there are some criteria, i.e. firstly, central things. That means ... that I only do the highlights, specific things .... They should at least once have heard the word *mbira* as it is simply central, together with some important principles underpinning it. (Britta Sweers, Rostock, 24 November 2003)[13]

Besides a concern with the canon, many ethnomusicologists critiqued world music survey courses for their tendency towards information overload. Students are simply faced with too many new countries and their musics. Some ethnomusicologists have thus advocated a narrowing down of surveying 'big' cultures, notably Jeff Todd Titon who refers here to his widely used textbook *Worlds of Music: An Introduction to the Music of the World's Peoples* (Titon, 2002):

> In those days there were only two textbooks available: one by Bruno Nettl called *Folk and Traditional Music of the Western Continents*, and another by William Malm that chiefly covered Asia, Indonesia, China, and Japan. I thought those textbooks were superficial and unsatisfying in their treatment. I did not use them and I didn't know any ethnomusicologist who liked them .... The only kind of introductory textbook that I thought would have integrity was one that, instead of surveying a lot of music superficially, concentrated in some depth on the musical cultures of *a few* representative human groups. I proposed that I invite a small group of ethnomusicologists to collaborate with me on a textbook that would consist of case-studies. (Jeff Todd Titon, personal email communication, 15 May 2003)

While the comments show that some ethnomusicologists feel apprehensive about world music surveys, others strongly advocate the educational value of such courses,

---

[13]   Das ist eine Einführung in die Weltmusik, so es kommen einige Kriterien dran, und zwar einmal zentrale Sachen, d.h. ich mache in dem Fall nur die Highlights, die speziellen Sachen .... Sie sollen wenigstens einmal das Wort *mbira* gehört haben, weil das einfach sehr zentral ist, und halt einige wichtige Prinzipien, die dahinter stehen (Britta Sweers, Rostock, 24 November 2003).

suggesting that broad surveys are highly suited to students who are sceptical about musics other than Western classical art music (Shahriari, 2005). Such a positive stance is reflected in the following statement by an ethnomusicologist who describes how a world music survey led her towards developing a completely new perception of the diversity and beauty of musical sounds from around the world:

> I was introduced to Cantometrics as an undergraduate when no ethnomusicology was taught in Montreal and I'd never heard the word, or imagined that music I liked to listen to was a discipline. It was one of those general world music try-to-cover-it-all courses which people increasingly put down for superficiality and which I loved, and opened innumerable new worlds for me. Some I followed up intensively, some less, some not at all. But I HEARD them. The professor was a piano teacher with no advanced degree and no courses in ethnomusicology (Phil Cohen). He invented the course, and arrived at every class with a huge stack of LPs under his arm. The first thing he told us was 'you don't have to LIKE it all, you have to LISTEN to it and try to understand it'. He himself – who played only 'classical' piano – would always stand transfixed when any LP was on, and his very body language made us all listen to try to hear what was so special about what he was hearing. He said the same of Cantometrics, which he explained at length, with examples: he said it was brilliant and quite possibly very flawed, but that the point was listening and thinking, not deciding whether it or any other system or methodology would solve everything. That was quite possibly the best course I ever had in my life, and I wouldn't exchange it as an introductory course for anything more 'in depth'. The WAY of listening and thinking about material created its own depth, so the breadth of material covered, which many would put down as leading to superficiality, was essential. There was no systematic sequencing either, we never knew what to expect from that stack of LPs under his arm. (Judith Cohen, email to SEM-list, 13 October 2004)

Perhaps for similar reasons, most UK and German ethnomusicologists offered at least one world music survey course at introductory level. Many students tended to enjoy studying such a broad, introductory and vastly interesting course, which 'definitely functions to broaden students' horizons as far as teaching music as a world-wide phenomenon and also showing them how various cultures produce music' (Jesse C., email to SEM-list, 14 October 2004). Such courses seem particularly suitable to stimulate students' interest in music of other cultures and to raise their awareness about many different ways of making music. Even Rüdiger Schumacher who seemed so sceptical about world music surveys stated that 'I have realised that under certain circumstances, one can awaken [students'] interest …

in such a course ... [for instance] in the framework of a summer university where
one tries to awaken interest in potential future students' (Köln, 22 July 2004).[14]
For similar reasons, Britta Sweers advocated that students need the opportunity
'to gain a general impression, also a listening impression of masses of musics ...
possibly many different things. This is rather like a colourful plate [referring to a
plate of sweets, nuts, raisins, etc found in Germany during the Christmas season]
... where everyone chooses something themselves, and takes something with them
.... This is the best foundation education' (Rostock, 24 November 2003).[15]

Regional and area studies
Some ethnomusicologists felt that exposure to fewer cultures or countries within
a larger region has greater educational value, as it allows for more in-depth study.
Regional and area studies, which occurred particularly in subsequent years of
study, were regarded as enabling students to become more completely immersed
in the music and its cultural meanings and functions. At the University of Bangor,
students progressed from a world music survey at level 1 to more specific, regional
studies at levels 2 and 3, since Caroline Bithell was able to 'develop [my] own
specialisms, so I teach one course on the Mediterranean and Africa .... So we
diversify a bit more in the second and third year. (Bangor, 8 October 2003). Equally
at SOAS, second- and third year students 'usually focus on the music culture of a
selected area or areas: Africa, the Middle East, South Asia, Southeast Asia, or East
Asia' (Handbook 2003/04, The Department of Music, SOAS). A similar model
existed at Queen's University Belfast with modules designed to develop from a
more general geographical world music course at level 1 towards increasingly
specific regional and other courses in subsequent years. This is very similar to
German higher education: while courses in the Grundstudium seemed fixed and
the same for all students, thus providing a solid foundation in musical studies,
courses in the Hauptstudium built upon different regional areas. Increasingly
specialising, most such courses concentrated on one region or geographical area
while approaching music cultures more in-depth, which necessitated a higher level
of intellectual engagement by students. Some courses developed from a general
introduction to the region's culture and music towards more specialised case
studies, whilst others reflected a succession of different topics pertinent to that
particular region:

---

[14]   Aber ich hab festgestellt, man kann eigentlich unter Umständen Interesse wecken,
wenn man so einen Kurs meinetwegen im Rahmen ... einer Sommeruniversität anbietet, wo
man versucht, auch das Interesse bei möglichen künftigen Studenten zu wecken (Rüdiger
Schumacher, Köln, 22 July 2004).

[15]   Ich habe viele verschiedene Beispiele in der Vorlesung, damit sie mal einen
allgemeinen Eindruck, auch Höreindruck bekommen von einer Masse an Musik ...
möglichst viele unterschiedliche Sachen. Das ist eher ein bunter Teller, wo ... jeder für sich
etwas rausgreifen kann, und irgendwas mitnimmt .... Das ist die beste Grundlagenbildung
(Britta Sweers, Rostock, 24 November 2003).

I wanted to go into depth rather than into breadth in general …. So I picked particular vocal styles and looked at them in detail …. The module as a whole aims to give students a general broad insight into African music, to give them a sense of the richness of styles of musical activity across Africa, and functions of music in particular parts of Africa, a sense of Africa as a living, vibrant place that is not just jungle with … people banging drums in it. And also to show how in many parts of Africa, again my favourite theme of politics, how the political situation has impacted on music, how history has impacted on music. Again, Africa is a very rich continent, demonstrating all of that as well. (Caroline Bithell, Bangor, 15 October 2003)

As already indicated, there exists a symbiosis between ethnomusicologists' specialisms and the foci of the regional and area studies offered (see also Shelemay, 2003). As a result, 'the courses that [ethnomusicologists] teach are quite different to those that they studied, simply because [they] worked around specialisms …. Here at Bangor there is a policy that ties together scholarship and research, and education' (Caroline Bithell, Bangor, 8 October 2003). This is echoed by Rüdiger Schumacher who 'so far offered relatively little, or actually nothing, about Africa; that is not really [his] area'.[16] Instead, 'my teaching emphasis is on the music of Asia, geographically taken; and thematically, the area of sacred music …, epic song and also music theatre … [as] my own research specialism is … Southeast Asia, Java and Bali' (Köln, 22 July 2004).[17] Meanwhile, Hae-kyung Um explained that 'area studies depend on people's specialism …. This will probably evolve from there …, a kind a dialectical relationship between the people who are teaching there and what the institution could facilitate' (Belfast, 18 November 2003). Regional area courses thus typically reflect and are shaped by the ethnomusicologist's area of research and specialism, yet not all research specialisms are deemed suitable for an entire course. Jonathan Stock, who had just completed a book on Shanghai opera, felt that this area of research expertise was less suitable as a focus for an entire regional course. Explaining that 'there is the research that we do generally, that informs everything we do in our teaching, and then there are rather specific research subjects … that might only come up as a lecture', Jonathan Stock further suggested that:

Shanghai opera … might come up as a lecture now, or once a year … but probably won't turn into a whole module …. I suspect, given the kind of intake that we get, which is people with a classical music background, that if we put

---

[16] Ich hab bisher relativ wenig, oder offen gestanden eigentlich gar nichts zu Afrika angeboten; das ist nicht so mein Gebiet (Rüdiger Schumacher, Köln, 22 July 2004).

[17] Für mich [ist] der Lehrschwerpunkt die Musik Asiens, geografisch gesehen; und thematisch, der Bereich Sakralmusik …, Epengesang und auch Musiktheater …. Meine eigene Forschung in erster Linie natürlich Südost-Asien, Java und Bali (Rüdiger Schumacher, Köln, 22 July 2004).

on a course on Chinese opera ... we'd probably only get two or three students, but if we put on the music of East Asia, we might get nine or ten. So it's a more viable class size. (Jonathan Stock, Sheffield, 13 October 2003)

Undoubtedly, regional area courses can facilitate a deeper engagement with a particular music culture. Yet some ethnomusicologists, notably Rüdiger Schumacher, felt that such courses still resembled some 'kind of survey ... [of] big topics like Central Asia ... or Bali ... [which is] again a survey of a very large and very rich music culture .... One could thus ... be much more detailed' (Köln, 22 July 2004).[18] For this reason, some ethnomusicologists instead advocated themed approaches for the transmission of world musics at universities.

Themed courses
Themed courses are typically organised around conceptual and critical foci, whereby course contents are designed on the basis of succession of (often independent) themes and issues. The latter may include identity, politics, dance or 'epic song, ... music theatre or sacred music' (Rüdiger Schumacher, Köln, 22 July 2004),[19] whereby thematic discussions also often occurred in regional area courses. For example, at SOAS themed courses focused on the topics of 'music, shamanism and healing; or music and religion' (David Hughes, SOAS, 11 November 2003). Such courses may reflect ethnomusicologists' more direct engagement with particular concepts and ideas, past and present. Indeed, themes are frequently introduced during national and international conferences and publications aimed at an exclusively ethnomusicological audience and readership, so that 'it would be more useful ... [to discuss] key-issues ... which come out of a conference as a conference theme now and then' (Hae-kyung Um, Belfast, 18 November 2003). Course content changes may thus reflect and be modelled upon shifts in contemporary academic discourse and debate. Themed courses typically require in students a higher level of coherent and independent thinking, and thus occurred most frequently at subsequent levels of undergraduate study. Themed courses are particularly suitable in addressing the role music plays in people's lives and communities, thereby taking an anthropological approach. The focus on key issues can also encourage students to think critically and to broaden their musical outlook, leading students not

---

[18]   Es sind ja auch insofern Überblicksveranstaltungen .... Ich mein das sind schon große Themen wie Zentralasien, die ich nehme. Gut, ich hab jetzt in diesem Semester als Vorlesung *Musik in Bali*. Da könnte man sagen, das ist ein kleines Thema. Aber es ist in dem Sinne auch wieder ein Überblick über eine sehr große und sehr reiche Musikkultur. Also man könnte bei sehr vielen Themen noch sehr viel stärker auf's Detail gehen und das untersuchen (Rüdiger Schumacher, Köln, 22 July 2004).

[19]   Überregionale, vergleichende Kurse [sind] einem bestimmten Thema, einem bestimmten Gegenstand gewidmet .... Das können Epengesang sein, ... oder Musiktheater, oder Sakralmusik (Rüdiger Schumacher, Köln, 22 July 2004).

only towards deeper musical appreciation, but also towards an understanding of the cultural processes people construct through music (Shelemay, 2001). Themed courses also enable cross-cultural comparisons, thereby unifying musics from different origins and providing an inclusive framework for all musical traditions. Themed courses facilitate a more integral stance towards the world's musics on the grounds of relevance, rather than musical quality. The organisation into themes thereby allows for considerations of the multifaceted and dynamic nature of culture around the globe whilst tracing cross-cultural musical currents globally. Rüdiger Schumacher included themed courses in the undergraduate curriculum by:

> ... selecting a specific theme, a specific question, and making cross-regional comparisons. For example, in the last semester, I have offered a *Hauptseminar* about extra-European music theatre, well, the concept, the connection between music and theatre ... to look at the concept of theatre [and ask] how is this evident in different cultures. One usually gets strong contrasts, also in the presentation [performance]; on the other hand, one always has a connecting [theme], the question about theatrical characteristics. Thus it is not as loosely connected as in 'big' world music surveys. (Rüdiger Schumacher, Köln, 22 July 2004)[20]

Interestingly, some ethnomusicologists also included Western art or popular musics in themed courses, often advocating that familiarity with music may help students to move into meaningful discussions of more unfamiliar ones. According to Andrew Killick, 'it is dangerous to present too much stuff that's new at one time. If I want to bring out a theoretical point, I would rather do it by using examples that are already familiar' (Sheffield, 28 November 2003), a point echoed by Jonathan Stock who 'include[d] Madonna songs because they [students] are already familiar with them, and ... that might make it a bit easier for them to have views and to form views on ... how Madonna creates identity' (Sheffield, 10 November 2003). Both ethnomusicologists cautioned about transmitting to students too many new ideas and musics and instead relied on more familiar musical examples in more challenging theory courses whilst including diverse musical examples to reflect the discipline's inclusivity of subject matter. Yet there also exists some criticism, specifically around the idea that the wide range of musical examples included in

---

[20] ... sich ein spezifisches Thema, eine spezifische Fragestellung auswählt, und die unter Umständen überregional vergleichen kann. Beispielsweise im letzten Semester hatte ich ein Hauptseminar gemacht über außereuropäisches Musiktheater, also das Konzept, die Verbindung von Musik und Theater, das Theaterkonzept einmal betrachten, wie ist das in unterschiedlichen Kulturen ausgeprägt. Man bekommt dann sehr starke Kontraste, auch in der Präsentation; man hat auf der anderen Seite immer ein verbindendes, also die Frage nach dem Theatercharakter. Also es ist nicht so unverbindlich wie sonst im großen World Music Kurs (Rüdiger Schumacher, Köln, 22 July 2004).

themed courses may seem bewildering to students. At the same time, themes may mean completely different things to different people (Wade, 2004). There is also an implicit danger that such courses impart eurocentric perspectives on the world's music cultures, which may put into question the autonomy and sovereignty of music cultures not from the West.

Ethnomusicology courses

It has been suggested so far that ethnomusicology courses typically occurred at higher levels of study. For example, ethnomusicologists at universities in Belfast, Durham, Köln, Sheffield and London (SOAS) incorporated ethnomusicology courses in later years or offered blended courses that amalgamated the study of world musics with theories in ethnomusicology. Such courses necessitated from students higher levels of academic comprehension and critical thinking, whilst often involving the conduct of a small, independent ethnographic fieldwork project that aimed at a more nuanced approach towards blending theory and practice. Such ethnomusicology courses introduced students to the core concepts of the discipline, including relevant ethnomusicological literature. At the University of Durham, I encountered a 24-week course entitled *Introduction to Ethnomusicology*, which explored the works of ethnomusicologists so as to introduce the history of ethnomusicology and the discipline's theoretical models. This course included not only the works of Erich von Hornbostel, Curt Sachs, Alan Merriam, Bruno Nettl, Anthony Seeger, Martin Stokes, Ali Jihad Racy and John Blacking, but also studies of hermeneutics, copyright law, semiotics and nationalism theory (Music Department Handbook 2003/04, University of Durham). According to some undergraduate students studying on this module, this focus on concepts and theories was deemed extremely challenging and daunting by many (group interview, Durham, 23 October 2003).

A similar approach existed at the University of Köln where two ethnomusicology courses *Einführung in die Musikethnologie 1 & 2* (Introduction to music-ethnology 1 & 2) focused intensively (in fact, far more intensively than in ethnomusicology courses in the UK) on the history and theory of ethnomusicology. The first course started with discussions on European expansionism in 1500, leading through romantic and imperialist eras to the beginnings of comparative musicology. This discipline was studied in great depth, illuminating its methods of transcription and analysis, classification and the origins of *Kulturkreislehre*. The course moved on to the founding fathers of cultural anthropology in America (Boas, Malinowski, Radcliffe-Brown, Mauss), illustrating cultural-area-theory, discussing studies in Europe after 1945 and finally arriving at ethnomusicology and the anthropology of music, studying scholars like Charles Seeger, Mantle Hood, Alan Merriam and Richard Waterman. The subsequent course followed with discussions about bi-musicality and the question of musical universals, moving on to neomarxist, cognitive and hermeneutic approaches to musical study. This was followed by ethnography and thick description, symbolic anthropology and performance theory, and structuralism and post-structuralism. The course also discussed the crisis of representation and writing-culture-debate, gender studies, postcolonial studies and black studies, cultural studies and the popular, coming to a conclusion about new directions, such as the music industry, world music and globalisation.

Elsewhere, the approach was consciously to avoid in-depth ethnomusicological history and challenging terminology at undergraduate level. Many ethnomusicologists in the UK and Germany agreed that such courses are rather daunting and ambiguous to certain students who would rather learn about world musics. Caroline Bithell even deemed it important to change the module title in order to avoid the term itself:

> I changed the title of modules from 'ethnomusicology' to 'Music of ...'. A first-year module called 'Introduction to ethnomusicology' ... sounded a little bit too technical to students, and they have this misconception that it is about organs because of the organology bit ... so we just shifted the emphasis a bit, more than the content really ... although I did start condensing some of the theoretical and methodological issues ... not leaving them out, but to find different ways to do it. So, for instance instead of four lectures at the start about the aims and methods of ethnomusicology ..., I changed some of these things into a seminar later in the course, after they had a few fireworks to keep them happy. (Caroline Bithell, Bangor, 8 October 2003)

Ethnomusicologists generally agreed that theoretical ethnomusicology courses may best be placed at postgraduate level as these students bring higher levels of commitment and preparedness towards more challenging and intellectually stimulating subject matters. The progression from Masters to doctorate level also reflects a move away from instructor-led transmission of ethnomusicological concepts and methods and towards highly student-centred active learning through independent reading and research. This will be the focus of the following discussions, which illustrate the transmission of ethnomusicology at postgraduate level of study.

Progression at Postgraduate Level

Studying about the discipline of ethnomusicology, its concepts, history and methods characterised students' experiences at postgraduate level. Whilst such ethnomusicology courses were varied across UK and German universities, they can be categorised into three broad types, including (a) theory courses, (b) practice-oriented courses and (c) hybrids thereof, thus placing differing emphases on the study of pivotal texts in ethnomusicology, the practical preparation of students for doctoral research in ethnomusicology, or a combination of both. An underlying concern with progression was pivotal in these courses. Theory courses, for example, often moved from generic, introductory discourse on ethnomusicology as a discipline towards more specialised, thematic discourse. At Queen's University Belfast (QUB), a course entitled *Key Readings in Ethnomusicology* 'started with a very historical [topic] and then went through different kinds of issues .... each issue built on the previous one and accumulated knowledge' (Hae-kyung Um, Belfast, 18 November 2003). This idea of progression was equally significant in more practice-oriented courses, which often moved from generic research training towards more specialist performance practice as a tool for research. The level of students' autonomy in the learning process also progressed as their studies became increasingly independent and self-directed, particularly when preparing a Masters thesis (in the UK) or *Magisterarbeit* (in Germany), and during subsequent doctoral research. Postgraduate theory courses in ethnomusicology thus required from students higher levels of commitment towards independent and self-directed study with the ethnomusicologist facilitating students' learning.

Theory courses in ethnomusicology typically introduced students to the ethnomusicological literature of eminent scholars in the field. At the University of Sheffield, an introductory module entitled *Postgraduate Readings in Ethnomusicology* aimed at 'introducing students to a cross-section of the literature in English for the discipline of ethnomusicology. The history of the discipline is surveyed followed by an examination of principal techniques and issues in current research' (Module Handout, Postgraduate Readings in Ethnomusicology, University of Sheffield, 2003). Students were provided with a comprehensive reading list of approximately six journal articles or book chapters per topic, which had to be read in preparation to each session. Topics typically included: what is music?; historical perspectives (comparative musicology, anthropology of music, ethnomusicology); fieldwork; insider/outsider views; transcription and analysis; etc. Besides selective literature on ethnomusicology's concepts, history and methods, such courses also often focused on more contemporary themes and issues, including identity, language, gender and globalisation, to name a few examples. Although such theory courses were often reading-based, some courses also included technical training and more practical, hands-on sessions, specifically on the topics of fieldwork, transcription and analysis. Such practical training is pivotal in ethnomusicology, and many universities offered postgraduate courses that were conceived as a foundation for doctoral work in ethnomusicology. Besides one or two modules on theoretical issues in ethnomusicology, these degrees placed significant emphasis on practical, hands-on skills required in ethnomusicological fieldwork. At Goldsmiths College London, the MMus in Ethnomusicology also included the 'performance of fieldwork' and the use of video as a research tool.

While most taught postgraduate courses focused on ethnomusicology as their subject matter, there was one noteworthy exception at the University of Sheffield, which offers a MA in World Music Studies (through Distance Learning). This course not only focused on the study of world musics, but also on a thorough and distinctive training in ethnomusicology:

> World Music Studies has been designed to progress logically from an introduction to the study of world music and the research skills involved, through increasingly specialised, technical and critical studies, to the completion of an

original research project that contributes new knowledge to the field. (Course Description, University of Sheffield, 2005)

A few other postgraduate courses in ethnomusicology at SOAS, Goldsmiths and Durham equally focused on world music studies alongside theoretical courses in ethnomusicology. These were usually regional area or themed world music courses and also included (in some instances, for example SOAS) courses in anthropology, language or performance. Generally however, postgraduate courses in ethnomusicology focused most and foremost on ethnomusicology as a discipline, and in particular its paradigmatic concepts, history and methods.

Progression and Ethnomusicological Texts

As discussed throughout this chapter, the ethnomusicology curriculum is underpinned by notions of progression, and this was equally evident in ethnomusicologists' use of literature and textbooks. At undergraduate level or *Grundstudium*, students typically engaged with introductory world music textbooks, which mirrored the tripartite categorisation of undergraduate world music courses, as these were written either as world music surveys or regional and area studies books, or followed a themed approach. The first type of textbook in the form of a world music survey was frequently used in earlier years of study, as these provided a broad introduction to traditional musics within their cultural contexts, often accompanied by CDs or websites containing listening examples and further materials. Caroline Bithell found that 'students seemed to quite like the Elizabeth May book and the Jeff Todd Titon book ... [which] is quite nice also because of all the CDs' (Bangor, 9 October 2003). Yet world music survey textbooks were also often criticised for their obvious limitations, particularly in the light of superficiality, as such books 'claim to cover everything, [yet] they inevitably have shortfalls. This is particularly evident in the *Garland Encyclopedia*; in some places, it is very nicely detailed and contains a lot of important information. Yet when one looks for detailed information, one recognises again and again, yes, there is nothing written about [selected topics]' (Rüdiger Schumacher, Köln, 22 July 2004).[21] Reflecting on the textbook *World Sound Matters* (Stock *et al.*, 1996), David Hughes, though finding it a wonderful resource, critiqued that 'the examples from Japan ... are very poorly done, they are very misleading .... It just shows the

---

21   [Solche Bücher] enthalten eine ganze Reihe von sehr wichtigen und detailierten Untersuchungen, aber weil es den Anspruch hat, alles zu umfassen, greift es notwendigerweise zu kurz. Das ist besonders deutlich auch durchaus zu sehen bei der *Garland Encyclopedia*; in manchen Stellen ist es wirklich sehr schön detailiert und enthält eine ganze Reihe von wichtigen Informationen. Wenn man dann aber detailierte Informationen sucht, dann stellt man immer wieder fest, ja, darüber steht nichts drin .... Es lässt sich nicht vermeiden, dass man Lücken hat (Rüdiger Schumacher, Köln, 22 July 2004).

difficulty of doing this' (SOAS, 11 November 2003). Another criticism emerged from the risk of canonising music cultures for study, for example in *Worlds of Music* (Titon, 2002), although Jeff Titon had a different view:

> I think if *Worlds of Music* has been canonical, it has been so in another way: it has taught generations of students to think about musical cultures in some depth … and … the ways in which individuals within musical cultures experience music … That is, it has been canonical in establishing a particular approach to the study of people making music. (Jeff Todd Titon, personal email communication, 15 May 2003)

Textbooks adopting regional and area study approaches were often deemed more suitable. An excellent example is Wade and Campbell's *Global Music Series* (2003), which contains numerous volumes that facilitate more in-depth study of specific music cultures. Students particularly valued the fact that each volume grew out of the author's research specialism, which made the music culture more real and alive and enabled students to gain a deeper appreciation of ethnomusicological fieldwork in different settings. Meanwhile, textbooks adopting a themed approach are useful for their cross-cultural and interdisciplinary approaches (Shelemay 2001:xiii), which can enhance students' heightened levels of critical thinking, although 'structuring the course as in Shelemay's *Soundscapes* may have the disadvantage that the music can be nothing more than an example' (Caroline Bithell, Bangor, 8 October 2003). For this reason, themed textbooks have been criticised, including 'the book by … Kay Kaufman Shelemay … [because] it is impossible to include so much in one book' (Rüdiger Schumacher, Köln, 22 July 2004).[22] Ethnomusicologists questioned particularly the musical discontinuity evident in these themed books, together with the predominant focus on culture. Meanwhile, textbooks that have as their focus musics as a primarily sonic art have also been criticised on the basis that the study of the world's musics should also encompass emotions, movement and human interrelations. Besides textbooks on world musics, other recommended textbooks focused on ethnomusicology as a discipline, which included texts by Bruno Nettl and Alan Merriam, although these books were usually utilised in subsequent years due to their academic and intellectually challenging contents:

> Bruno Nettl's *Twenty-Nine Issues and Concepts* works OK, but is quite complicated for a lot of people to take in and deal with in one year, even for native speakers, certainly also for myself …. Nettl doesn't treat his book as a textbook intentionally, so it's hard to read it as a textbook …. Although it's

---

[22] Auch das Buch von der … Kay Kaufman Shelemay ist auch sehr stark kritisiert worden. Das geht auch eigentlich nicht, alles in ein Buch reinzupacken (Rüdiger Schumacher, Köln, 22 July 2004).

useful, however, Nettl's book is tricky to use as a kind of stand-on-its-own resource. (Jonathan Stock, Sheffield, 13 October 2003)

At postgraduate level or *Hauptstudium*, the core literature centred around more theory and method-based ethnomusicological handbooks or ethnographic monographs. At entry postgraduate level, introductory textbooks presented to students the discipline's history, subject matters, methods and other pertinent issues (examples include Bohlman, 2002; Myers, 1992c; Nettl, 1983, 2005). As courses progressed, students were increasingly required to engage with more specialised texts that deal exclusively with the history and scope of ethnomusicology (including Nettl and Bohlman, 1991; Shelemay, 1992), the discipline's anthropological direction (including Merriam, 1964) or the discipline's ethnographic methods (including Barz and Cooley, 1997, 2008). At higher levels of postgraduate study, students normally encountered ethnographic monographs by eminent scholars in ethnomusicology, including John Blacking (1973), Anthony Seeger (1987), Timothy Rice (1994), Paul Berliner (1981) or Thomas Turino (1993). These texts featured frequently on students' compulsory reading lists, yet this raised problems for the many postgraduate students whose first language was not English. Ethnomusicologists have thus to consider 'how to make the ideas of ethnomusicology accessible to people whose native language is … very different from English … who are really having a hard time trying to extract the ideas from the readings' (Andrew Killick, Sheffield, 3 November 2003).

It is important to note here that this brief section is by no means an exhaustive representation of books on world musics and ethnomusicology utilised by ethnomusicologists across UK and German universities. Thus, whilst some examples of textbooks in the form of world music surveys, regional/area studies and themed approaches, as well as books with a focus on ethnomusicology as a discipline were mentioned, ethnomusicologists across universities utilise a whole array of other books and textbooks at undergraduate level of study that adopt these formats. Equally, postgraduate studies are typically underpinned by a far wider variety of theory and method-based handbooks and monographs than those mentioned in this brief section. The point here is to highlight the fact that the use of ethnomusicological texts in the form of books and textbooks often reflects the idea of students' progressive learning from basic, introductory knowledge of the world's musics and towards more complex, in-depth concepts about ethnomusicological theory and fieldwork paradigms, whilst the latter may bring some problems in comprehension, specifically for students whose first language is not English. Indeed, a more thorough, in-depth analysis of the current usage of ethnomusicological texts, both in English and other languages, would make interesting future research in ethnomusicology pedagogy so as to shed light into a further dimension of the disciplining of ethnomusicology at universities.

More generally, this chapter has argued that the transmission of ethnomusicology reflects Western ideas of progression, evident in the separatist approach in which the subject matter is divided into alternative subjects for academic study together with a steady increase in theoretical discourse and intellectual challenge, and in the move from instructor-led towards increasingly student-focused pedagogical learning approaches as students progressed through their undergraduate and postgraduate studies. Another pertinent theme in the transmission of ethnomusicological knowledge emerged from ethnomusicology's concern with music in and as culture. This is the concern of the following chapter, which illustrates how ethnomusicology's anthropological orientation impacts on the transmission of ethnomusicology's history, subject matters and methods.

Chapter 2
Transmitting Ethnomusicology, Expressing Culture

Modern ethnomusicology is signified by certain canonic approaches to the study of and writing about musics (Bohlman, 1992a, 1992b), which ethnomusicologists wish to understand in and as culture (Merriam, 1964).[1] This anthropological orientation to the study of ethnomusicology and world musics appeared to be significant at universities in the UK and Germany, as many ethnomusicologists transmitted ethnomusicology as the anthropology of music:

> Ethnomusicologists try to discover what people, music-makers themselves, think is part of their music, and why they are doing it, and what's it all about, what's at the heart of it for them. We are very easily distracted by details of notes and specialist stuff, that we as specialists can measure and weigh and compare, whereas in fact many of the people who are … creating music … it's about words, or feelings, or emotions …. I guess, in an ideal course, I would repeat all this stuff at the end to emphasise again that these are humans making music, and it's all about humanity, not really about the music. The end point is about humanity. (Jonathan Stock, Sheffield, 6 October 2003)

This anthropological focus even shaped and impacted on the title of a world music survey course offered to students at the University of Bangor on the basis that:

> Ethnomusicology is part ethnology and musicology, so I want to keep the anthropological side strongly prominent in using the title 'music cultures' … avoiding the ambiguous term 'world music'. (Caroline Bithell, Bangor, 8 October 2003)

The strong anthropological orientation of ethnomusicology transmission at universities in the UK and Germany is particularly noteworthy as most ethnomusicology courses and courses of study are situated in Schools or Departments of Music. An exception occurred at Queen's University Belfast (QUB) where ethnomusicology is situated within the School of Anthropological Studies and was described by the Head of School as the anthropology of music:

---

[1]   In this chapter, 'modern ethnomusicology' refers to post-1950s developments in the disciplining of ethnomusicology. The term 'modern' should not be equated to modernism.

> I don't really worry about whether we'd call it anthropology or ethnomusicology
> .... It is clearly important that students of human society and culture learn about
> music ... because it's a big part of some people's lives .... That's why I think
> ethnomusicology is actually better placed within an anthropology department
> than it is within a music department because I think it's important to understand
> [music] within its wider social and cultural context ... the role that music plays
> in people's lives. (Kay Milton, Belfast, 19 November 2003)

I found that the emphasis on the anthropological study in ethnomusicology at QUB had significant implications at the time of my research, namely that students without any musical background were able to study ethnomusicology in contrast to those students applying at QUB's School of Music who were required to pass an entrance examination consisting of performance, theory test and sight singing. This in turn affected module contents (musical transcription and analysis, for instance, were not compulsory) as well as the level of performance skills (not) required in world music ensembles. At the University of Köln, a more formally verbalised, yet seemingly similar anthropological emphasis existed, whereby the focus of *Musikethnologie* was first on context and second on the types of musics studied: 'Subject of ethnomusicology is music in its cultural and social context. Thereby the music of Africa, America, Asia, Australia and Oceania form the field of work' (study rules 29/2003).[2] There was also a more pronounced emphasis on the objective, logical, almost scientific study of musical elements, instruments, musical styles and genres. This kind of approach was characteristic of work in comparative musicology in the early twentieth century, which focused predominantly on the study of tonal systems and the classification of musical instruments. German ethnomusicologists indeed still derive much of their approach from this discipline with its emphasis on 'transcription and analysis of musical sound' (Rüdiger Schumacher, Köln, 22 July 2004).[3] Such an emphasis was expressed primarily in course descriptions that aimed to provide a comprehensive musical overview. The University of Köln course description for *Musik in Bali,* for example, illustrates this:

> After a detailed study of Bali's cultural history and the fundamental
> characteristics of its music, these lectures will at first investigate the features
> of the numerous kinds of instrumental ensembles and their music in regard to
> instrumental line-up, tuning and function of instruments [and] in their ensemble

---

[2]   Gegenstand der Musikethnologie (ME) ist Musik in ihrem kulturellen und sozialen Kontext. Dabei bilden die Musik Afrikas, Amerikas, Asiens, Australiens und Ozeaniens, die europäische Volksmusik und die Populärmusik das Arbeitsgebiet (Studienordnung 29/2003, Köln).

[3]   ... die alte, gut-deutsche Musikethnologie, die letztendlich noch auf die Berliner Schule zurückgeht, also viel wichtiger eben Transkription, usw, und Musikklanganalyse (Rüdiger Schumacher, Köln, 22 July 2004).

playing, formation, repertoire, use and function. The musical overall picture will be completed through a detailed discussion of the different forms of vocal music making, particularly of sung poetry, as well as of the variety of dance and theatre traditions. (University of Köln, Annotated list of lectures summer semester 2004, page 3)[4]

Rüdiger Schumacher confirmed that:

> *Musikethnologie* is historically an area, which is of course closely connected with the early developments of comparative musicology .... Traditionally, a very strong emphasis on structural analysis of music as sound, and indeed a comparative perspective .... This has ... already changed .... In my opinion, the anthropological direction has already become much stronger. At the moment here, it balances itself slightly out. (Rüdiger Schumacher, Köln, 22 July 2004)[5]

Comparative musicology has thus become less influential on musical studies in German and European music ethnology (Bohlman, 1992a:129). Meanwhile, Britta Sweers, trained in the Anglo-American tradition similarly 'shows the central points in the music ... [as in] comparative musicology .... I prefer showing musical examples, transcriptions. I mean these are musicians; they can read music' (Rostock, 25 November 2003), while at the same time placing significant emphasis on the contextual study of musics, enabling students to gain a relative understanding of music cultures.[6] The uneven emphasis on anthropological approaches or those

---

[4]   Am Anschluss an eine einführende Betrachtung der Kulturgeschichte Balis und der fundamentalen Charakterzüge der Musik werden in dieser Vorlesung zunächst die Merkmale der zahlreichen Instrumentalensemble-Arten und ihrer Musik hinsichtlich instrumentaler Besetzung, Stimmung und Funktion der Instrumente im Zusammenspiel, Formbildung, Repertoire, Gebrauch und Funktion untersucht. Das musikalische Gesamtbild wird vervollständigt durch eine detaillierte Behandlung der verschiedenen Formen vokalen Musizierens, insbesondere der gesungenen Poesie, sowie der Vielfalt von Tanz- und Theatertraditionen (Universität zu Köln, Kommentiertes Vorlesungsverzeichnis Sommersemester 2004, Seite 3).

[5]   Musikethnologie ist von der Geschichte her eine Richtung, die natürlich mit den frühen Entwicklungen der Vergleichenden Musikwissenschaft sehr eng verbunden ist. Dadurch dass Marius Schneider die ersten Jahre hier war, und seine Schüler gewissermaßen auch in dieser Tradition ausgebildet worden sind, also insofern eine sehr, also von der Tradition her, sehr starke Ausrichtung auf Strukturuntersuchungen von Musik als Klang, und durchaus auch eine, ja, vergleichende Perspektive. In der Praxis hatte sich das eigentlich schon unter meinem Vorgänger doch deutlich gewandelt, der beispielsweise sehr enge Kontakte zu John Blacking hatte, usw. Da ist meines Erachtens auch die anthropologische Ausrichtung sehr viel stärker schon geworden. Das hält sich jetzt ein bisschen die Waage (Rüdiger Schumacher, Köln, 22 July 2004).

[6]   Da ich auch aus diesem anglo-amerikanischen Raum komme, ist für mich eigentlich diese Mischung sehr, sehr wichtig, d.h. einerseits zentrale Punkte der Musik zeigen,

deriving from comparative musicology seemed also to model and shape the contents and methods pertinent to the transmission of ethnomusicological knowledge. For example, course contents on historical perspectives in ethnomusicology resembled an uneven emphasis on different periods in the history of ethnomusicology, such as the German tradition, the European folk tradition or the American perspective. Course contents also often revolved around specific kinds of music, usually traditional non-Western styles, which seems to stem from the subject matters typically studied by comparative musicologists. Yet there was also considerable emphasis on students' active learning through musical participation, rather than just objective and passive knowledge transmission in formal ethnomusicology classes. Such transmission methods seem to resonate with the methods and approaches taken by most ethnomusicologists who – through their anthropological orientation – often wish to understand the meaning behind music making through the experiential portion of the ethnographic process. The transmission of ethnomusicology at universities can thus be traced back to the methods and subject matters pertinent in early comparative musicology or be found in modern ethnomusicology's anthropological tendency. Both influences will be turned to in the following section, beginning with discussions on the differing historical perspectives encountered in the transmission of ethnomusicological knowledge.

Historical Perspectives in the Transmission of Ethnomusicology

Ethnomusicology courses, both in the UK and Germany, frequently contained studies on the historical development of the discipline of ethnomusicology. Whilst this focus was often one among many other pivotal key issues studied, entire ethnomusicology courses discussing historical perspectives were rare. At Queen's University Belfast, for instance, the course *Key Debates in Ethnomusicology* included four history-related sessions with topics such as: looking at the 'other' (as in earliest oriental music studies); looking at 'self' and each other (as in comparative musicology); pioneers in (American) ethnomusicology; British ethnomusicology and British musicology. Interestingly, there existed broad consensus among ethnomusicologists on the 'important' historical periods in the development of ethnomusicology, although the transmission of such topics was also often shaped by ethnomusicologists' concepts and beliefs, and the country in which they transmitted ethnomusicological knowledge. The latter is specifically noteworthy of consideration, which was marked by a bipartite

---

also … ich denke mal, das ist auch die deutsche Seite wiederum, also die Vergleichende Musikwissenschaft …. Ich zeige auch gern Musikbeispiele, Notenbeispiele. Ich meine, das sind Musiker; die können Noten lesen …. Und den Kontext finde ich eigentlich selbstverständlich …. Der ist, denke ich auch für die Musiker sehr wichtig … Material …, mit dem sie sich selber relativieren können … und relativ erleben (Britta Sweers, Rostock, 25 November 2003).

division in approaches, best described as the German – American and European – American historical perspective on ethnomusicology. The following section will illustrate how these viewpoints are transmitted by ethnomusicologists in the UK and Germany.

The German – American Perspective

As noted earlier, at German universities there often existed a strong affinity towards comparative musicology in the formal transmission of ethnomusicological knowledge. Almost half of the course *Einführung in die Musikethnologie 1* at the University of Köln focused on transmitting this approach. Interestingly, the Freie Universität Berlin called its course of study *Studiengang in Vergleichender Musikwissenschaft* (course of study in comparative musicology). In world music courses there also seemed to exist a noticeable emphasis on comparative musicology, evident in a concern with classification and the objective analysis of musical sound, while focusing on universal schemes, tracing music evolution or mapping global culture areas (Cooley, 1997:8). Students also learnt that the methodologies used for the systematic collecting of (folk, exotic or primitive) musics were based on field and laboratory work. This is not to claim that German music-ethnologists are unaware of or uninterested in anthropological emphases, yet besides an interest in anthropological approaches, the German tradition of comparative musicology seemed strongly to pertain to German ethnomusicology.

American-derived ethnomusicology, by contrast, has emerged in opposition to comparative musicology. At the University of Durham, the undergraduate course *Introduction to Ethnomusicology* dealt with the emergence of this new discipline by moving from discussions of early theorists (Erich von Hornbostel, Curt Sachs, Jaap Kunst) towards discussions of later theorists (Alan Merriam, Charles Seeger, Bruno Nettl, John Blacking, Ali Jihad Racy). Interestingly, this course transmitted history in such a way so as to directly link German comparative musicology with American ethnomusicology. This focus on two periods in the history of ethnomusicology, namely German comparative musicology and American anthropology of music was also evident elsewhere. Andrew Killick who had trained as an ethnomusicologist and educator at American institutions provided a student handout entitled *American Ethnomusicology and the Berlin School*. The handout's title and content reflected the view that disciplines other than comparative musicology had played a minor role in the emergence of modern ethnomusicology. This view suggests that modern ethnomusicology emerged in American academia as a direct counter-development to German approaches. Both the Berlin School and American ethnomusicology were transmitted as directly intertwined without many external influences (see also Bohlman, 1992a:129). When such a view was transmitted by an ethnomusicologist, students learnt that since the 1950s ethnomusicology moved away from comparative musicology and its modern-era science paradigm towards more experiential forms of fieldwork. They learnt that ethnomusicologists distanced themselves from classification, description and explanation of music structures and instead valued music as embedded within society and culture. Students thus learnt that the anthropological approach aims at understanding what music means to its creators and listeners by studying music in and as culture. At the same time, however, this historical perspective has also been criticised for being American-centric, notably by ethnomusicologists in Europe.

The European – American Perspective

European ethnomusicologists often emphasised and acknowledged the 'hidden voices' that contributed to the development of current ethnomusicology, whilst criticising their absence in the ethnomusicological discourse.[7] Some ethnomusicologists suggested that 'ethnomusicology largely ... coheres to the journal [*Ethnomusicology*], I suppose, and the society [SEM], at least in their [American] world view .... It means that people who are outside that get a little bit left out of the story .... I think it is more dangerous in the English language' (Jonathan Stock, Sheffield, 13 October 2003). Rüdiger Schumacher agreed that:

> There is [not] much discourse ... which illustrates [the history of ethnomusicology] holistically ... [and] reflects on or looks at the ideology of ethnomusicology, which shows how certain music-ethnological approaches are committed and connected to different intellectual periods in time .... Local, regional traditions ... are not so well-known, or perhaps deliberately silenced by some because the general historical overviews of ethnomusicology usually ... [include] comparative musicology in Berlin ..., whereby at times this is rather illustrated as monstrous or abstruse. And then it only [concludes] with the developments after the second world war in the US, and otherwise *tabula rasa*. And that I cannot imagine. We have called this 'hidden voices', question mark. There are thus many voices, which have not yet entered consciousness .... In many countries in the Eastern European region other people have developed their own valuable methods for research and presentation .... That is, in my opinion, necessary [for a] well-balanced history of ethnomusicology, and not just to select the so-called international highlights. (Rüdiger Schumacher, Köln, 22 July 2004)[8]

---

[7]   For example, the programme of the XXI European Seminar in Ethnomusicology, organised by ethnomusicologist Rüdiger Schumacher (Köln; August 2005) included five sessions (containing 15 papers) on *Hidden Voices – European Traditions in Ethnomusicology*, which acknowledged the (hidden) European contribution to modern ethnomusicology.

[8]   Eines dieser Themen geht um ... Traditionen der europäischen Musikethnologie, also vor allen Dingen lokale, regionale Traditionen. Man könnte auch sagen, nationale Traditionen, die nicht so bekannt sind, vielleicht auch bewusst von manchen totgeschwiegen werden, weil die allgemeinen Geschichtsüberblicke der Musikethnologie sehen ja so aus, da steht eben ein bisschen über die Vergleichende Musikwissenschaft in Berlin ... drin, wobei das manchmal ein bisschen als monströs oder abstrus dargestellt wird, und dann

Some European ethnomusicologists therefore transmitted to their students the ways in which ethnomusicology has also absorbed influences from other disciplines, including the European folklore movement. At the Hochschule für Musik und Theater Rostock, the study of European folklore appeared frequently in lectures and classes, which reflected the ethnomusicologist's own specialisation in British folk music. One session focused on Bela Bartók's *Mikrokosmos* and included examples of his field recordings that have informed Bartók's composition, emphasising that a fuller understanding of this music necessitated (besides musical analysis) also contextualisation. At the University of Sheffield, meanwhile, students learnt that the development of ethnomusicology has been shaped by numerous disciplines, including the European folklore movement and early studies of Native American music. Providing a concise overview to draw comparisons (Figure 2.1), Jonathan Stock wished to avoid the danger of transmitting an American-centric historical perspective on ethnomusicology. This more holistic view on the development of modern ethnomusicology discards the notion that the predominant influence came just from American anthropology. Instead, Jonathan Stock also emphasised the difference in fieldwork and folksong classification in the European folklore movement that tended towards scientific approaches in order to collect, compare and explain music as object for musical analysis:

I wanted to make clear … that we come from different places, and that it works differently in one country or continent than in another …. Overtly American concerns… are not the only concerns … [i.e.] von Hornbostel is only important as he has influenced those guys in New York, and so on, which is … kind of selective history …. I think, to an extent they [American ethnomusicologists] are right [to suggest that modern ethnomusicology is 'American'], but only to an extent …. If you were Italian, or French, or German, or whatever, you'd be reading the national journals in those places, and it would be very easy for them to turn to their local language research, whereas perhaps in English … we turn to English-language research, which is all by Americans anyway … so we slip most easily into that mistake. (Jonathan Stock, Sheffield, 13 October 2003)

---

heißt es nur eben die Entwicklung nach dem 2. Weltkrieg in den USA, und sonst *tabula rasa*. Und das kann ich mir nicht vorstellen. Das haben wir dann genannt 'Hidden Voices' Fragezeichen. Es gibt also sehr viele Stimmen, die bislang noch nicht ins Bewusstsein gedrungen sind …. Dass in vielen Ländern im osteuropäischen Bereich ganz andere Leute ganz wertvolle eigene Methoden auch der Forschung und der Darstellung entwickelt haben, das ist eigentlich gar nicht bisher in's Bewusstsein vorgedrungen. Das ist meines Erachtens notwendig, wenn man wirklich eine ausgewogene Geschichte der Musikethnologie schreiben will, und eben nicht nur die sogenannten internationalen Highlights rausgreift (Rüdiger Schumacher, Köln, 22 July 2004).

	Fieldwork	Cross-cultural comparison	Insiders' voices	Music-focused
Folklore movement	X			X
Comparative Musicology		X		X
Historical Musicology			X	X
Anthropology/ Native American studies	X	X	X	X
Modern Ethnomusicology	X	X (certain aspects)	X	X

Figure 2.1   Summary of key-points on the historical perspectives of ethnomusicology by Jonathan Stock; University of Sheffield, 13 October 2003

Interestingly, the concerns and approaches of folklorists somewhat resonate with those of comparative musicologists, both stressing so-called 'scientific' approaches and the 'authentic' in music.[9] This latter concern with tradition was also often significant among current ethnomusicologists, both in their research and the transmission of ethnomusicological knowledge at universities.

Transmitting Musics from Here and Now? Ethnomusicology's Subject Matters

Many early ethnomusicologists agreed that their subject matter included all musics, except popular entertainment music and Western art music (Kunst, 1959), and many have until recently maintained this focus on musical authenticity and so-called authentic traditions (Feld, 2000:10). However, a concern with tradition and authenticity is nowadays widely criticised for its blatant romanticisation of the native and natural in contrast to the civilised and modern (Frith, 2000:308). Modern ethnomusicology's subject matter thus encompasses not only authentic non-Western styles, but also art and commercial popular musics. Whilst early ethnomusicology was thus characterised by discovery and exploration, today's

---

[9]   Folklorists' concern with collecting, analysing and classifying so-called 'traditional' folk music has of course opened up in recent years, and nowadays folk scholars and musicians also often regard fusion music (folk rock, electronic folk, etc) as a legitimate subject matter.

'ethnomusicological research is less a discovering research ... simply because today, one does not just travel relatively blue-eyed into the world ... to discover something ... completely new, that nobody has ever heard ... and documented. Instead, it is concrete, very specific questions based on an existing foundation, which initiate research. Thus this general [notion of] discovery ... plays a lesser role in modern ethnomusicology' (Rüdiger Schumacher, Köln, 22 July 2004).[10] Despite these shifts in the discipline's scope and focus, some ethnomusicologists still today wish to explore and discover older repertoires characterised by recognised aspects of the tradition:

> When I set out to do my fieldwork, I didn't know how much music I would still find ... with its primary functions intact ... I had read about musics dying out .... People kept saying it's like a swansong; it's breathing its last breath. But then I would arrive at these fairs, half way up a mountain in the middle of the night and just find lots of people singing, improvising and .... I would ask: 'What's that song you just sang?' and they would say: 'It's about last year about...' It was still happening! ... To find that it was happening for real was deeply satisfying at lots of different levels, particularly since it seemed quite happily to coexist with what was at surface level in the towns ... the cosmopolitan .... But then in particular, they were still creating, often quite deliberately, spaces and contexts where they can operate in the old way, which seemed to be in space and time apart from the cosmopolitan. (Caroline Bithell, Bangor, 8 October 2003)

Similarly, much educational discourse is based on world musics that are folk or traditional, which results from the fact that ethnomusicologists write about the often traditional musics they specialise in. Examples include writings by Jonathan Stock (1991, 2002b) who examined possible ways of teaching traditional Chinese *erhu* music in schools or colleges, whilst Robert Kwami (1995) proposed a particular framework for teaching traditional West African music in educational institutions. Some ethnomusicologists discussed the transmission of Indian (traditional) art music in the West (Farrell, 1992), while others evaluated pedagogic methods for transmitting non-Western traditional musical instruments, such as the *mbira* (Marx, 1990; Klinger, 1996) and *tabla* (Farrell, 1997), also offering suggestions for transferring traditional teaching methods from India (Farrell, 1986) and Ghana (Wiggins, 1996) into Western formal education. Student textbooks often similarly focus on so-called traditional world musics. Thus certain other types of music have

---

[10]   Die musikethnologische Forschung ist heute weniger eine entdeckende Forschung ... einfach weil man heute nicht mehr relativ blauäugig in alle Welt fährt, und jetzt will ich mal entdecken was es gibt ... was ganz Neues, was noch nie jemand gehört ... und dokumentiert hat. Sondern es sind heute eben doch sehr konkrete, sehr spezifische, auf einem bestimmten, bereits existierenden Fundament aufbauende Fragestellungen, die die Forschung bewegen. So dieses allgemeine Entdecken spielt in der Musikethnologie eigentlich weniger eine Rolle (Rüdiger Schumacher, Köln, 22 July 2004).

until recently been absent in educational discourse written by ethnomusicologists, among them Western art music and European folklore. Ethnomusicologists instead often focus on foreign cultures, a focus that can uphold binary oppositions between self and other.

Yet how are modern ethnomusicology's claims to a more inclusive stance negotiated and realised in the transmission of ethnomusicology? Here, I found that ethnomusicologists' focus of research (e.g. traditional foreign musics) indeed modelled the subject matters transmitted at universities, as world music courses were dominated by musics that are traditional and not from the West. At the University of Durham, I encountered an emphasis on 'the study of types of music that do not belong to the Western art-music tradition (i.e. oriental, African, Irish folk, etc.) …, including ethnic musics' (Music Department Handbook 2003/04), whilst at Rostock, 'art music is normally rarely covered in a lecture' (Britta Sweers, Rostock, 24 November 2003).[11] Where the subject matter was more open and did include popular music, for instance, this was often uneven in emphasis by comparison to more traditional styles. Some ethnomusicologists explained that the East Asian music course at SOAS 'has maybe twenty percent of pop music in it …, which is a matter of staff interest' (David Hughes, SOAS, 11 November 2003), and 'the way I put everything together very much reflects my own interest' (Hae-kyung Um, Belfast, 18 November 2003). In contrast to world music courses, ethnomusicology courses did include popular and Western musics more frequently, yet still reflected a rather separatist approach that differentiated between traditional and popular styles. Yet whilst an element of popular musics was evident in these courses, only a handful of courses were entirely based on popular styles. In some instances, discussions of popular musics were discussed in one or two sessions, whilst in other instances, popular musics occurred more frequently throughout a course, for instance in *Music in Africa* at the University of Wales (Bangor) where Caroline Bithell strongly advocated the inclusion of popular musics:

> When I first designed that module, I was also thinking of appealing beyond the little ethno-group who had taken the first year course as a pre-requisite, and I was looking more towards the popular music people as well, who also come at it to some extent from a sociological perspective, although they also do pop music composition too. So it is in that social, political area as well …. I thought it was an ideal continent to present, not so much in a sort of ethnomusicological ghetto or exotic ghetto … looking at the variety of musics, not just traditional music, or folk music …. There is much scope to bring in popular music as well …. So it is part of a move to get it out of the ethnomusicology box … which is important politically, in particular not to see Africa as 'traditional' and the rest of the world as moving on … so going against some of those prejudices. (Caroline Bithell, Bangor, 15 October 2003)

---

[11]   Dass eine Vorlesung auch Kunstmusik behandelt, ist normalerweise eher selten (Britta Sweers, Rostock, 24 November 2003).

In Germany, Rüdiger Schumacher similarly offered a course in world music or 'world beat ... and particularly ... how it is to be understood ... [including] the important mechanisms of production, distribution and reception ... and genre-specific topics, such as *Rai* and *Salsa*' (Köln, 22 July 2004).[12] Britta Sweers, meanwhile, felt that 'as it is an introduction to world music, the idea simply is, on one side that they are enabled to listen to the traditional, but then also that what so to speak can be heard at the outer surface. That means, with *mbira, isacathamiya* etc, I have of course also played Paul Simon ... so that they can realise the different levels, and relate these to one another' (Rostock, 24 November 2003).[13] By focusing more often on popular styles in students' encounters with world musics, ethnomusicologists wished to challenge students' preconceptions while making the music more real and relevant to these novice learners. Some ethnomusicologists even argued that the transmission of ethnomusicology should begin with a discovery of students' own musics and then extend to the expressions of others. They advocated a movement from the local to the global so as to transfer knowledge from known to new musics (Campbell, 2004:128; Killick, 2000:14). Some courses indeed reflected this approach, which also integrated examples of Western musics, both from art and popular genres. Jonathan Stock, for instance, included musical examples for ethnographic illustrations taken from 'here and now' on the basis that 'students may still have the impression that ethnomusicologists only study foreign people' (Sheffield, 6 October 2003). Such emphases on transmitting all musics, including musics at home and contemporary musical styles reflect modern ethnomusicology's distancing from earlier models of comparative musicology and folklore studies by moving towards an anthropological approach for musical understanding. Caroline Bithell agreed that 'the central defining point is looking at ... music ... in the context of the people who are making that music .... For me it is actually the people being there that is important in being an ethnomusicologist myself' (Bangor, 1 October 2003). Meanwhile, Jonathan Stock intentionally blended all kinds of musics in *Seminars in Ethnomusicology*:

> The main point of this session was to convey that music is socially constructed, and because society differs from place to place, so too does their music ....
> I deliberately chose different music: traditional, religious, irreligious, popular, classical ... to cross time periods and continents ... in order to raise consciousness.

---

[12] World music als Kurs ... world beat ... und zwar ausgehend von den wichtigsten Grundlagen was wollen wir darunter verstehen ... die wesentlichen Mechanismen von Produktion, Distribution und Rezeption ... und genre-spezifische Sachen, wie *Rai* und *Salsa* (Rüdiger Schumacher, Köln, 22 July 2004).

[13] Da es eine Einführung in die Weltmusik ist, ist die Idee einfach, dass sie einerseits das Traditionelle zu hören bekommen, und dann aber auch das, was man sozusagen an der Außenoberfläche hört, d.h. bei *mbira, isacathamiya,* usw. Dann habe ich auch natürlich Paul Simon gespielt ... so dass sie die unterschiedlichen Ebenen auch wahrnehmen können, und das in Bezug setzen können (Britta Sweers, Rostock, 24 November 2003).

> To include many different examples makes the point that if we don't know what
> music is, then at least we've got an open mind. (Jonathan Stock, Sheffield, 30
> September 2003)

It is clear from these discussions that many ethnomusicologists applied the
anthropological emphasis in the transmission of ethnomusicological knowledge. It
is based on the idea that music is a human expression. Modern ethnomusicologists
thus discard an emphasis on subject matters for study and instead value the
particular approaches suitable for understanding people making music (Titon,
1997:91). The aim of research is to assert the extent to which music is meaningful
to the people involved in its performance. Yet the occasional focus on more
traditional, non-Western musics in the teaching of ethnomusicologists reflects the
work of earlier ethnomusicologists whose concerns were still very similar to that of
comparative musicologists (Merriam, 1977:192,195). Thus some ethnomusicology
and world music courses may still have to accommodate contemporary issues and
phenomena, such as globalisation and hybridisation. Although this occurs, it is
only rarely integrated well within courses, resembling a separatist approach that
divides musics into clearly defined categories. While some ethnomusicologists
may have become more interested in hybrid musics in their research, they have
yet to design more hybridised and holistic world musics courses. A model for
the transmission of ethnomusicology that more strongly acknowledged notions of
intercultural exchange would also mirror more current discourse on globalisation
and locality.

Learning Ethnomusicology by *Doing*

Ethnomusicologists often advocated that 'ethnomusicology is what
ethnomusicologists do' (David Hughes, SOAS, 11 November 2003), and in their
research, ethnomusicologists often use active participation both as listeners and
makers of music, whilst stressing the experiential portion of the ethnographic
process. Music education too is believed to be most effective when entailing active
musical participation and involvement, and in their roles as teachers and educators,
ethnomusicologists often engaged students in hands-on musical experiences. They
stressed that the greatest value in learning about world music for students is to be
actively involved in it, as it can lead towards deeper respect for the special skills
required, improve students' listening and motor skills, and transfer more broadly
to a deeper awareness of music's role in and as culture. Such an experiential and
reflexive learning is often deeper and longer-lasting for students, and resonates
strongly with modern ethnomusicology's anthropological orientation. From this
emphasis on *doing* in the transmission of ethnomusicology, together with the variety
of learning activities aiming at students' active involvement, a tripartite model will
be derived in this book that groups these activities into listening, performing and
constructing ethnomusicology. The model thus highlights the experiential portion

of students' active and (in some cases) social knowledge construction. It is also the first comprehensive model for ethnomusicology pedagogy in higher education.

There already exist educational frameworks, specifically in the area of music education (Boyce-Tillman, 1996:73; Swanwick, 1979:55), whilst some also focus more specifically on world music in school education (Skelton, 2004; Wade, 2004). Yet none of these models has yet been fully recognised in music pedagogy nor applied widely in higher education, although there are attempts to think along such lines. Witzleben (2004), for example suggests that Rice's (1987) tripartite approach to studying musical traditions can be applied to the transmission of ethnomusicology at Western universities, while Patricia Shehan Campbell has proposed a field of study called world music pedagogy that merges the disciplines of ethnomusicology and music education (Campbell, 2004). Nonetheless, there is currently no widely accepted model for ethnomusicology education, which is further evident in the recent founding of the *Arbeitsgruppe Musikpädagogik und MusikEthnologie* (Forum for music pedagogy and ethnomusicology) by German music-ethnologists and educators on the basis that 'intercultural music pedagogy resembles a focal point in discourse. Until now however ... there has hardly emerged music-pedagogical research and conceptualisation in Germany that is informed by modern music-ethnology' (Invitation letter by AMMe, Bielefeld, 12 March 2006).[14] For this reason, a model for the transmission of ethnomusicology is needed that encompasses students' active experiencing of ethnomusicology through listening, performing and constructing. Focusing on doing rather than on the subject matters for study, the model resonates with what ethnomusicologists essentially do in their work. Such a model involves students actively in the experiential portion of the learning process, reflecting a concern with an approach to understanding people making music. Consequently, the model provides a particularly suitable framework for the book in illustrating students' multifaceted experiences during their exposure to activities involving listening, performing and constructing ethnomusicology.

Learning by Listening

Listening to music activates people's minds and bodies to enter into a deeper involvement with it, and ethnomusicologists often placed considerable emphasis on students' listening experiences as they themselves have often become acculturated with non-literate, oral musical traditions. Learning about music as sound reflects

---

[14]   Liebe Kolleginnen und Kolleginnen, Interkulturelle Musikpädagogik nimmt eine zentrale Stellung in der öffentlichen Diskussion ein. Bisher sind jedoch in den Disziplinen Musikethnologie und Musikpädagogik in Deutschland nur wenige Erkenntnisse gewonnen worden, und auch eine praktische Umsetzung ist noch nicht erfolgt .... Umgekehrt hat eine seitens der modernen Musikethnologie gestützte musikpädagogische Forschung und Theoriebildung in Deutschland bisher kaum stattgefunden (Einladungsbrief der AMMe, Arbeitsgruppe Musikpädagogik und MusikEthnologie, Bielefeld, 12 March 2006).

ethnomusicologists' concern with the listener and belief in the importance of informed and accurate listening for music making (Blacking, 1973:10). Learning through listening at universities typically included live and recorded world musics performances on the basis that 'acquiring familiarity with the sounds of the musics of the world is an important objective of the course' (Options book 2004/05, Music Department, Goldsmiths College of London). Listening helped students to open their ears to the timbres of instruments as well as the melodic and rhythmic components of the music. As a result, ethnomusicologists often disregarded musical notation and analysis as a sole means for musical understanding:

> From my point of view, analysis is much more about listening. Looking at the thing on paper ... helps you to work out the patterns but I want them to listen to the textures you can't put on paper. (Caroline Bithell, Bangor, 22 October 2003)

Whilst listening to musical aspects is clearly central to a deeper musical understanding, listening to ethnomusicologists in lectures and seminars was yet another means for students actively to participate in the learning process. This form of listening enabled students to search for meaning behind the music and to move beyond mere musical understanding towards recognising concepts of identity, authenticity and democracy in the music cultures they encountered. These observations have informed the book's second part, which opens with Chapter 3 illustrating students' listening experiences in the context of their personal and musical identities, and perceptions of self and other. The theme of listening to ethnomusicology continues in Chapter 4 by explaining students' (often) preconceived ideas of authenticity and tradition, which were reinforced at times by the physical, material, literate and sonic spaces, as well as ethnicity of the ethnomusicologist encountered at university. The subsequent Chapter 5 illuminates how listening to ethnomusicology impacted on students' move towards tolerance and compassion and a heightened sense of democracy, which will bring Part II of the book to a close.

Learning by Performing

Direct participation in music making often complemented the more theoretically-based listening to ethnomusicology. It is a form of ethnomusicological learning that seeks an understanding of people's rich and intertwined experiences through direct exposure in musical activity. Educationists have long recognised the value of performance for developing musical understandings. To many ethnomusicologists, however, learning by performing is also a way of sharing the cultural and individual experiences of a music culture (Blacking, 1973:54). Performance practice was thus widely valued in ethnomusicology programmes in the UK and Germany, although institutional constraints often hindered its full integration into the curriculum. As a result, performing ethnomusicology also involved seeing-hearing-trying of musical instruments and occasional workshops led by guest musicians (Chapter 6), resembling *animation* that often generated heightened levels of enjoyment in students. Whilst this will be the concern of the opening chapter of Part III, the subsequent Chapter 7 will focus more directly on longitudinal performance practice, which also included learning to perform as a technique for research. Often culminating in a final performance, this form of performing ethnomusicology emphasised music-as-music and often triggered performance anxiety in students. Since the emphasis on students' enjoyment and anxiety is so pivotal in the discussions of Chapters 6 and 7, Chapter 8 has been included here to illustrate the ways in which these emotions can be explained and understood as socially and culturally constructed. Chapter 9 will then provide a contrasting example of performance practice through performance ethnography and a focus on music-as-culture. More generally, Part III will locate performing ethnomusicology along a tripartite continuum so as to highlight students' differing experiences during the discovering of material culture (Chapter 6), expression and from (Chapter 7), and value (Chapter 9) in university education.

Learning by Constructing

It is often argued that the deepest-level musical learning results only from musical composition, yet the research revealed that musical composition in a non-Western style was typically absent in UK and German higher education. Nonetheless, there existed alternative, equally creative learning activities, and these included the constructing of musical transcriptions, the writing of ethnomusicological texts and the making of ethnographic films. Transcription, ethnography and ethnographic film are central to ethnomusicology as a discipline and will thus inform the discussions on the constructing of ethnomusicology in Part IV of the book. Opening the discussions on musical transcription is the role of Chapter 10, which will illustrate ethnomusicologists' emphasis on different transcription approaches with the aim of gaining an emic understanding of music and culture. This will be juxtaposed to students' approaches, which reflected an appropriation of world musics into Western musical paradigms, and thus their eurocentric perspectives to non-Western musics. Constructing ethnomusicological texts, the focus of Chapter 11, was another pertinent activity during students' learning, which required them to conceptualise their fieldwork experiences in a local community or culture, during which they connected with real musicians and audiences while writing an ethnography. The discussions will illustrate students' strategies for data analysis and interpretation, and explicate numerous factors that impacted on these strategies, including the reading of ethnomusicological discourse, ethical considerations, supervisors' feedback and examiner recommendations. The chapter will conclude how constructing ethnography impacted on students' attitudes and perspectives, and triggered a transformation through their critical reflections on self and others. Chapter 12 will be concerned with the mediation of fieldwork experience through ethnomusicological uses of film and video in formal ethnomusicology education. In the opening of the chapter it will be argued that whilst ethnomusicologists frequently seek out various visual media to bring music cultures alive in the university classroom, little attention is currently paid to constructing ethnomusicological film so as to allow students to mediate their own fieldwork experiences in audiovisual ways. The first part will focus more generally on the use of film and video in the university classroom, including the kinds of film and video used in formal world music classes and the pedagogical strategies employed by ethnomusicologists. A brief section will also show how and to what extent film and video has the capacity to mediate fieldwork experiences by enabling students to pay attention not only to musical sounds but also to the visual dimension of a given music-cultural practice. The second part will then focus on ethnomusicological filmmaking, opening with discussions on the ways in which ethnomusicological filmmaking is formalised in the ethnomusicology curriculum at one institution. Subsequent discussions will focus on the experiences of one student in constructing an ethnomusicological film, whilst illustrating the considerations taken during the filming, editing and structuring of the film, as well as reflecting on the process of filmmaking. The chapter will close with an assessment of the value of ethnomusicological uses of film and video for ethnomusicology education by assessing their impact on students' attitudes and perspectives towards world music cultures.

PART II
Listening to Ethnomusicology

Listening provides firsthand encounters with a broad representation of the world's musical expressions. In its simplest form, listening means hearing music. Yet listening may also refer to hearing the voices of people making music and looking for meaning behind the music. Truly listening to these voices has the capacity to generate deeper understanding, appreciation and respect for music and its makers. This is the concern of the chapters presented here, which will illustrate students' often complex and entwined listening-based experiences as they try to make sense of particular educational encounters. More specifically, Chapter 3 will examine the relationship between students' experiences of listening to the world's musics and their makers, and the impact of those experiences on students' sociocultural identities, demonstrated in their expressions of taste and motivation. The discussions will take into account that existing experience can inform the process and contexts of listening, and these experiences differ for each individual as they emerge from personal motivational and interpretational relevancies, even while they are shaped by social processes. Students' experiences will thus be situated within the broader social and cultural contexts in which they are embedded. This same idea is followed in Chapter 4, whilst focusing on the role played by ideas of authenticity in directing students' listening experiences of the world's musics. The final Chapter 5 will consider the impact of students' musical experiencing on moves away from canonising – the institutionalisation of certain music cultures for study over others – and towards expressing a form of global democracy, a belief in equality between all people and their musics. Does ethnomusicology have the capacity to increase students' awareness, tolerance, understanding and acceptance of the world's different cultures, its peoples and their music? How does listening to ethnomusicology produce sense and convey meaning to students? Overall, it is argued that whilst students' concepts of identity, authenticity and democracy are socially and culturally constructed, they are at the same time shaped and modelled by their experiences of listening to ethnomusicology.

Chapter 3
Listening to Music, Experiencing Identity

During students' experiencing of the world's musics in ethnomusicology classes, the concept of identity emerged as a particularly pertinent theme. This was evident in students' imagining of belonging to particular social groups. Music can indeed represent a source for the construction of a coherent sociocultural identity and become an object in which groups of people can see their central values held and reflected (Stokes, 1994, 2003a). The connection that existed between particular groups of students and 'their' musics was specifically constructed and negotiated through students' expression of musical taste. As a result, certain musics included those with similar and excluded those with different musical preferences. Music was thus either integrative or disintegrative, whilst playing a pivotal role in forming social relationships or separating between different groups of students (see also Barber-Kersovan, 2004). Musical taste may be understood in two ways, namely by referring to people's critical judgements about artistic works so as to differentiate between 'good' and 'bad' music, or by describing people's aesthetic choices that work symbolically to reflect their sociocultural identities (Leonard and Strachan, 2003b:373). The first view assumes that taste is 'natural' and governed by autonomous psychological or biological factors; taste is personal and idiosyncratic. The second view, by contrast, suggests that taste is artificial and socially shaped. It advocates that aesthetic judgement is informed by the social identity of the audience, reflected in its social status, class, age, race, gender, political and religious persuasion, and geographical location. Both views will be considered in the following discussions of students' musical taste as a mediator of sociocultural identity.

Taste as a Natural Concept: 'Good' and 'Bad' World Music

At its most basic level, music is a symbol of identity through its sound, which contains and resonates with distinctive meanings and memories. For example, sound can convey a sense of time, place and tradition through instrumentation, rhythms or special playing techniques. Further layers of meaning may be derived from the lyrics, melody, instrumental practice, performance style and dance accompanying the music. Westerners, for example, are often said to prefer music that is fast in tempo, and that evolves around tonal centres (consonance), has regular rhythm and a clear melody (with many different pitches), and that contains regular phrasing, bright timbres and high complexity (Shehan, 1986; Brittin, 1996; Fung, 1994, 1996; LeBlanc *et al.*, 1999). Westerners apparently also prefer instrumental to vocal musical styles (Fung, 1994). Yet whilst broad generalisations about people's musical preferences must be treated with caution (the following discussions will exemplify that it is difficult to sustain sweeping generalisations about people's aesthetic musical choices), I indeed found that connections existed between groups of students and different kinds of world musics. For example, the majority of students 'enjoy[ed] listening … particularly to Latin American music' (Carolina, Bangor, 15 December 2003) because of 'the catchy rhythms. Latin music itself is interesting' (group interview, Sheffield, 7 November 2003), a view also supported by other research into students' musical listening preferences (Fung, 1994, 1996).[1] Similarly, some European musical styles were preferred by many students for their 'clear, Western melody and [apparently] less complex rhythms', whereas Eastern European music sounded 'out of tune' (Rebecca, Sheffield, 17 October 2003) and was thus less preferred.

Sub-Saharan African music, by comparison, was frowned upon by some students, even though Fung (1996) argued that Westerners prefer this music, a view supported by Shehan (1986) on the basis that the music's structural organisation into repeated verse-refrain resonates with Western music. Yet when confronted with Ghanaian drumming, the group of Sheffield students expressed strong dislike and commented that 'it's all so awful' (Andrea, Sheffield, 10 October 2003). They seemed to prefer melodic rather than rhythmic musical examples that had a 'clear' tone and texture. Graham further commented that 'I find the instruments quite irritating, especially the little metal bits [referring to the rattling metal parts, beer bottle tops and other additions found on some African musical instruments] …. If you could take off all these metal bits and make it a purer tone, I'd like that much rather!' (Sheffield, 17 October 2003). Meanwhile, African popular music was more frequently welcomed by the students because 'it has a regular phrasing, there is a clear melody and the instruments are cool. The rhythms in African pop music are really interesting … I don't like any weird instruments' (*ibid.*). To Graham's surprise, he even enjoyed listening to the music:

> That bit on African pop music wasn't bad actually. It was a lot better than I thought it's gonna be. It did sound quite good. When he said, it would be an example of African pop, I thought 'Here we go …' [with a derogatory tone of voice]. (Graham, Sheffield, 17 October 2003)

During their encounters with Asian musics, students expressed mixed views as to their preferences, even though Fung (1996) found that Westerners typically dislike Asian music. For example, the traditional Taiwanese ensemble at the University of Sheffield was quite unpopular, many students strongly disliking the sounds and

---

[1]   Fung's research seemed appropriate for comparison to the results presented in this book, as his research included non-music majors and students on a fundamentals class for education majors aged 18 to 36 (1994), and music majors and non-music majors at undergraduate level aged 18 to 69 (1996), of whom the majority were American.

timbres of the music. Graham, again, claimed that 'I hate the timbres so much that I would never join this ensemble. I just couldn't stand the sound. I get a headache …. It's just not nice. It's horrible … It's just a horrible tone' (*ibid.*). Sian agreed. This kind of music was 'difficult to listen to. It is actually horrible to listen to with its loud, continuous reed instruments' (Sian, Sheffield, 24 October 2003). Students' dislike for this particular genre was clearly a response to the 'unusual' timbres and textures often found in Asian musics (see also Shehan, 1986). Yet to other students, Asian musics were hugely interesting. Christopher, a young male student, expressed strong interest in Japanese culture and court music, which 'pleases and affects me. It's not about musical characteristics but its atmospheric character. The music uses the pentatonic scale, has no harmony and moves quite slow. It is atmospheric and does something to me …' (Sheffield, 20 November 2003). Meanwhile, West Asian (Middle Eastern) musics were also perceived differently by different students, depending obviously on the kind of music encountered. Iranian classical music performed on the *santur* appealed strongly to most of the Sheffield students, as 'it sounded familiar …. It sounded really nice because it had a pure sound …. Yeah, the sound was very clear, unlike African music which is buzzing …. It sounded tonal …. It was easier to listen to. I would like to know whether all *santur* music sounds like that, whether it's always such an easy listening' (group interview, Sheffield, 24 October 2003). Other Middle Eastern musics, by contrast, were often disliked due to the microtones, heterophonic texture, embellishments, irregular rhythms and wailing melodies.

Taste as a Result of Familiarity

The previous discussions show that it is ambiguous to derive broad generalisations about students' aesthetic choices with regard to large-scale musical categories like Latin American, African, Asian, including Middle Eastern musics. Yet at the same time, the research conducted with UK and German students revealed that at times there existed certain patterns in their aesthetic choices, and these seemed to be shaped by social and other outside pressures. It is thus questionable whether musical taste is a natural concept, as students' preferences were subject to outside forces. This included musical familiarity, as students tended to prefer world musics that resonated with Western styles and idioms, often commenting that 'I like music that has a pretty melody and sounds familiar, that has some familiarity to Western scales and is memorable' (Rebecca, Sheffield, 17 October 2003):

> I liked best the music of Latin America and some sub-Saharan African music. I found it harder to listen to Asian music because it's much further from our music. Asian music seems more … we are more exposed to Latin and African music, I guess. You probably never hear Chinese music. (Rebecca, Sheffield, 19 December 2003)

> Non-Western music is the sort of thing I find difficult to listen to. I need to study
> it a bit more before I begin to appreciate it. (Emma, Durham, 27 October 2003)

Students were clearly unsure about musics with which they were totally unfamiliar.
They experienced these musics as meaningless (see also Budd, 1992:162).
Meanwhile, in approaching a musical transcription exercise, a group of Sheffield
students selected examples that they liked and believed to be easily transcribed.
Here, a 'likeable' and 'easy' example was typically a musical track that sounded
familiar to Western music:

> I chose this example because I thought it would be easier to write down, because
> some of them I can't imagine how to transcribe them. (Rebecca, Sheffield, 17
> October 2003)

> I picked it, because it sounded fairly easy to transcribe for a start, and it was one
> that I liked and I could listen to. (Christopher, Sheffield, 20 November 2003)

> I have chosen a piece from Papua New Guinea because I felt that this would be
> fine to go ahead and transcribe. (Edward, Sheffield, 24 October 2003)

> I have picked a flamenco piece for voice and guitar because I am a guitarist ....
> It doesn't sound ridiculously hard ... so hopefully I can work it out. (Graham,
> Sheffield, 24 October 2003)

Students regarded an 'easy' musical example to consist of a melody with
accompaniment, and that was melodic, rather than rhythmic. Tuning also played a
role, as students chose examples with a clear, Western-tuned melody. 'It was one
I thought ... I could probably pick up because there is not much going on. There
is just one instrument, two sounds. One sound is fairly constant, it doesn't really
change much, and then the other sound above that, it's just picking the rhythms
and notes up' (Christopher, Sheffield, 20 November 2003). Clearly, what seemed
familiar and felt good also often appeared to be safe. Familiarity created in students
a feeling of comfort, thereby somewhat legitimising the possibility of becoming
attracted to the music. Personal experience of and familiarity with musical styles
were thus important, as 'it's music that I have personal feelings for, not music that
I'm quite distant from .... It makes it a lot more interesting to learn about' (Mary,
Liverpool, 15 March 2005). Meanwhile, to students who were already familiar
with other cultures, the world's musics seemed far more accessible:

> I have chosen all modules in Asian musics because I've got some experience
> from my travels.... In my travels I went to East Asia and Southeast Asia, so I
> thought I've got some experience of these cultures ... and know what it's like.
> (Eva, SOAS, 11 November 2003)

I have chosen [the module] *Music Cultures* because I like Arabic music. I studied *oud* in Iraq before I came here and I've played some Afro-Cuban music on guitar and some percussion. (Mark, Bangor, 15 December 2003)

I chose this module *Music in Africa* to get more of an insight into the continent I love, and to the music that moves me so much. I lived in Kenya for the first five years of my life. Africa has always been in my blood and I have travelled all over. My parents live in Malawi at the moment. (David, Bangor, 15 December 2003)

Those students who already had experiences with some of the world's cultures and musics were also more likely to express preferences towards newly encountered musical styles. Listening to these newer musics during their university studies in turn led towards familiarity with and thus preference for these styles. During this process, newer musics became more understood and valued as a result of transmission and exposure (see also Shehan, 1986:154). In other words, listening leads to experience, whilst experience leads to preference for musics of other cultures (Brittin, 1996:329). Students indeed confirmed this claim:

I learnt to play the *tabla* during my studies. At first, I didn't really like Indian music. I found it too repetitive. But now that I started the *tabla*, I got more into it. I like Indian music much more now. (Alexandra, Goldsmiths, 11 February 2004)

At GCSE I hated *gamelan* but actually studying it and watching that video snippet made me reconsider! (John, Manchester, 9 May 2005)

Hae-kyung Um equally felt that at first listening encounter, 'most students find it extremely uncomfortable because they don't know what to hear, what to make of it …. Then they really begin to hear what makes the music like that. They even begin to enjoy the heterophony, which is not very comfortable for many people' (Belfast, 18 November 2003). Familiarity with musical styles and idioms heightened students' preferences for new musics, either through the music's resemblance to Western styles or through students' experiences of newer musics. Yet whilst students' aesthetic musical choices may be a result of familiarity, they are also shaped by outside social and cultural pressures. The next section will focus on this idea whilst illustrating taste as a sociocultural construct in students' negotiation of identity.

Constructing Difference through Music: Taste as a Social Construct

Students' musical aesthetic judgements are often socioculturally shaped, namely by peers, parents, teachers and institutions (Shehan, 1986:158), as well as social values, popular fashion and personal whim (Blacking, 1987:123). For example, George reflected that 'my parents bought me a *shakuhachi*; they are very supportive' (York, 6 May 2004), whilst Xavier found that 'my interest in ethnomusicology was very powerfully defined by this friend of mine …. This conversation was a very powerful experience in my life …. It inspired me to study ethnomusicology' (Goldsmiths, 12 February 2004). Taste can thereby function at a symbolic level for people to distinguish between and express themselves in different social positions (Bourdieu, 1984). Among university students, peer approval played a significant role in shaping musical taste, which in turn led towards students' assimilating into a particular peer group. The group of Sheffield students, for example, agreed on their dislike of African traditional music by stating: 'Who would actually listen to or buy this?', agreeing that they would never do so. Graham pulled a face while commenting, 'Imagine you say to your mates "Look what CD I've got"', which resulted in all the other students' laughter (group interview, Sheffield, 10 October 2003). Clearly, peer judgement impacted on individuals' sense of self-affirmation (see further Pitts, 2005) and played a significant role in shaping students' musical tastes. They tended to listen to and enjoy the same music listened to by other students they liked, or with whom they identified. This is further exemplified by the fact that many students found it difficult to deal with the rather 'unfamiliar encounters' (John, Manchester, 9 May 2005). Students often described their non-Western encounters as weird, different and in some way other. Since most students are novice learners of musics outside the European tradition, they thus found it problematic to think about and deal with the unfamiliar in music (see also Gammon, 1999:5). Listening to a whispering song from Burundi, for instance, Rebecca depicted her experience as 'freaky' (Sheffield, 17 October 2003), thereby somewhat mystifying the other in music (see also Nettl, 1992a). Other students commented that:

> I felt it [the music] was really weird at first, because it's so different from everything else …. I think it's so different to Western music …. I just thought it was a weird topic. (Adrian, Durham, 27 October 2003)

> I still find it quite difficult to listen …. It's just really mysterious …. It's just really different. (Emma, Durham, 27 October 2003)

While some students rejected these 'weird' musics, others retained a deliberate sense of distinctiveness through their musical openness, thereby negotiating and constructing a particular identity that differed to the other students. This, of course, required a certain level of self-confidence by these students:

> I have chosen all world music modules … because I just like to be different …. I don't care if I am different. I am interested in it and don't care what people say. So world music is just another thing that's different …. I find some students a bit boring because they just sit in and watch telly all day, and then they go out

at night. I have a life …. I have done *samba* all day last Saturday … and when
I come back from *samba*, I am thrilled, and my friends look at me like …. But
I think it's their loss. I think they don't get as much out of life …. I think that
variety is the spice of life. (Alice, Bangor, 8 October 2003)

Students who readily accepted and appreciated the world's musics often saw
themselves in the light of 'otherness' and 'alternativeness'. Proud to possess a sense
of adventure, these students often mentioned that they liked travelling, meeting
new people and learning foreign languages, being fascinated by different ways
of life. Rebecca, for example, imagined that 'it would be really cool if somebody
asked, and I would say "Oh, I play violin and Indian sitar" (Rebecca, Sheffield, 20
February 2004). George had a similar opinion to Rebecca:

> This course is really important to me, but to other students it's probably less
> important … because of my interest in other languages and cultures. That made
> it more important to me. Also the fact that I like travelling sparked my interest,
> whereas some people just did it because they had to and didn't put much effort
> into it at all. (Rebecca, Sheffield, 5 March 2004)

> … nobody else plays the *shakuhachi*. That's quite unusual …. I don't just feel
> more comfortable, but it's nice to be doing something that is different …. Most
> students find me playing the *shakuhachi* slightly strange; most haven't heard
> of the instrument …. What I like about the *shakuhachi*? I like the slowness, the
> different qualities of the sound, the kind of meditative character. (George, York,
> 6 May 2004)

This negotiation and constructing of difference seemed to be reflected in the global
music market, which has since the 1980s increasingly promoted 'world music'
as an exotic product of the music industries and media in the West. Such exotic
musical products that presume 'an Other' (Guilbault, 2001:178) appeal only to
certain types of consumers (Leonard and Strachan, 2003b:374), and are thus
marketed with particular sensual, mystical and attractive attributes that confirm
that these musics are *different*. People who consider themselves to be different and
outside the norm, and who tend towards being alternative, hip or even antagonistic
feel drawn towards these musics. This was equally true for students encountering
courses on non-Western musics. For example, Harnish (2004:131) found that many
of his American students associated playing in the *gamelan* with 'being cool'.
Compared to 'mainstream students' (*ibid.*:126), he found that these students dress
more casually and colourfully, use more alternative body jewellery, frequently
participate in other arts and are more likely to smoke, take on a more open stance
towards contemporary and electronic music, unusual food and anti-capitalist
popular culture (*ibid.*:137), all symbols and mediators of a particular sociocultural

identity. Some scholars even suggested that *gamelan* attracts homosexuals as a voice of marginalised peoples (Brett, 1994; in Harnish, 2004:137).[2]

The UK and German students who liked world musics similarly revealed different outlooks in life combined with a liking for travelling, alternative music, food and lifestyles. For example, Christopher, a male student from Sheffield with interests in Japanese culture, including martial arts, *daiko* drumming and *gagaku* court music wore long hair and unconventional clothing, enjoyed travelling and languages, and liked Asian foods. In some instances, students' construction of difference was further enhanced by the physical divide between university departments, and, with it, the distinction between the transmission of world music and Western art music. That places can carry pivotal intrinsic connotations for students to negotiate difference was particularly evident at Goldsmiths College London where ethnomusicology was physically (if not administratively) situated in a different building. Physical and social separation from mainstream music students resulted in students' strong and positive feeling of social belonging and group identity. The following statements summarise students' experiences at that particular university:

> That's good that this department is detached from the music department, because I feel we are the weirdoes, you know, the strange people … because we are in a small house outside … and have no contact with them and don't talk about classic Western music …. I don't go to classical concerts by the music department …. No, I don't like them anymore. I used to like them …. I feel depressed when I go and find it too stuffy. (Anna, Goldsmith, 11 February 2004)

> I really enjoy the atmosphere because we are only a small group of students … like a family and we discuss our problems. John [Baily] is always there, always trying to help. (Shu, Goldsmiths, 13 February 2004)

> It's like a family here … John Baily is like the Godfather to all of us, that's really nice. It's like a family house where you can go and talk …. This building is just for ethnomusicology and anthropology …. We have nothing to do with the music department. (Alexandra, Goldsmiths, 12 February 2004)

---

[2]   And it is not only students who perceive themselves in this way. Ethnomusicologists apparently also often perceive themselves as different and as the most alternative of academics (Solís, 2004b:4). Emma described one UK-based ethnomusicologist as follows: 'I think ethnomusicologists are different to the musicologists …. They … have been brought up in this Western culture, and … have got some sort of relationship with another culture …. So he's got this sort of interest in something a bit different' (Emma, Durham, 27 October 2003).

Shaping Factors

The previous section has shown that there exists a correlation between students' social identity and their musical preferences. This, in turn, is often shaped by demographics such as race, gender, religious orientation, class and age. For example, people with non-Western backgrounds who live in the West apparently have higher affinity for non-Western musics, whilst adolescents typically prefer performers representing their own race and gender (Brittin, 1996). Meanwhile, women apparently have broader musical tastes than men (LeBlanc *et al.*, 1999). At universities in the UK and Germany, I observed some variants to this. For instance, in classes on Indian Bollywood *filmi* music, female students (whatever their ethnicity) often readily identified with and related to the kitschy and romanticised plots and fantastic settings, while male students despised these plots strongly, particularly the often macho-like appearances of the male hero actors. Religion too impacted on students' musical choices, as in one instance, a Chinese female student refused to participate in a Taiwanese ensemble due to its association with Buddhist temple ceremonies, explaining that 'I am from Hong Kong .... I am Christian, but this is music for a different religion ... for funeral .... I don't like that because of my religious background. I don't feel comfortable' (Andrea, Sheffield, 3 October 2003). Ethnicity was another pivotal factor in students' aesthetic choices. For example, Chinese undergraduate students often explicitly disliked non-Western (including Chinese traditional) music as many of them are trained in Western art music, which they regard as 'serious' musical training in contrast to non-Western styles that are often seen as an unpleasant, distracting experience (see also Witzleben, 2004:142). Shu explained that 'I have only been listening to classical music before ... for fifteen years .... People back home in China like my mom ... think that world music is not music .... They find the melody of this kind of music not very pleasant' (Goldsmiths, 13 February 2004). Upon listening to the world's musics for the first time, Melanie revealed that:

> I was just fed up after I have listened for several minutes, because it was African music. The people were shouting. It was not really music in the common way. The music is quite annoying. Music [to me] is a nice melody ... Western classical music. Their vocals were not really singing. (Melanie, Sheffield, 10 October 2003)

Clearly, ethnographic study can bring a more nuanced understanding to the preferences that students evince in response to listening experiences. While such brief observations of shaping factors, such as ethnicity, gender and religious orientation would require a more substantial investigation, the following discussions only focus on social class and status, as well as age and life experiences. Both issues crystallised as pivotal, yet it must be noted that such categories are never clearly bounded and frequently overlap with one another. The separation of these issues thus reflects a concern with clarity in the discussions that follow.

Social class and status

Life-style choices and consumption patterns can reflect cultural hierarchies and status, whilst taste in music has the potential to affirm one's class (Bourdieu, 1984:34). Aesthetic judgements may thus be actively constructed and recreated in social relations in order to reproduce hegemony (Bourdieu, 1986). This is also linked to educational level whereby the 'higher' educated classes apparently reject the ordinary objects of popular culture (*ibid.*:35). This may explain some students' aesthetic judgements about the world's musics, as they conveyed a connection between their own (imagined or desired) belonging to a certain social status and class, and their somewhat chauvinist musical taste (see also Blacking, 1987:133). With increased experience through education and enculturation into the Western art music culture, it often became more difficult for these students to accept new, contrasting models or systems of music. Since many of these students assimilated values associated with the Western art music canon as legitimate for consumption (Bourdieu, 1984:40), many of these students felt 'a bit sceptical at first' (John, Manchester, 9 May 2005), as to them this new, unfamiliar music sounded strange and different. Melanie mentioned that 'I find this music quite exotic. I am more used to Western classical music, even pop, jazz and more modern music. With [this] music I am just not comfortable' (Sheffield, 6 October 2003). This music was also often associated with people of lower social status with non-Western cultures being regarded as traditional and primitive:

> I just get really curious as to things like – and this is gonna sound really really awful – but do they have CDs and listen to music on CD players? Because the view that we get is that they don't, you know. Are they more modern than that? (Mary, Liverpool, 15 March 2005)

Most students brought a romanticised quest in seeking the traditional other in music, often commenting that 'I expected more traditional music …. That's why I liked the session on Pygmy music most' (Alice, Bangor, 15 October 2003). The efforts of ethnomusicologists to make unfamiliar musics accessible through carefully designed lessons and practical work may even feed these assumptions. Encounters in world music ensembles, for example, seemed to strengthen some students' concept that the world's musics may be simple and easy to learn because the performance context and music seemed less serious than that of Western art music. Three students from across universities commented that:

> I thought a lot of people enjoyed playing in the *gamelan* but didn't take it all that seriously. I felt that people who took it felt it was a bit of a break and just something enjoyable. But nobody continued it. (Diane, Birmingham, 29 January 2004)

> It feels to me quite relaxed, maybe it's just the way it is played, sitting on the floor. It's not strict performance in the sense that it's laid-back, not so formal

with people dressed up in suits and things like that ... That feels more relaxed to play, and fun. (Stephanie, York, 17 May 2004)

On one side, it is also very important for me to have – besides this other, strict classical – also something, which enables you to let go. (Jennifer, Rostock, 24 November 2003)[3]

While the majority of students were careful about making their aesthetic judgements explicit, some were clearly vociferous in communicating more derogatory value judgements, especially students studying at the German music conservatory. Jennifer replied to my question why she selected the introductory course to world music by saying, 'Well, you probably want to hear something nice from me now!' (Rostock, 24 November 2003).[4] She went on to express a very strong sense of hierarchy as to what constitutes an appropriate subject matter for study:

Did this perhaps inspire you to buy a world music CD and listen to it? No, no, and I won't do this either [in the future]. Well, as a school music teacher I can do well without this. (Jennifer, Rostock, 24 November 2003)[5]

Kathrin, another student at this conservatory, similarly felt that the course was 'not important ... It is all well and nice and interesting, but it is not really important' (Rostock, 24 November 2003).[6] Their experiences of world musics did not seem to have any impact on their general outlook on music. Upon asking whether the world music course had made any difference, Jennifer replied 'no, as I already said, I simply find this very, very interesting, also to see how the different people [folk] – sometimes you only know, yeah, there are the Indians – well, to find out, what kind of music they make .... No. Interest in strange music has not yet been woken in me' (Rostock, 24 November 2003).[7] Meanwhile, UK students majoring

---

[3]   ... das ist für mich auch einerseits sehr wichtig, dass man neben diesem anderen, strikten klassichen auch noch mal was hat, wo man sich einfach mal loslassen kann (Jennifer, Rostock, 24 November 2003).

[4]   Tja, Du willst jetzt bestimmt was tolles hören! (Jennifer, Rostock, 24 November 2003).

[5]   *Hat Dich das vielleicht inspiriert, eine world music CD zu kaufen und anzuhören?* Ne, ne, das werd ich auch nicht machen. Also, als Schulmusiklehrer brauch ich damit gar nicht anzukommen (Jennifer, Rostock, 24 November 2003).

[6]   ... und so wichtig is das eben alles nicht. Das ist zwar gut und schön und interessant, aber es ist nicht wirklich wichtig (Kathrin, Rostock, 24 November 2003).

[7]   Nö, also, wie ich schon gesagt hab, ich find das einfach sehr, sehr interessant, auch zu gucken, wie die einzelnen Völker – manchmal weiß man ja nur, ach, da sind die Indianer – also zu erfahren, was die für Musik machen ... Ne, Interesse an einer fremden Musik hat das noch nicht geweckt (Jennifer, Rostock, 24 November 2003).

in Western art music similarly felt that experiencing the world's musics had no real impact. Mary explained that:

> World music .... I don't think that I can fully get a grasp on it, because I don't enjoy it enough .... It's not something I actively want to sit and listen to ... so I think playing it continually might send me over yet .... I think in terms of musicianship, it's not greatly gonna effect my musicianship .... I don't particularly like to deviate from classical music .... It not necessarily had that much of an impact on my own personal musicianship .... It's not something that I'm gonna carry on to study ... and once I've done it, I have done it. (Mary, Liverpool, 15 March 2005)

Nevertheless, if some students appeared lax in their attitude towards world music courses, others described them as fun and different from the norm. A few students even stated that they had chosen to study world musics because they were 'fed up' or bored with the seriousness of studying Western classical music. Final-year Bangor-student Alice commented that 'classical music .... It just bores me .... I think when you get to Uni, you had so many years of Haydn, Mozart and Beethoven .... The music is always the same; it goes Andante, Allegro, and whatever. The titles don't grab you for a start .... I can't think about anything worse than going to a concert and seeing in the programme *Haydn String Quartet, Opus number whatever* .... I can't stand this conventional stuff anymore' (Bangor, 3 October 2003). Some postgraduate ethnomusicology students shared this same opinion:

> I have studied classical music, Bach, Beethoven, and all this serious stuff. Ethnomusicology is a bit different, and it's nice to learn about all those different cultures, things that aren't the same as in our culture, things that are not so serious [as Western classical music]. I find this really interesting .... The thought to write a dissertation on Bach chorales couldn't be any more boring. (Eva, SOAS, 11 November 2003)

Even some Chinese students, who often voiced critique towards non-Western and Chinese traditional music at undergraduate level, deemed world musics suitable for postgraduate study, even when choosing to focus on 'a Chinese composer of Western classical music with Chinese elements' (Celine, Sheffield, 30 April 2004). These examples show that there exist connections between postgraduate and general music undergraduate students and 'their' musics. It was also often students with self-doubts in their musical ability and talent in Western art music (see also Kingsbury, 1988) who – in the highly competitive atmosphere of Western art music culture – may have turned to ethnomusicology as an alternative to a classical performance career.

Age and life experiences

As implied earlier, students' aesthetic musical judgements were also shaped by their age and life experience. Younger students often 'sit in the lectures because they feel they have to' (Emma, Durham, 27 October 2003), whilst commenting that 'I possibly will listen to more non-Western music when I am older' (Adrian, Durham, 27 October 2003). Students of a more mature age, meanwhile, brought with them more dedication and commitment to study, and also seemed to value and appreciate the world's music to a larger extent. According to Jane and Patrick, two mature postgraduate students from two different universities:

> The fact [is] that I understand a lot more … beyond what [younger students] understand. You can tell by what they say, their responses …. The understanding gained through life is so valuable. I would not have liked to do this at their age …. I really feel that I can make a contribution. If I had come straight from school, I don't know …. I think you have to be involved with and like people to understand life …. It's communication, it's interaction, and I really think that this is the difference to undergraduates …. They haven't seen the world yet …. I have noticed with the younger graduates, they have a very narrow view to how things are … not just musically. (Jane, Liverpool, 15 March 2005)

> I am doing this because I want to do it. In a way, coming to it at this age, I've got an advantage because it is what I want to do, so I'm committed to it, whereas a lot of the kids in the first year … were there because their parents wanted them to be there, or they didn't know what else to do with their lives …. Another advantage is I've got a lot of life experiences, so I can relate it to stuff they haven't seen yet. (Patrick, Belfast, 19 November 2003)

Celine, another mature student reflected on her professional life in Hong Kong, which 'made me more aware of other cultures. Multiculturalism became part of my own identity, you know, a kind of globalised identity without boundaries' (Sheffield, 30 April 2004). More mature students often brought with them a rich array of life experiences, enabling them to accept and appreciate difference in musics more easily. Diane, a former undergraduate at Birmingham Conservatory who aimed at becoming a professional flautist, juxtaposed her disinterest in world music during her studies with her recent (that is, several years after her degree and into teacher training) interest in world musics:

> I don't really know why I didn't take any interest in it, to be honest, because now I'm coming to look at it again [as part of her teacher training] and find it quite interesting. But maybe it's just that my whole ideas have changed now and I'm not as focused on becoming a flute player, realising that it might have been a bit too specialist all on the flute, and I have come to realise that it's of no use now for my PGCE, absolutely none …. When I found out about all the different things that this course covered, I realised how narrow my musical education was

.... I felt a bit embarrassed, to be honest ... about my lack of overall musical knowledge. (Diane, Birmingham, 29 January 2004)

As the discussions show, younger students often wish to become better performers or composers and to pursue a performance career in Western classical music. Yet those students who more fully understand the limited opportunities available to classically trained musicians (the majority of students become school teachers and professionals in non-music-related careers) seemed to have a higher level of intrinsic motivation to study world musics. More openness towards world music emerged when students wished to pursue a career as professional music teachers, whereby these students often selected a wider range of music courses in order to gain a broader musical knowledge and understanding. In order to prepare adequately for this profession, Stephanie, a final-year undergraduate student, selected a module on Indonesian *gamelan* (amongst others), whilst undertaking independent research into the role of the *gamelan* in music education. A final quote illustrates that:

I try to do a wide range of modules ... [because] I want to have broad knowledge at the end of my degree ... not just classical stuff .... I thought to take the opportunity to learn about things I wouldn't normally be able to learn about .... My plan at the moment is to do a teaching certificate PGCE, maybe to go into primary school teaching. (Stephanie, York, 17 May 2004)

More generally, it was interesting to note that connections exist between different student groups at universities and 'their' musics. This chapter thus sought to shed some light into the ways in which students' musical tastes and preferences reflected, modelled and resonated with their sociocultural identities. Yet it must be noted here that – as always in locally-specific ethnographic research – the discussions may not be representative of the entire student population in the UK and Germany. Nonetheless, the chapter has shown that in some instances, students' musical taste is a sociocultural construct, as it is shaped by other factors, such as social class and status, age and life experience, thereby bringing some understanding to the preferences that students evinced in response to listening experiences.

Chapter 4
Listening to Music, Experiencing Authenticity

The previous chapter has shown that connections exist between musical preference and social identity, and that some students were intrigued by 'the other' in their listening encounters. Yet recent debates have raised questions about music education in the West, criticising (the often staged and managed) musical transmission for potentially constructing traditionalism and authenticity (see also Solís, 2004b:16). Western perceptions of authenticity have their roots in the European Romantic search for the native and real (and therefore authentic) in contrast to the newly industrialised life that marked the era of modernity (Frith, 2000:308; Gebesmair and Smudits, 2001:112).[1] In relation to world musics, authenticity thus typically refers to traditional and folk musics, and also ethnomusicologists often value older, more traditional musical repertoires rather than newer musical styles (see also Solís, 2004b:16). This concern with authenticity shaped and modelled the content of musical transmission at universities, whereby some ethnomusicologists sought to reduce the differences between the original and instructional culture.

Yet students' experiences in the West obviously differ to those which emerge through complete exposure in a non-Western music culture, as the instructional culture can never be a true replication of the original culture. Some ethnomusicologists were thus less concerned with 'authentic' musical transmission. For example, Neil Sorrel at York University encouraged students freely to explore the instruments of the *gamelan* instead of adhering to the 'traditional' ways of transmission, namely learning the two tuning systems *slendro* and *pelog*, followed by learning to play a Javanese piece. Other methods were similarly deemed unsuitable for these novice learners who were encouraged to use cipher and Western staff notation (instead of adhering to the oral-aural tradition) and to use Western terms (instead of traditional terminology) (Figure 4.1). Learning to play only one instrument (instead of all, as in the traditional way), students participated in weekly workshops and were required to practise individually (instead of gaining precision through coordination and cooperation of ensemble members). Students learnt to perform the *gamelan* without having completely to adhere to traditional means of instruction. Yet the ethnomusicologist also maintained some

---

[1] At that time, cultural purity rather than hybridity became the measuring device for authenticity. As a result, Europeans began collecting folk music and music from exotic, faraway places outside their homelands thinking that 'real' traditional musics were dying out.

culture-specific notions, such as taking off shoes, explaining to students that 'in many cultures people take off their shoes entering someone's home. Indonesians think you are [impolite] if you don't take off your shoes. It is only the ... British who keep their shoes on all the time. There are also other codes of behaviour' (Neil Sorrel, York, 26 April 2004).

By comparison, Inok Paek at Sheffield University aimed at transmitting Korean *kayagŭm* performance in rather traditional ways by kneeling on the floor without shoes, not stepping over the instruments, orientating on the instrument with and without traditional Korean notation, singing the Korean symbols during playing, and using traditional terminology for instruments and music theory. Paying attention to individual students with other students in the group watching and listening resembled another, more traditional way of transmitting *kayagŭm* performance. Due to institutional constraints, however, the methods had also to be adjusted: the ethnomusicologist tuned the instruments herself, an activity she would traditionally pass on to an assistant; students had also to rely on spoken and written explanations rather than learning by doing only; students continued with individual rather than collective lessons due to time restraints. It was thus impossible to transmit this non-Western music culture without adapting to the conditions of the Western education system. This was also true at the German conservatory in Rostock where Brazilian music was transmitted in rather Western ways, namely by partitioning the rhythms into shorter, more manageable sections:

> The workshop leaders have dealt with this very 'teacher-like' .... They have thousands of handouts ... which exactly show when to play .... The *meringue* and other styles ... are literally dissected and taught like a typical German teacher would do [laughing] .... But it makes much sense; it is, of course, the case that we aren't Brazilian, and therefore we need methods, which students can understand, which they are trained in and can subscribe to. (Wolfgang Schmiedt, Rostock, 25 November 2003)[2]

The transmission of non-Western musics in the Western institution obviously necessitates a certain degree of Westernisation, both of the music itself and the methods used for transmission. Whilst students' musical learning was often aided by instructional books and texts, which may otherwise not form part of traditional

---

[2]   Die workshop leader ... (ein Schlagzeuger und ein Saxofonspieler) haben sich sehr lehrerhaft damit auseinandergesetzt .... Die haben dann tausend Zettel, die sie verteilen, und dann steht da immer ganz genau drauf, wann du die *claves* spielst; dann musst du das immer so machen. Wenn's in Brasilien ist, musst du das aber ein achtel vorher machen .... Die *meringue*, und wie sie alle heißen, werden also im einzelnen seziert, und wie ein deutscher Lehrer so was beibringt dann auch vermittelt [lacht] .... Das macht aber auch viel Sinn; es ist ja so, dass wir halt hier keine Brasilianer sind, und da brauchen wir Methoden, die die Studenten verstehen können, worauf die trainiert und abonniert sind (Wolfgang Schmiedt, Rostock, 25 November 2003).

Figure 4.1   Neil Sorrell demonstrating on the *rebab* during a *gamelan* rehearsal at the University of York, 10 May 2004

learning, the transmission methods typically shifted away from repetitive, intensive exposure and towards more formal, explicit instruction. Ethnomusicologists thus often suggest that authenticity is incompatible with the reality of Western education (see also Johnson, 2000; Skelton, 2004:169). Some scholars have even put into question the concept of authenticity altogether (Leonard and Strachan, 2003a:164). They often argue that the world musics are only less authentic or even inauthentic in the framework of an essentialist and dichotomous understanding of authenticity. For this reason, authenticity has increasingly been regarded as an ideologically concept that is socially and culturally constructed.

Authenticity as an Ideological Construct

Musical experiences work at many different layers of meaning, and to many students, certain musical and extramusical signifiers, including the physical, material, sonic and literate spaces, together with the ethnomusicologist's ethnicity, shaped and modelled their ideas of authenticity, tradition and the exotic other. Beginning with the physical spaces in which students had musical encounters, this section will illustrate how students' perceptions resonated with and reflected such constructed ideologies of authenticity.

The Physical Space as Signifier of Authenticity

The physical context in which students had non-Western musical experiences in the higher education institution was marked by particular objects, informality and lack of hierarchy. Obviously, the physical spaces of musical encounter can never be an exact replication of the original space. Yet some ethnomusicologists sought (whether deliberately or not) to authenticate students' listening experiences in such formal surroundings, and this included displays of non-Western items and artefacts or alternative teaching methods that emphasised difference:

> I arrived at a small terrace house .... The small room ... contained a normal-size kitchen table .... There were ... lots of photographs of mainly Afghan musicians, of whom I recognised a few from the film *Breaking the Silence* ..., and quite a few instruments, including two *rubab*, some long-necked lutes, and other instruments from Afghanistan or India. Walls were covered with pictures, which looked a bit like *ragamala* paintings, Chinese wallplates, and other stuff; all together, a small cosy room reminding me that I am in an ethnomusicology course. (Fieldnotes, Goldsmiths, 10 February 2004)

Marked by my own (past) quest for otherness and difference, my fieldnotes depict the teaching space at Goldsmiths College whilst particularly highlighting the non-Western artefacts. The experience of discovering that ethnomusicology and thus the musics transmitted in this space must be in some way different and other (and thus authentic) provided me with great pleasure. During conversations with the Goldsmiths students, I found that they similarly paid attention to the many 'ethnic things, like the carpets from Persia …, lots of pictures of famous Afghan musicians …, *tablas* and other instruments …, Green tea from Asia …, the burning of incense sticks' (group conversation, Goldsmiths, 12 February 2004). These artefacts and items even enhanced students' perceptions of being the 'different weirdoes' (see previous chapter), which led towards some kind of imagined authenticity about the world musics encountered here. In some instances, ethnomusicologists used incense and 'ethnic' table decorations, whilst in other instances I also observed personal accessories, including native necklaces, earrings and wristbands, which signified affiliation to another, different music culture. Students often found such accessories interesting and different to the norm. Clothing similarly impacted on students' perceptions, commenting for instance that 'I really like how he respects the tradition … with what he wears' (group discussion, Sheffield, 12 December 2003). Here, students referred to a *kora* teacher from the Gambia who dressed in the traditional Islamic *dishdasha* or *djellaba* (robe) and cap (Figure 4.2). These garments signalled to students instantly that both the teacher and the musics they listened to were authentic as the musician who looked right resembled to them the same origin as the music he transmitted. Yet this also potentially alienated the students from the teacher in their spectatorship position, a stance of gazing at the other.

In another instance, students experienced a heightened sense of authenticity when playing in a *gamelan* ensemble as this was exhibited in an ethnological museum, the Rautenstrauch-Joest-Museum für Völkerkunde Stadt Köln.[3] The *gamelan* ensemble formed part of the exhibition of collected artefacts and exhibits from around the world. One student playing in the ensemble described the instruments as 'ethnic exhibits … but at the same time a real example from an unknown folk' (Lydia, Köln, 20 July 2004).[4] During the rehearsal break, students handed me a leaflet advertising the museum's *gamelan* workshops whereby the text deliberately romanticised the idea of exploring [*erkunden*] a strange music culture [*fremde Musikkultur*]. Wondering [*bewundern*] at such an other indeed constructed a sense of orientalism and exoticism:

> *Gong, kempul, kenong, kethuk, saron, kendhang, boning* – these are the illustrious names of *gamelan* instruments from the Indonesian island of Java, which can be admired in the Rautenstrauch-Joest-Museum … Yet the gongs, big gongs, metallophones and drums not only please the eye, they may even be played under expert instruction. In this way, visitors … have the opportunity,

---

[3] See also http://www.museenkoeln.de/rautenstrauch-joest-museum/default.asp?s=& tid=&nr=&kontrast=&schrift=-&mus=rjm.

[4] Ich spiele im gamelan ensemble. Das ist im Museum für Völkerkunde … und ist ein ethnologisches Austellungsstück … aber gleichzeitig ein echtes Beispiel von ungekannten Völkern (Lydia, Köln, 20 July 2004).

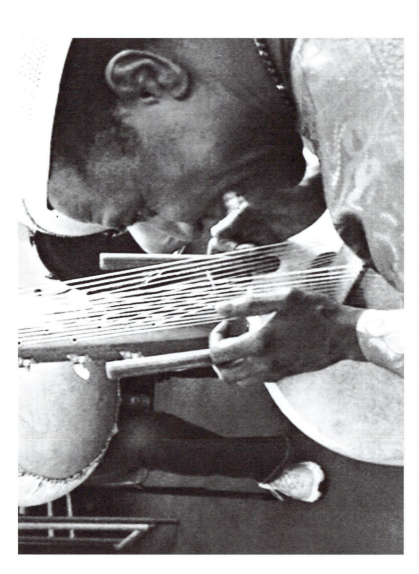

Figure 4.2   Seikou Susso leading a *kora* workshop in traditional clothing at the University of Sheffield, 5 December 2003: See also Seikou Susso's website http://www.seikoususso.freeuk.com/.

to explore an exhibit ... [and] to experience and understand a strange music culture. (Leaflet; Rautenstrauch-Joest-Museum für Völkerkunde, Stadt Köln; 22 July 2004)[5]

To the students, the particular physical space – the ethnological museum – in which they listened to and played *gamelan* music signified notions of tradition and the other, which in turn validated concepts and ideas of authenticity.

The Material Space as Signifier of Authenticity

Students also placed significant emphasis on their encounters with an imagined authentic material culture. Their first experiences with ethnomusicology often occurred through course or module handbooks, which sometimes included visual imagery. Module handbooks projected at times a concern with simple or old cultures, signified by images of half-naked people playing unusual instruments or African drums (see also Krüger, 2007:98). To students, such images may have directly impacted on their expectations of studying more traditional musical styles, rather than learning about modern and popular musics. For example, the first-year course handbook at QUB contained an image of two creatures (Figure 4.3). During an informal conversation among first-year students, some jokingly commented that the image reminded them of 'cave drawings ... or extraterrestrial aliens' (group conversation, Belfast, 18 November 2003). Such readings may signal to students that their subject matter for study entails somewhat primitive or primeval people, and creatures not from here.

Students also often related in similar ways to images on CD covers when listening to world musics. In my own classes on *Music and Semiotics,* for instance, the CD cover of *Timbuktu* (2002) by Malian musician Issa Bagayogo was projected onto the whiteboard (see also Krüger, 2007:99). Behind an earthy background, the cover depicts a close-up, frontal shot of the musician's face that stares directly at the viewer. Students revealed powerful, discomforting reactions: a certain expected social distance and safety towards the other seemed reversed through the immediate intimacy experienced by them. The frontal angle of the musician's face together with his assertive facial expression seemed to confront students directly. The musician seemed to gaze at them, thus contradicting students' expectations of being in the spectator position themselves. Students suggested that 'he must be a modern musician living in the West .... I'd say his music is probably quite

---

[5]   *Gong, kempul, kenong, kethuk, saron, kendhang, bonang* – so lauten die klangvollen Namen der Gamelan-Instrumente von der Indonesischen Insel Java, die man im Rautenstrauch-Joest-Museum bewundern kann ... Die Gongs, Kesselgongs, Metallophone und Trommeln erfreuen jedoch nicht nur das Auge, sie dürfen unter fachkundiger Anleitung sogar gespielt werden. So ... haben [die Besucher] Gelegenheit, ein Ausstellungsstück... zu erkunden, [und] eine fremde Musikkultur zu erfahren und zu begreifen (Leaflet; Rautenstrauch-Joest-Museum für Völkerkunde, Stadt Köln; 22 July 2004).

SCHOOL OF ANTHROPOLOGICAL STUDIES
THE QUEEN'S UNIVERSITY OF BELFAST

SOCIAL ANTHROPOLOGY
&
ETHNOMUSICOLOGY

LEVEL ONE

HANDBOOK

2002-2003

Figure 4.3   Undergraduate course handbook for students of Social Anthropology
and Ethnomusicology; Queen's University Belfast, 16 November
2003

modern', which in turn made the musician appear 'less authentic … in terms of African traditional music' (in-class conversation, Liverpool, 15 March 2005). It is interesting to note that only recently, my music students commented similarly on the cover of Youssou N'Dour's album *Joko: From Village to Town* (2000), which also depicts a close-up, frontal shot of N'Dour's face, and which evoked associations with urbanism and modernity to them. In contrast to such experiencing of modern African musicians, students also encountered more prejudiced portrayals of African music culture, specifically in world music textbooks (for examples see Asselineau *et al.*, 1994:114; Locke, 2002:140; Turino, 2004:187; Miller and Shahriari, 2006:231-6). Such images typically depict half naked, dark-skinned people in rural environments playing percussion instruments who are spatially positioned at some distance to the spectator (another good example of this is the front cover of Malcolm Floyd's edited volume *World Musics in Education,* 1996a; see also Krüger, 2007:100). Such depictions created more formal kinds of imaginary relations, placing the other at a safe distance and reaffirming students' spectator position at the other. The images themselves signified authentic African music culture, confirming that students had encounters with 'more traditional music' (Alice, Bangor, 15 October 2003) and 'folk music' (Jennifer, Rostock, 24 November 2003),[6] also suggesting that 'I can picture them all dancing to it and having a good time' (Christopher, Sheffield, 20 November 2003). Another student even suggested that 'all African people dance naked around the fire' (Lora, Bangor, 8 June 2006). Such images reaffirmed students' romanticised concept of African musics to be traditional (as opposed to modern), and thus authentic.

So far I have shown that what seemed modern (instead of traditional) to students was often regarded as inauthentic. Such reading was strongly informed by students' musical and extramusical preconceived ideas, regardless of whether they listened to traditional or more modern non-Western music. To exemplify this with another example, in my classes on *Music and Gender*, students listened to the popular music of international Israeli pop icon *Ofra Haza*, whilst viewing the CD cover of the album *Shaday* (1988) (see also Krüger, 2007:101). Referring to the ornate jewellery on the fingers, hands, wrists and head of the singer, together with her heavy black eye makeup, students described her as wearing 'jewellery and eye-shadow typical for women in the Middle East' (in-class conversation, Liverpool, 29 March 2005). Other signs further authenticated students' prejudiced views of gender roles in the Middle East. For example, Haza's downward look apparently had 'a certain expression of angst in her face' (in-class conversation, Liverpool, 29 March 2005), which seemed to evoke notions of feminine vulnerability. Folding her hands as if symbolically to cover her face (like a veil) further supported students' preconception of 'the oppressed woman in the Middle East' (in-class conversation,

---

6   Ich find das total schön, dass das hier, gerade mit den musicalischen Schwerpunkten, also auch das volksmusikalische, dass man das so mitkriegt (Jennifer, Rostock, 24 November 2003).

Liverpool, 29 March 2005). This imagery reaffirmed students' prejudices about authentic Middle Eastern music when listening to Haza's music.

Musical instruments were also a means through which students negotiated and constructed concepts of authenticity. At most universities, students experienced at least one non-Western musical instrument, which typically included the African *kora* and *mbira*, Middle Eastern *zurna*, *ud* and *darabukka*, Asian lutes, zithers and xylophones, and indigenous American flutes, to name but a few. The more these instruments differed in shape, size, decoration or playing technique to students (by Western standards), the more students found them interesting. Students often viewed such instruments as unusual and exotic objects that were intriguing and inspiring. Students often felt drawn to these instruments both visually and aurally. Reflecting on her first day at university, Carolina remembered that 'when I looked around on the Open Day ... there were different instruments out on display, which were all so different ... so it looked interesting and sounded fun' (Bangor, 15 December 2003). Yet musical instruments were only perceived as authentic if these seemed unspoiled by Western influences. In one instance, students scrutinised the West African *kora* and put into question its authenticity when they realised that the tuning pegs on the instructor's *kora* resembled those of the Western guitar (Figure 4.2). This was also true when students discovered the Zimbabwean *mbira*'s sound resonator to be decorated with Coca Cola and Budweiser bottle tops to add a rattling effect to the soundscape. Meanwhile, Rebecca who participated in a gospel choir outside her university studies discontinued singing because 'it doesn't seem as African as it could be ... The music is very Europeanised with harmony, etc' (Sheffield, 28 November 2003). These examples reflect students' construction and deconstruction of authenticity depending on the level of perceived cultural purity or hybridity.

The Sonic Space as Signifier of Authenticity: Music-as-Sound

In the previous section, I suggested that the often older, traditional repertoire resembled difference and otherness, thus authenticity to students. Yet which particular musical aspects enhanced such an ideological construct? Students regarded world musics to be authentic when they listened to distinctly different sounds. Such sounds typically contained discrepancies that sounded both out-of-tune and out-of-time by Western standards (Keil, 1994b:98). The further out the pitches, textures and timbres sounded, the more different these musics appeared to students. In order to illustrate the ways in which musical structures mediated particular social meanings, it is possible to break down these structures into its musical elements, including perspective, time, interacting sounds, voice quality and timbre (Van Leeuwen, 1999). Each musical element carried semiotic value for students, which helps to explain students' ideological construction of authenticity during listening to world musics. Before discussing these, it must first be noted that the same signifier – as always in semiotics – may be used at different levels, so that the following interpretive descriptions are by no means exhaustive. Instead what follows is a snapshot of those issues that were pertinent to students.

Perspective

Musical sound created perspectival relations between the sounds represented and students' perceptions. For example, sounds heard in the foreground of a piece of music seemed in closer distance and were thus noticed more intensely by students. In a class on *Music and Semiotics*, students listened to a Chinese folk song played on Western cello, *pipa*, *erhu* and *sheng*, accompanied by a strong *tabla*, bass and percussion section,[7] a musical example that clearly reflects processes of blending and hybridisation.[8] Yet to many students, this piece evoked experiences of authentic Chinese music, commenting that 'the music sounds Chinese …. I don't know why … maybe because of the way the melody is played on the cello or the other instrument [*erhu*]' (in-class discussion, Liverpool, 15 March 2005). Students' judgements derived from noticing the melody in the foreground, which was indeed based on a Chinese folk song in a pentatonic scale and utilised stereotypical embellishments, such as slurs and ornaments. The Western and non-Chinese elements were largely ignored by students, as these sounded in the background and thus seemed less significant in students' (de)constructing of authenticity. This example illustrates the Western phenomenon of exaggerating seemingly exotic elements in the sound of non-Western music. It shows how music that is aimed at a Western market plays around with expected characteristics of a musical tradition by stressing its difference and exoticism (see also Nettl, 2005:440).

Meanwhile, other more hybrid musical examples were experienced as inauthentic. Listening to Thomas Mapfumo's *chimurenga* popular songs, some students suggested that 'this isn't really traditional music, although he uses the traditional instrument *mbira* and sings in their traditional African language …. He uses too many Western electric instruments … that makes it sound, I don't know … like music for the city and not traditional' (in-class discussion, Bangor, 10 October 2005). Hearing the electric sounds of electronic instruments in the foreground – sounds that have also more generally been described as crowded and homogenised (Tagg, 1990) – thus evoked in students images of modern, urban environments. Musical inauthenticity was also perceived during chants in praise of the Taliban in Afghanistan that typically feature heavy reverb on the male vocals (Baily, 2004:21–2), which some students described as 'artificial and unreal' (Samantha, Bangor, 10 October 2005). Music played in quiet, rural places, by contrast, was imagined as sounding purer, clearer and authentic, as in the aforementioned Chinese example. All these examples show that students associated natural and pure sounds with

---

[7]   Yo-Yo Ma's arrangement of a Chinese Traditional *Blue Little Flower*; from the album *Silk Road Journeys: When Strangers Meet*; Sony Music Entertainment 2004.

[8]   Chinese music is characteristically free-flowing and less percussive, is traditionally not played on the Western cello, nor used to combine the three aforementioned Chinese folk and art instruments, and never traditionally utilised the Indian *tabla*.

authentic, rural music in contrast to artificial, electrically modified and crowded sounds, which were seen as inauthentic and associated with urban environments.

Time

The musical concept of time also shaped the ways in which students constructed concepts of authenticity, specifically when musical time differed to familiar time signatures, which are often governed by regular, unvarying, constant machine-like beats with a stress on the first note of each measure or phrase, usually in duple or triple time. Listening to examples of Eastern European folk music, students instantly noticed the irregular, asymmetric rhythmic metres, commenting that 'to Western ears, they have strange time signatures like 5/4 or 7/8 …. It just doesn't sound right …. It sounds funny' (Christopher, Sheffield, 20 November 2003). Such metres carry semiotic value by reaffirming otherness and difference. Similarly, Indian classical music appeared strange due to the unmeasured and continuous drone upon which melodic and rhythmic phrases are built, which students associated with medieval music and thus constructed a concept of authenticity that is rooted in the past. Music in the Arabic-speaking world also often features drones, and some students commented that 'the Egyptian arghul is played with circular breathing technique … that produces a constant drone sound … it sounds a bit medieval' (group interview, Sheffield, 31 October 2003). Drone sounds have indeed become so uncommon in the West that their meaning potential can point away from urban, regulated human patterns that are so characteristic of modern Westernised lifestyles. Hearing a continuous, unmetred drone authenticated students' experiences with these musics.

Interacting sounds

Listening to interacting sounds also carried semiotic value to students. Antiphony, for example, was typically associated with African traditional music, which to some 'expresses the social interaction between people in African villages … Here [in the West] we often hear only one voice like in pop or rock' (Rebecca, Sheffield, 10 October 2003). Listening to a Malian *Griot* Song in a class on African music, students picked up on the divided gender roles and commented that 'the male voice seems to be the leader because he sings first and is followed by the female voice … Maybe women are secondary to men in African villages' (group interview, Sheffield, 10 October 2003). The example reaffirmed students' assumptions about traditional gender roles whilst authenticating it as African music. Meanwhile, listening to *Kuli* panpipe music from Latin America, students learnt about the ways in which the music reflects the complementary, equal roles men and women play in this society. Some students commented that 'I find it really interesting how the three panpipes create one melody … and how men and women are equal …. One player alone would not make much sense' (group discussion, Sheffield, 7 November 2003). That this reflected difference and otherness was particularly emphasised in comparison to the gendered inequalities pertinent in some Western classical music. In another instance, this time a class on *Music in Southeast Asia*, students listened to the simultaneously interlocking and heterophonic texture of *gamelan* music. One student grasped that 'the texture reflects how each player is equally important in the music … It seems far less elitist than our music' (Stephan, Sheffield, 30 April 2004). In egalitarian societies there indeed exists a stronger sense of belonging to a larger whole, which is reflected in the musical texture of *gamelan* music. By highlighting this difference in interacting sounds, students experienced *gamelan* as authentic non-Western music.

Voice quality and timbre

Students' listening encounters of different voice qualities and timbres also connoted particular meanings in regards to authenticity. In contrast to Western music that often features a perfect, clean and polished voice, much world music was far from such smooth and sweet vocal qualities. A whispering song from Burundi, for example, sounded 'freaky' (Rebecca, Sheffield, 17 October 2003), whilst Mongolian diatonic or throat or overtone singing 'is not my taste at all. It sounds somehow weird and unnatural. I just wonder how one person does that' (Kathrin, Rostock, 24 November 2003).[9] Students could not relate such sounds to human actions, as the pitches moved outside the normal range of the human voice. The meaning potential here arose from the music's not-human, supernatural or even extraterrestrial qualities, an otherness that in turn authenticated students' listening experiences of such music. Meanwhile, singing in Spanish *flamenco* music was described by some students as being 'hoarse, rough … and sandy' (group interview, Liverpool, 15 March 2005), voice qualities also associated with the harsh living conditions of rural country people, which reminded them of 'people with weather-beaten faces' (group interview, Liverpool, 15 March 2005), again constructive of authenticity. By comparison, listening to Indian classical *khyal*, one student compared the rapid vocalisation section towards the end of a performance to 'cats screaming …' (Craig, Liverpool, 17 November 2004).[10] This student expressed an indirect derogatory value judgement by implying a lack of refinement (by Western standards) and a comparison to music that somewhat sounds primitively animalish, so as yet again to construct otherness and authenticity in music. Register was another striking dimension of voice quality and timbre. For instance, listening to the extremely high falsetto voices in Chinese opera, which were traditionally sung by males, some students laughed and commented that 'this sounds really bizarre … it just seems really weird, at least to us' (group interview, Liverpool, 15 March 2005). In the West, the masculine voice is usually associated with the lower registers so that higher regions can become ambiguous in gender terms. Yet higher voices sounding in Chinese music authenticated it to students.

---

[9] Obertongesang mag ich überhaput nicht. Es klingt irgendwie komisch und unnatürlich. Ich frag mich nur wie einer alleine das macht (Kathrin, Rostock, 24 November 2003).

[10] This observation was made in a lecture on the music of India, during which students watched the following VHS: *Khyal: Classical Singing of North India,* Video Cassette Ethno VC 1; with accompanying texts by Martin Clayton and Veena Sahasrabuddhe; Open University, 1998.

Listening to Chinese rock music, the higher voice of contemporary rock singer Cui Jian sounded right as it resembled the same ethnicity as Chinese people: 'I can see that the higher voices somehow fits with ... the smaller Chinese people' (group interview, Liverpool, 15 March 2005). In relation to Western rock music, however, students commented that 'it is just funny to think that Chinese audiences think of his voice as being hoarse and aggressive' (group interview, Liverpool, 15 March 2005).[11] Such examples reflect both directly and indirectly the ways in which students authenticated non-Western musics during their listening experiences of these different musical styles.

The Literate Aspects as Signifier of Authenticity

The literate aspects were another means to enhance students' constructing of authenticity. Cipher notation, often used for *gamelan* ensemble practice across universities, was frequently perceived by students as authentic Indonesian notation. Yet cipher notation is a Western invention, introduced to Indonesia by colonialists in the early nineteenth century, which has in the meantime become normalised and thus authentic of Indonesian culture. Nonetheless, students actively constructed ideas of authenticity when the notation was deemed indigenous and original, and differed to Western staff notation. In a class on *East Asian Music*, students encountered Chinese notation and instantly commented that 'this is an example of original Chinese notation for the Chinese zither' (Stephan, Sheffield, 20 February 2004) (Figure 4.4). Equally, playing in a Taiwanese ensemble, one student reflected on the notation and associated his experience with authentic musical transmission:

> We are learning through traditional Taiwanese teaching methods. We are learning to read the Taiwanese score, which looks like Chinese symbols, and we are learning the notes and what they are called on the page as opposed to the Western equivalents. (Christopher, Sheffield, 20 November 2003)

The absence of notation altogether was also often considered as authentic, as formal music learning in the West typically places value on the literate aspects of speech and sound. Oral-aural instruction occurred, for example, in the aforementioned Taiwanese ensemble at Sheffield University, whereby students began by learning to sing the score (this, however, is not a traditional Taiwanese method as players learn to play the melodies first on little recorders.) To the Western students, the instructional methods seemed considerably different to musical learning in the West. They felt that the methods were close to tradition, which resulted in their experiencing of authenticity:

---

[11] I refer particularly to observations made during listening to Cui Jian's CD *The Power of the Powerless*; World Beat (label), 2 November 1999 (release date).

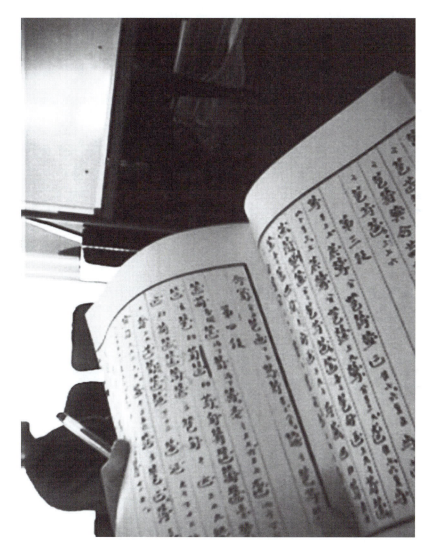

Figure 4.4   Chinese notation for *qin*; University of Sheffield, 20 February 2004

> I played the oboe-like instrument …. It's really traditional the way we learn …
> it was really hard though. First of all though, before we played them, we had to
> sing the rhythms, because it tires you out if you play too much …. We just sang
> the pitches, and each note has a different name like *gong* and *teh* and stuff. And
> then we played them … and then we played the percussion instruments, the big
> gong and the cymbal things …. You don't really read the music; you just pick it
> up as you go along. So each week you get better. You just pick it up and watch
> what other people do. (Sian, Sheffield, 31 October 2003)

In another instance, students participating in a Klezmer ensemble at SOAS had
authentic experiences during their oral-aural learning, described in my fieldnotes
as follows:

> The teacher sang a short section of a tune, inviting students to simply copy … by
> singing the tune, internalising and feeling it in order to let this experience float
> over to the instrument. Feeling was stressed permanently during the rehearsal
> and the sound … making it sound 'Jewish'. How? By the use of ornamentation,
> dynamics and downward slide …. A comparison was made to Gypsy music
> which uses an upward slide, showing the happy nature of Gypsies. However the
> downward slide symbolises the sadness associated with the Jews …. Students
> then copied the vocal part and tried it on their instruments. There was no notation;
> learning was done aurally …. She closed her eyes when playing and moved her
> whole upper body. Most students adopted the movements …. The atmosphere
> felt intensely emotional. The quality of the ensemble was not perfect, but this
> did not seem to matter. Instead she placed the biggest emphasis on sounding
> 'Jewish' and to play with feeling. (Fieldnotes, SOAS, 11 November 2003)

The constant emphasis on feeling and emotion led towards particular associations
with authentic Jewish music culture. The teacher verbalised and visualised her
own musical emotions with certain patterns of sound and body movements so as to
enhance a sense of authenticity. Klezmer musicians indeed often use extremes of
expression to convey a kind of Jewish sentimentality, and Jewish styles of playing
are distinct for their particular dynamics, phrasing, trills and *Krekts* (groans) and
vibrato (see also Netsky, 2004). In the ensemble, students learnt how accurately
to capture this feeling, sound and technical language, including the use of precise
trills, ornamentation and rhythmic nuances. Students expressed these constructed
meanings by swaying their bodies to the music, closing their eyes and applying the
appropriate technique to their own playing. This enabled students to come close to
an authentic experience of Klezmer music.

Students thus often constructed concepts of authenticity by emphasising the
different and traditional ('old') features of a music culture. Participating in world
music ensembles, students often highlighted that the oral-aural transmission 'feels
more relaxed [due to] the way it's played: sitting on the floor. It's not strict … it's
laid-back; not so formal with people dressed up in suits' (Stephanie, York, 17 May

2004). Stephan agreed that oral-aural learning is 'so relaxed ... It's almost like an honesty, a sort of down-to-earth nature and quality about it that took me aback ... It's not pansy ... Western music feels a lot more inaccessible ... the music itself excludes a lot of people who feel they do not really understand it' (Stephan, Sheffield, 30 April 2004). Meanwhile, Alexandra implied a powerful dichotomy between fake and real, suggesting world musics to be equivalent to 'real' folk musics:

> In Western classical music ... I feel they are fake. They just go on stage, bow ... come in and out. It's like a fake performance, whereas folk music you just go there and play ... and you play for eighteen hours ... you just feel it ... you don't 'make it'. (Alexandra, Goldsmiths, 11 February 2004)

Ethnicity as Signifier of Authenticity

The ethnomusicologist's ethnicity also enhanced students' imagined authenticity, as a native teacher appeared strange and personified cultural difference. Such a teacher embodied immediate authenticity (Trimillos, 2004). Theresa described her teacher with astonishment, commenting that 'she is really fascinating .... Sometimes I don't understand what she is trying to say but ... I just find her really interesting' (Belfast, 19 November 2003) (Part III, Figure III.1). The native ethnomusicologist was also often assumed to be better qualified to provide cultural knowledge:

> Getting people from there who know what they are doing and have experienced that would be much more authentic. It's exciting to see someone from that place playing their instrument. It makes it more real if they bring their culture to us, instead of us delving into their culture .... It's more of an active process, instead of formal lectures .... I don't know though whether you learn more from it. It's probably just more exciting. (Rebecca, Sheffield, 5 March 2004)

> It's good to have actually a musician ... from that culture ... to know what they are talking about and to appreciate what it's like. (group interview, Sheffield, 12 December 2003)

A native ethnomusicologist was thus seen as an expert who can contribute original experiences and anecdotes, thus having an almost sacred position as the musical insider who culturally knows (Trimillos, 2004b:38). A native ethnomusicologist was also granted immediate credibility as master musician. For example, after a guest session by an Iranian ethnomusicologist during which he demonstrated the *santur* and *daf*, students commented 'I just thought, Wow! Amazing! He is such an incredible performer! It was really fascinating!' (Rebecca, Sheffield, 20 February 2004). Many students voiced their appreciation of the excellent standard of playing during such demonstrations, yet they had in fact no knowledge of the music and its demands on the performer. In a similar instance during a class on *Music in Japan*, an English ethnomusicologist demonstrated Okinawan folk songs with a female from Okinawa. After the class, I found that to students only the native guest's presence authenticated their experiences of Japanese music. The host ethnomusicologist had a different view:

> They [students] could observe a session like today in the East Asian module, where we had an Englishman who had been to Japan, learnt a lot of Japanese music and one of the students in the module was Japanese but she was learning from him. And she was obviously far more familiar with Western instruments and music. So, an example like that could lead students to think about the questions of what is authentic after all! (Andrew Killick, Sheffield, 7 May 2004)

Whilst the majority of ethnomusicologists in the UK and Germany are Caucasian, they seemed to gain credibility (in the eyes of their students) through their work as subject specialists and intellectuals, as 'he really knows the stuff ... he has so many books in his office ... he seems to know everything' (Christopher, Sheffield, 20 November 2003). In many instances, students held 'their' ethnomusicologist in 'unquestionable and very high esteem' (Roger, Sheffield, 8 December 2003). Such assumptions obviously require challenging:

> I feel that there is an issue of authenticity that students seem to think that for whatever reason those who come from another culture than ours are automatically musical insiders, regardless of their background. Yeah, students often have that perception and it is one that needs to be challenged. (Andrew Killick, Sheffield, 7 May 2004)

By seeking and mystifying the other in their listening encounters with ethnomusicologists, students' attitudes indeed reflect romanticised concepts of authenticity. As shown throughout the chapter, the physical, material, sonic and literate spaces signified authenticity through associations with rural tradition, simplicity, emotion and enjoyment. The emphasis on cultural purity (rather than hybridity) in music cultures not from the West was a powerful means by which students experienced a sense of authenticity that is rooted in European Romantic philosophy of the early nineteenth century. It illustrates that authenticity is a socially and culturally constructed concept.

Chapter 5
Listening to Music, Experiencing Democracy

The previous chapters have illustrated the ways in which students sought and mystified the other in music through constructing concepts of difference, otherness and authenticity. Yet listening to world musics also enhanced in many students more tolerant attitudes towards people whose beliefs, values, behaviours and practices are often significantly different to their own. This is the focus of this chapter, which illustrates the relationship between the transmission of ethnomusicology and its capacity to enhance more democratic views in students. Ethnomusicologists typically approached this by avoiding processes of canonisation of certain music cultures, even though world musics were often taught by surveying a range of selected music cultures, an approach increasingly criticised for creating a canon of music cultures for study. Yet whilst ethnomusicologists have to accept – due to institutional constraints – that they may create new kinds of canons manifested in the form of selected course contents, they often utilise transmission strategies that help to discard canonisation, the institutionalisation of certain musics over others (see also Koskoff, 1999:547–9). Ethnomusicologists are thus often less concerned about their content selection in university courses and classes, and instead focus on the transmission of certain beliefs and perspectives that instil in students that all people have equally important and meaningful musical values and lead them to approach the different world musics with open-mindedness, fairness and compassion for all kinds of differences.

This shift in emphasis towards the transmission of values and beliefs in formal education resembles a kind of democratisation movement that aims at promoting social tolerance in students while enhancing a belief that all people and their musics are equal (see also Woodford, 2005a, 2005b). Intending to transmit musics from the perspective of more than one single dominant culture, this view advocates pluralistic perspectives and greater postcolonial and democratic awareness. The terms canonisation and democratisation may thus be understood as opposites, with ethnomusicologists often seeing themselves as part of the democratisation process. With these discussions in mind, this chapter illustrates the ways in which the transmission of non-canonical, more democratic concerns impacted on students' values, perspectives and beliefs. It will show why many (but not all) students expressed democratic social and musical values, conveyed through their growing belief in equality between all people and their musics, whilst others held on to certain eurocentric musical and cultural values. This chapter thus focuses on the relationship between particular listening experiences and their capacity to enhance more democratic views in students.

Disciplining World Musics?

Listening to world musics in survey classes, students seemed to bring with them certain motivations, principal among which was a concern with musical mapping, categorisation and therefore disciplining in order to gain a global overview of all musics. Another tendency amongst many students was a quest for musical canonisation, that is an assumption that the musics and instruments chosen for study by the ethnomusicologist must be more important and valuable for study than others that were not included. Learning about the *mbira*, for instance, the first-year Sheffield students assumed that they studied such a canonical musical instrument and thought that 'the *mbira* must be important in African society. Yes, I imagine it's a serious instrument because he [Andrew Killick] actually showed us it. I don't think he would show us a joke' (group interview, Sheffield, 17 October 2003). The same students also preferred sessions that dealt with the classification and categorisation of world musics and musical instruments. A session entitled *China: Tradition and Innovation* that focused on comparisons between Chinese and Indian categorisation systems for musical instruments was well received by students, as they found it logical and easy to understand. Seeking an overview of the musics covered in this course again illustrates students' tendency towards musical disciplining and canonising:

> I feel that the lessons are a bit specific in one area. For instance, today it was all about bagpipes …. It seemed too specific really. We need to know about European music in general …. We are supposed to know about European music. (Graham, Sheffield, 19 December 2003)

> Last week was really interesting, but it was very specified to Iran and we ought to do the rest of Asia as well. It just seems a bit specific …. So is it not better to do a broader thing in the actual lectures? (Joanne, Sheffield, 19 December 2003)

> I didn't feel I really got to know, for instance, African music as a whole. It seems we were doing it too vaguely …. I would have liked to do more on Latin America because we did the whole continent in one lesson and … that didn't seem to cover the whole of Latin America. (Rebecca, Sheffield, 31 October 2003)

Yet whilst many students brought such initial motivations to their musical studies, there were also students who were more critical towards canonical assumptions about the course content, such as Alice, although she similarly conveyed an underlying wish for general overview and classification:

It may be good to have a summary that brings all lectures together, that makes clear why she has chosen these topics. It's such a massive continent, and I think that the topics she chose were quite representative, quite important parts. Probably, but I don't know .... What I'm trying to say is that I don't know how important these topics are, or whether they are just favourite topics. I don't know how they fit into the bigger picture and whether these are topics [the ethnomusicologist] thinks are important. (Alice, Bangor, 22 October 2003)

Ethnomusicologists were well aware of the problems that may arise from such perspectives. In order to avoid the mapping or categorising of world musics into global culture areas and universal schemes, thereby giving students a sense of having covered the most important global cultural areas, some ethnomusicologists thus often opened up the subject matters for study by utilising a wide range of musical case studies. Yet this often led students to feel overwhelmed and disorientated. Liz commented that 'there is so much out there to listen to, it's easy to get lost' (Manchester, 9 May 2005). Listening to examples from Greece, Bulgaria, Bosnia, Turkey and various other examples in a session on the *Music of Europe* seemed equally confusing:

Listening examples are better for us to comprehend the ideas, but if he plays too many examples from the CD, we easily forget. There is so much information coming at you, I suppose. (Andrea, Sheffield, 31 October 2003)

This country-jumping makes me get lost. He went from Eastern Europe, then from Iran to Egypt, then to France, then to England. That's why I got lost. (Joanne, Sheffield, 31 October 2003)

Students' experiences of musical overwhelmedness arose not only from listening to a wide range of musical examples, but also from more formal instructions on the cultural, historical, geographical and other aspects of the music culture. The following are selected quotations to exemplify students' experiences across universities:

I thought that the sessions were a bit crammed ... more than we actually needed ... It's too much .... There is too much information to take in .... It is too much information. It's a crash course in a really massive subject and it doesn't really work! It seems quite daunting. (group interview, Sheffield, 19 December 2003)

I found it quite frustrating the fact that you do a different continent every week, and you need to rush through it, and you don't get a chance to really appreciate the music of each culture. (Adrian, Durham, 27 October 2003)

> I think the course in general tries to cover too much …. It's all interesting. I think the problem with the course is that you get so much information. (Lauren and Alice, Bangor, 22 October 2003)

> I have really enjoyed the wide variety of topics we have covered in the course …. The amount of information we were given in each lecture is quite overwhelming though! (Thomas, Manchester, 9 May 2005)

Students felt that there were too many cultures addressed, examples listened to, topics discussed and technical terms explained in order to remember it all. Adrian linked it to 'having to be multilingual because there were so many different terms' (Durham, 27 October 2003). Meanwhile, Joanne found this experience 'quite awful, horrific, daunting and off-putting' (Sheffield, 20 February 2004). Yet it is important to point out here that such perspectives do not necessarily represent the views of the entire student population in the UK and Germany. It would be interesting to determine whether students at SOAS, the University of Köln and QUB have similar experiences whilst studying on more specialist world music programmes where students may generally be more committed and willing to accept more intensive courses and classes in world musics. Nonetheless, students' experiences of information overload are noteworthy, as they also had a significant positive impact by evoking in students a sense that there is genuinely no clear canon of music cultures for study. Babette, for instance, recognised that this approach 'could include anything' (Bangor, 15 December 2003).

Yet students' more eclectic musical experiences may not fully explain their expressing of more democratic beliefs and values, and humanistic and tolerant attitudes towards the world's peoples and their musics, a position encountered among many students across universities. Instead, Roger felt that there exists a connection between studying music in and as culture and its impact on students: 'Studying world music helps, for instance, ease racial tensions … but only when students really understand why this music is important to different people' (Sheffield, 8 December 2003). Students' democratic musical desires thus seemingly resulted from ethnomusicology's anthropological emphases.

Experiencing Music In and As Culture

Ethnomusicology is variously a sound-centred study of music (Hood, 1971) or a sociocultural study of music (Merriam, 1964, 1977). Referring to this debate, Neil Sorrell specifically emphasised the latter perspective, as 'it actually is important and interesting when you learn about the sociocultural context of music too …. It does just … give you a completely different perspective. It helps you get a lot of things right …. How you perceive music and how you think about it' (York, 6 May 2004). Ethnomusicologists indeed often wish to understand music as expression of human experience in the context of social and cultural organisation, a focus also observed across UK and German universities. For instance at Bangor, a course on *Music in Africa* required students to 'discuss the ways in which the music of the pygmy peoples of central Africa can be seen to be a product of, and to operate in harmony with, both the natural environment and their lifestyle as a whole. What kinds of insights can the musical traditions of these peoples (groups such as the Aka, Bayaka, Efe and Ba-Banzélé) offer into other aspects of their culture?' (Assignment question 2003/04; course 'Music in Africa'; University of Wales, Bangor). This focus reflects the ethnomusicologist's concern with understanding music as a reflector and generator of social meaning, requiring students to understand music as a resource for understanding pygmy society. The question specifically focuses on pygmy cultural principles, such as the non-hierarchical, democratic structure of pygmy society as reflected in pygmy song structure. Thus students were not expected to understand music-as-music but to utilise musical analysis as a tool to understand a particular society and its values. Students thereby learned how people in other cultures construct cultural processes by and through music.

In another course on African music at Sheffield University, students similarly learnt that mythical beliefs resonate with and shape musical structures. According to Andrew Killick, drumming music is often cyclic and reflects African concepts about life as being a cyclic process. Rebecca found it particularly 'interesting to think about how African music is repetitive and circular instead of … linear. This made us think about their strong mythic belief in reincarnation … or the role of seasonal cycles in their society' (Sheffield, 10 October 2003). Meanwhile, in a course on Indonesian *gamelan* at the University of York, students learnt about shadow-puppetry and dance as a reflector of Javanese culture:

> One dancer is the hero; one is the bad guy. If you compare their movement, the bad guy is waving around his arms over his head. The hero never lifts his arms higher than his head and moves very slowly …. That can be explained with Javanese culture: the hero has gained his spiritual strength through meditation and that results in self-control. The bad guy has relatively no self-control and wastes a lot of energy. For the Javanese, the very controlled and calm state of mind is what they would aspire to …. If a Javanese observed you going crazy and becoming angry over a matter, they would find you pathetic and stupid …. The Javanese have expressions for things like that, for instance 'losing face' …. This is also reflected in the music: the word *(h)alus* means smooth and refers to music as well as situations. Another word *gagah* characterises the bad guy: it's about outburst of emotions, which is a 'no-no' thing, since it implies aggressiveness, impulsiveness. (Neil Sorrell, York, 26 April 2004)

Another approach towards a more anthropological transmission of music-as-culture involved introducing students to a cross-cultural theoretical vocabulary, including gender, theatre, politics, dance and musical elements, such as rhythm or texture. Organisation by themes that unified musics from different case studies enabled ethnomusicologists to address the role music plays in people's lives and provided an inclusive framework for many musical traditions, including Western and non-Western, traditional and modern. In my own course on *Music and Politics*, for example, students learnt about different types of musical censorship with case studies including religious (Islamic) censorship in Afghanistan; state control and censorship in the former GDR and Romania; market censorship by MTV through the banning of certain pop music videos; and religious (Christian) censorship of the Norwegian Hardanger fiddle. Such a thematic emphasis enabled the juxtaposition of examples on the grounds of relevance to the topic in question, thereby revoking processes of canonisation. Meanwhile, another transmission strategy was that of instilling in students an appreciation of the global process by which their own music has taken shape. This broad theme ran through the entire course *Music of the World* at Sheffield University, which enabled students to draw meaningful connections between the most diverse musics, while at the same time allowing for considerations of the dynamic nature of cultures and their musics. This emphasis on cross-cultural influences and their effects on Western homogenised global music also reflected ethnomusicology's more recent concerns with global processes. According to Andrew Killick:

> The module is also tied together by a historical thread running through each session. I try to teach students the bigger picture, not just to survey several music cultures, but to try to show them what this other music has to do with them; I try to show them historical connections. (Andrew Killick, Sheffield, 6 October 2003)

This approach allowed the ethnomusicologist to transmit that world music has a globally shared musical language and history whilst linking the entire course together under the umbrella of one commercial global music. Students clearly grasped this idea, as 'it made it very clear because ... the lecturer brought in the analogy to the tree .... The roots are the various types of music coming together in the trunk, which symbolizes Western global pop music. It amalgamated all these different musics' (Graham, Sheffield, 24 October 2003). Students also showed an appreciation of the broader processes of cross-cultural influences and saw world musics in a far broader light. This in turn led them to be more tolerant and open-minded towards these musics. Approaching music in a way that abandoned the distinction between self and other, the ethnomusicologist democratised students' perceptions:

> I think studying world music widens our perspective on music. It's true that we think of music as a tune, or varieties of Western music. But if you went to a place and heard Birdsong, would you think of that as music? I think it is very important for us to become aware of the cultural places .... It is really good to study world music because it's widening our outlook on different people! (Rebecca, Sheffield, 10 October 2003)

This same teaching approach occurred at other universities where students grasped the importance of studying what music means to its creators and listeners. Music became seen as an expression of culture and a resource for understanding society (see also Cook, 1999:213). In this process, students comprehended the ethnomusicological concept of music in and as culture:

> We've talked about culture, and we've talked about the dance and how they express themselves .... I think that a lot of the music comes around because of the culture. So that's why we maybe focus more on the culture than we do on the music. In some instances, the music must be a bit of a by-product of what the culture is inflecting. They've got the music because of the culture .... Culture has not come from the music. (Mary, Liverpool, 15 March 2005)

> Music is not just a system by itself, but rather a reflection of the culture and society from where it was born. That is a far more important idea! It gives music a meaning, a point and a reason! (Steven, Sheffield, 30 April 2004)

> Ethnomusicology is the study of human beings and music. It's not only about the music of one particular country, one nation. Studying ethnomusicology, studying music in culture and humans .... I am not only interested in music itself, but also in the culture. (Shu, Goldsmiths, 13 February 2004)

Yet how did this cultural focus in students' musical experiences impact on their own attitudes and values? Does music, as Blacking claims (1973:xi), have the potential to enhance harmonious social relationships between people? Whilst ethnomusicologists like Blacking frequently argue(d) that exposure to world musics can increase awareness, appreciation and acceptance of the people whose musics are concerned, little research has yet been done on this series of claims (Fung, 1994:46). My research provides some insights that complement such debates. It revealed that the transmission of music in its cultural context impacted on students' experiences in two significant ways: first, it instilled in some students a broadened awareness of and deeper appreciation for other cultures and therefore higher valuing of these musics; second, encountering music as a human process helped some students better to appropriate their own culture and sociocultural identity. These insights are significant for understanding the relationship between ethnomusicological transmission and students' transformations, which are thus illustrated in the following section.

Towards Heightened Appreciation of the Other

Most ethnomusicologists believe that listening to world musics and understanding these within their cultural contexts 'gives students exposure to different sounds and different colour, which enriches their experience, their understanding of what musicality is!' (Hae-kyung Um, Belfast, 18 November 2003) Most students indeed commented on expanded musical perceptions, one suggesting that 'it has made me very aware of the other types of music which are around in the world and how different they are ... and it's made me more accepting of what's around' (Mary, Liverpool, 15 March 2005). Mary's latter reflection about heightened musical acceptance is particularly noteworthy as it shows that an ethnomusicological transmission of musics in cultural context broadened her musical horizons for all sorts of differences. Other students, such as Rebecca and Steven similarly found that an awareness of culture and people is of utmost importance so as to better appreciate and understand their musics:

> I feel we have to make an effort understanding other cultures .... It's not just us English who exist! (Rebecca, Sheffield, 5 March 2004)

> It would be a disgrace or almost rude not to study the music of someone else's culture. It's naïve to think that just because we are from the West, that's the only music that exists. (Steven, Sheffield, 30 April 2004)

Emma and Adrian also reacted to their music-cultural encounters positively and commented on their challenged and broadened views on music:

> I think it's just good to challenge the fundamentals of music and just to see that everything you've learnt so far, and everything you study in other modules, is really focused on Western music. And ... it's quite easy to forget that, and then suddenly you are challenged. Like he was talking today about the different tones and how Western music can stop you from appreciating non-Western music because how you've been brought up with that, and how you listen to tones like in Western music. (Emma, Durham, 27 October 2003)

> For me, it turned my world of music upside down .... I had no idea what music was, what music is, but I think it makes you sort of think twice, it makes you sort of realise that we [Westerners] are quite proud to think ... to have got it all sorted with harmony, the most important thing [in music]. But actually it can really limit how we listen to other music .... I hadn't really thought about that before .... It's really good how he challenges everything music is. (Adrian, Durham, 27 October 2003)

Meanwhile, Joanne experienced a broadened awareness and appreciation at the level of musical elements, suggesting that 'other cultures may not be so strict, and pitch doesn't matter so much. It's not just about our own little treble clef!' (Sheffield, 20 February 2004). Graham similarly commented on expanded views towards musical notation, conveying that 'we think of music as written, as strict. There is so much different and fascinating stuff, for instance how people read music' (Sheffield, 3 October 2003). Steven had eye-opening experiences that led towards heightened compositional freedom, suggesting that 'this course opened my eyes in regard to musical freedom. It doesn't have to be so strict. Your approach to music doesn't have to be bound by those [Western] rules. I now use more musical freedom in my compositions' (Steven, Sheffield, 30 April 2004). Clearly, studying world musics within their sociocultural contexts led some students away from eurocentric value judgements about other musics and towards increased tolerance for the musics that they encountered. In this process, students understood that music is always made with reference to its maker's unique standards and criteria. Steven, Melanie and Kathrin, for example, learnt that there are many ways of making music, which they came to regard as equally valuable and interesting, whether they liked or disliked the music:

> When listening to some of the examples, I didn't find them particularly good by Western standards because they sounded out of time or out of tune, not as strict. It was interesting to find then that within its culture, this piece of music would be regarded as very professional .... I try to make that transition. (Steven, Sheffield, 30 April 2004)

> It makes it more interesting to concentrate on the cultural background because the music itself is quite dull, not musical. But in the context of the culture or society it sounds more interesting, and I can understand better what they're trying to do. (Melanie, Sheffield, 10 October 2003)

> My preferences for the music itself differ; one region I like very much, another not so much, for instance overtone-singing [throat singing] is not my taste at all .... Anyway very interesting, whether I like the music or not. (Kathrin, Rostock, 24 November 2003)[1]

What students highlight here is that 'if we can understand more about the culture, we know why that kind of music is being performed' (group interview, Sheffield, 19 December 2003), and this understanding seemed to make their musical encounters more interesting and meaningful. Rebecca, more specifically, grasped that a country's development (e.g. economic, technological) and the availability of natural or other resources impact on the ways in which instruments are being made, which in turn helped her to appreciate the relationship between African musical instruments and music-making:

> We talked about how advanced the country is affects the music and how the instrument, the rattle-thing ... was made out of some kind of vegetable ... whereas in our country they'd probably make that in a different way. And, I

---

[1] Die Musik selber find ich sehr unterschiedlich; eine Region gefällt mir richtig gut, anderes wieder nicht so, zum Beispiel Obertongesang mag ich überhaput nicht ... Auf alle Fälle, sehr interessant, egal ob ich die Musik nun mag oder nicht (Kathrin, Rostock, 24 November 2003).

don't know, it's a completely different way of thinking because music is part of the community, instead of something that you just listen to. It's something that you do and you get involved in. (Rebecca, Sheffield, 10 October 2003)

Many students came to value world musics on their own terms by suggesting that 'African music is by no means simpler than Western music .... I think it's just completely different because music is society .... I don't think there is any way that we are above them. It's just a completely different culture' (group interview, Sheffield, 10 October 2003). To Christopher, musical complexity or simplicity was similarly irrelevant, commenting that 'Asian folk music, to Western ears just doesn't sound right .... But I don't think of it as right or wrong; I don't think of it in terms of tonality. It doesn't matter whether the music is complex or easy. It's about the people and what they regard as right and wrong!' (Sheffield, 20 November 2003). The musics listened to and studied in their cultural contexts instilled in students respect for the ingenuity of the people who perform it, evident in a final comment:

> You can't really define what music is the way we do, because there are so many different types and concepts of music .... It makes you think of music more on a grander scale .... It's a good way of opening your eyes to the world and becoming more interested in other peoples' cultures. (Rebecca, Sheffield, 4 March 2004)

Appropriating One's Own Culture

The previous section has shown that listening to musics and understanding these within their sociocultural contexts led towards greater appreciation of and tolerance towards *other* people and their musics amongst many students. Yet this approach to ethnomusicological transmission also impacted on students' awareness of their *own* culture and identity. That studying another people's culture and music can lead towards deeper understandings of one's own culture has long been recognised by ethnomusicologists (Blacking, 1973:ix–x), and John Baily similarly advocates that:

> I think also, that it should probably make you hear your own music in a different way, or think about it in a different way .... The more musics you look at around the world, the more you get a sense of the things that go on ... and then you can compare this to Western music and re-evaluate that in those terms .... Sometimes, it would be a good way of spotting students who think that Western music is the best music in the world .... You become more aware of why you say or think that .... It sharpens up the perception. (John Baily, Goldsmiths, 13 February 2004)

German ethnomusicologists, such as Britta Sweers agree that 'for musicians, this is a way, as John Blacking has already formulated, to get to know oneself differently, to see oneself in the mirror of another culture .... You have maybe more distance to your own culture as you look at it from the outside' (Rostock, 25 November 2003).[2] Hartmut Möller, principal at Rostock conservatory, equally felt that 'one only knows European music when one has also encountered non-European music, otherwise one just celebrates oneself and thinks this is so special, so valuable' (Rostock, 25 November 2003).[3] Studying someone else's music within its sociocultural context thus helped some students to appropriate their own culture and music, an experience they described as enriching and empowering. For example, Tina expressed that learning about musics within their political context resulted in 'rethinking the music I was listening to ... That was really good, and it does just influence your life a lot, you know' (Belfast, 18 November 2003). In other instances, students commented:

> This session helped us to understand the [African] culture a bit better ... about cyclical lifestyles, reincarnation, and all that .... The analogy to the [Western] orchestra in terms of hierarchy was quite interesting. This helped us questioning our own society a bit, something I have never done before. (Edward, Sheffield, 10 October 2003)

> What it has done for me? It has opened a lot of doors I didn't know existed .... Musicology wouldn't have opened the same doors .... The social influences, for instance ... and the actual social effect of that music in a concert .... It's just opened my mind. It's like a mind-blowing experience. (Roger, Sheffield, 8 December 2003)

> It has definitely made me think differently about both the tradition I am in and other traditions. (Thomas, Manchester, 9 May 2005)

Meanwhile, other students experienced a broadening perception of their own, syncretic identity. These students often highlighted the process of becoming critical self-reflexive musical learners through which they developed a more complete picture of their often complex life experiences. Patrick, for example, who had Irish ancestry and was raised in England, searched for his own Irish identity when learning to play Irish flute and participating in flute bands in Belfast whilst

---

[2]   Für die Musiker ist das wirklich eine Art und Weise – wie John Blacking das schon so schön formuliert hat – sich selber anders kennenzulernen, sich selber im Spiegel einer anderen Kultur zu sehen .... Du hast vielleicht mehr Distanz zur eigenen Kultur, weil Du sie von außen betrachtest (Britta Sweers, Rostock, 25 November 2003).

[3]   Man weiß eigentlich über die europäische Musik nur etwas, wenn man auch die nicht-europäische Musik kennengelernt hat, sonst feiert man sich nur immer selbst, und denkt, das ist so besonders, so wertvoll (Hartmut Möller, Rostock, 25 November 2003).

undertaking postgraduate research into Irish music during his ethnomusicological studies (Belfast, 19 November 2003). Meanwhile, Taiwanese student Celine only started appreciating Chinese music when studying at an English university, through which she rediscovered her own Asian identity:

> It is quite interesting to come all the way here to discover Chinese music .... This made me interested in it. I have realised that this helps me to understand my own identity ... being 'in-between' cultures .... I chose the *kayagŭm* workshop and feel very strange about that .... In China I would have never done this .... But here, I try to explore why I miss China, re-explore my own world and search for my own identity. I miss something that I should have paid attention to earlier .... I have neglected my own culture and music in the past, so although I'm Asian, I don't know my own tradition very well .... This is a really interesting feeling and experience because this is so close, but also so distant to me .... I wouldn't feel complete if I wouldn't try to understand my own culture too .... I rather feel somewhat ashamed because I am Asian and should know this but don't. Other students assumed that I know the instrument and music and gave me a strange look when I said that I didn't. (Celine, Sheffield, 30 April 2004)

Whilst Patrick and Celine (re)discovered their cultural and ethnic identities, other students developed heightened self-awareness of their musical identity. Sandra, for example, reflected on her past self-perception of lacking musical talent whilst studying amongst (what seemed to her) virtuoso performance students at a conservatory. Yet learning about ethnomusicology's inclusive, democratic stance towards world musics helped Sandra to understand her anxieties and concepts of talent and musical greatness in the Western musical establishment. This critical self-awareness and cultural contextualisation enabled Sandra to make sense of her own and equally valuable musical ability:

> I understand now why I got cold feet and didn't go to the conservatory .... I also understand why I didn't do music earlier. It was this, I had this elitist notion of musicians ... and now I know I wasn't that! ... Doing ethnomusicology was great because ... you realise that what we have, what I had, the Western art-view of music, it's only one view of music amongst other, possibly more acceptable views of music. So really, what I did find in ethnomusicology was this confirmation, liberation I've been looking for, so that now I would say I'm a musician! I'm not a virtuoso musician but I also understand now that I don't want to be a virtuoso. (Sandra, Belfast, 18 November 2003)

Teymoor similarly felt that there exists a connection between his ethnomusicological studies (and world musics as a human phenomenon) and increased self-awareness of his own musical identity:

My interest is non-Western music ... is my way to find myself. I am searching myself. That's what I'm doing. I'm searching myself in music ... because I think if you understand, if you recognise, study yourself, then you are getting to the roots of many things because ... we are all human. I think ethnomusicologists are doing the same thing. They are studying music as a human behaviour .... You are dealing with humans. When you are dealing with a human being, you are part of it .... Ethnomusicology for me is not the study of music of others, of others' music; it's the study of yourself. Yourself, and your music. Ethnomusicology for me is the study of myself in the point of view of music. (Teymoor, Goldsmiths, 10 February 2004)

Besides heightened self-awareness of students' own sociocultural and musical identity brought about by their ethnomusicological encounters, students also acquired a stronger appreciation of their own Western culture, including music. This was evident, for example, when students voiced explicit criticism about some cultural and musical practices to the extent that they described them as shocking and horrifying (by Western standards):

I am amazed about the difference between cultures. Sometimes they teach you things like yesterday [Iran during the Revolution], and told us all the things about how they were not allowed to play. That was really shocking. That made me realise that we are very lucky that we can play our music and everything. So we kind of learn [about ourselves] from other cultures. (Alexandra, Goldsmiths, 12 February 2004)

It was like the men watching the women make idiots out of themselves [referring to a documentary] .... How is that furthering what they [women] are trying to stand for? It made me a hell of a lot more thankful for my culture, despite the rules and restrictions that we have on our culture here. It's made me a hell of a lot more thankful that we don't go through things like that .... In regards to the actual music, it makes me a hell of a lot more thankful that we have so many different varieties of music in the Western world .... It makes me very thankful, despite the fact that we have S Club 7, or Britney, or whatever it is, we've still got good music, and we've got our classical history. (Mary, Liverpool, 15 March 2005)

Rightly so, these students found shocking some of the gross human injustices and discrimination that certain cultures practise against their own people. For example, in a class on music and politics in apartheid South Africa, students were horrified by the cruelties practiced against musicians who spoke out against apartheid.[4] Students showed similar reactions when listening to the stories of

---

[4]   I am particularly referring to students' reactions to watching the video documentary *Amandla! A Revolution in Four-Part Harmony* (2002, South Africa. Lee Hirsch); see further

Afghan musicians who suffered one of the strictest kinds of music censorship under the Taliban.[5] Learning about the misogynistic treatment of women in some cultures, Mary again commented that 'I didn't ever, ever think that there is so much discrimination between men and women. It was quite shocking to see how some of these women are treated and how they are expected to live' (Mary, Liverpool, 15 March 2005). Reflecting on these unfair cultural practices, students frequently praised Western democracy, freedom and equality, commenting that 'I am just glad that I live in a Western culture' (*ibid.*). Yet I also noted that some students' experiences were double-edged, playing onto their pre-existing stereotypes and leaving them to think that other cultures are traditional, primitive and backward. Ethnomusicological transmission may thus also have negative impacts by reinforcing students' perceptions of the West against the rest. Nonetheless, in many instances students did comment on mind-opening experiences and a heightened appreciation of other musics. They felt that the transmission of world musics within their contexts transformed their attitudes and values towards other as well as their own cultures. Students learnt to value diverse world musics on their own terms, whilst gaining a sense of respect for the ingenuity of the people who learn and perform these musics. As shown earlier, some students also reflected upon and better appropriated their own culture and/or identity. It seems, then, that the ethnomusicological transmission of music in and as culture has the potential to shape students' attitudes and perspectives towards equality and democracy. This finding is so pivotal that it will also be followed up and explored in subsequent chapters.

Reinforcing Difference and Otherness, or Deepening Appreciation and Understanding?

Whilst this chapter has been concerned with the relationship between ethnomusicological transmission and students' more democratic cultural values, Chapters 3 and 4 have illustrated that the transmission of ethnomusicology may not be ethnomusicological enough, as it tended at times to model, reinforce and resonate with students' ideas of orientalism and exoticism, difference and otherness. For example, during ethnomusicologists' appropriation of traditional world musics into formal Western education, musical and extramusical signs came to bear meaning to students that contributed to their constructing of authenticity and essentialism. Yet as shown in this chapter, students' encounters with music in and as culture and thus the role music plays in people's lives, seemingly transformed their attitudes and perspectives towards self and others. Here, students

---

www.amandla.com.

[5]   This observation was made with particular reference to the video documentary *Breaking the Silence: Music in Afghanistan* (2002, Afghanistan/UK. Simon Broughton); see further www.freemuse.org/sw6455.asp.

came to appreciate and value other musics on their own terms. They also better understood their own Western culture. This resulted specifically from teaching strategies that emphasised ethnomusicology's anthropological concern, rather than from transmitting eclectic case studies on world musics (although the latter indeed revoked canonical concepts of music cultures for study). It was thus the cultural experiencing of musics that enhanced in many students a democratised view of the world. They learnt that all people and their musics are inherently equal and equivalent in their own contexts (see also Koskoff, 1999:546). Some students described their experiences as holistic musical study. Even Jennifer at the German conservatory, often so critical of her experiences in world music, stated:

> I simply find it very, very interesting to see ... what kind of music they make, and ... then she also talks about the people [folk] themselves. And that is simply a holistic project, which I find very good. (Jennifer, Rostock, 24 November 2003)[6]

Meanwhile, Daniela felt that 'the discipline [of ethnomusicology] helps you to appropriate things, to comprehend the bigger picture' (Liverpool, 15 March 2005). As shown in this chapter, ethnomusicological study helped students not just to make sense of their own educational and life experiences, but also to develop heightened tolerance and compassion towards other cultures. They thus learnt the very values inherent in the discipline of ethnomusicology, namely equality, inclusivity and democracy. This shows that there exists a connection between ethnomusicological transmission and students' transformations, a fact that is particularly pertinent in a twenty-first century music education that places emphasis on such democratic values as freedom, creativity and contribution to society (see also Woodford, 2005a). Such an education ought to be the aim of ethnomusicological transmission and learning. The following chapters will share this same concern and illustrate students' musical and personal transformations within the context of performing ethnomusicology.

---

[6]   Ich find das einfach sehr, sehr interessant, auch zu gucken ... was die für Musik machen, und ... dann erzählt sie auch selber über die Völker was. Und das ist einfach ein ganzheitliches Project, was ich sehr gut finde. (Jennifer, Rostock, 24 November 2003)

PART III
Performing Ethnomusicology

Ethnomusicologists' quest for deeper cultural understandings is often accomplished by their direct engagement in musical participant-observation on the basis that musical performance can increase both the value and necessity of ethnomusicological fieldwork (see also Cooley, 1997). The performative aspects of culture that lead towards a kind of intrinsically musical and imaginative experiencing are thus pivotal in ethnomusicological research. Performing can sensitise the performing researcher to musical and extramusical aspects and can precipitate a sense of the music's style and aesthetics (Averill, 2004). Performance thus increasingly occupied a crucial position not only in ethnomusicological scholarship, but also in the transmission of ethnomusicological knowledge at universities. Yet little has been written about utilising performance at universities that sheds light into the ways in which students access the musical other. The most relevant publication by Solís (2004a, *Performing Ethnomusicology: Teaching and Representation in World Music Ensembles*) addresses mostly the ethnomusicologist's perspective. Performing ethnomusicology is therefore a particularly pertinent subject matter for the forthcoming chapters, as performance can lead students towards their perhaps most meaningful and conspicuous experiences during their encounters with world musics at university, enabling them fully to appreciate and understand another culture's music when transmitted in the classroom.

Most ethnomusicologists in the UK and Germany agreed that performing ethnomusicology at university is of great importance as it can enable students more deeply to experience and understand world musics, and enhance and broaden their view and understanding of the relationships between different musical sounds when transferred in the classroom. They often suggest that performance would enable students to acquire a certain kind of musical knowledge (see also Baily, 2001:86). Neil Sorrell specifically proposed that 'musical participation is the key to all musical understanding', and 'playing something is better than playing nothing .... You have to have a practical musical experience before things actually seem to matter .... Students should demonstrate a direct relationship to the music, and performing it is one way' (York, 10 May 2004). Active musical experiencing is thus important for students in order to gain a deeper understanding of the macro- and micro-processes of musical performance, claims also made by other ethnomusicologists:

This is yet another way of getting students to understand why things are different and why things are a certain way .... If you have a hands-on experience you start to appreciate it at a physical level. (Caroline Bithell, Bangor, 15 October 2003)

To students, it is simply important not only to hear the music and – based on that accordingly – through an analysis theoretically to deal with it, yet also to try it out at least once in praxis .... But there are things that are verbally formulated only with great difficulty, which can be better felt from own praxis. For example, the shifting hierarchical relationships in a Javanese *gamelan* are difficult to be verbalised theoretically. Yet when one has found out oneself, which instrument must listen to what other instruments, then immediately one can far better understand that. (Rüdiger Schumacher, Köln, 22 July 2004)[1]

Learning new ways of musicking (Small, 1998) can also impact on students' general musicianship. Valorising alternative systems and approaches to creativity, performance can provide students with choice and agency of musical alternatives, whilst developing skills and abilities necessary for general musicianship. For instance, longer-term performance training in Brazilian rhythms enabled students over time to 'feel the groove ... [and] to cope with rhythms in other [pop] bands' (Wolfgang Schmiedt, Rostock, 25 November 2003) and thus to apprehend the music operationally.[2] Performing ethnomusicology can also affect students' oral-aural musical awareness and enhance their ability to hear and listen to differing musical aspects. Indeed, students' development of oral-aural skills is important for discovering music's sonic structure and thus to understand musical sound analytically (Campbell, 2004:10). Ethnomusicologists also often emphasised that performing ethnomusicology is an important social activity for students. Performance can enable active collaboration, as the development of musical group competence is often shaped by democratic decision making. Some ethnomusicologists thus placed less emphasis on specialist training and musical

---

[1]   Für Studenten ist es wichtig, eben nicht nur die Musik zu hören und entsprechend darauf basierend über eine Analyse sich theoretisch damit zu beschäftigen, sondern zu versuchen, zumindest das auch in der Praxis einmal zu erproben. Nicht dass wir wollen, dass die jetzt gute Musiker in einem bestimmten Stil werden; soweit muss es gar nicht gehen. Aber das sind manche Dinge, die man verbal nur sehr schwer formulieren kann, dass sie die aus der eigenen Praxis empfinden. Beispielsweise das wechselnde Hierarchieverhältnis in einem Javanesischen *gamelan*, das lässt sich sehr, sehr schwer theoretisch formulieren. Wenn man aber selbst herausgefunden hat, an welchen Stellen welches Instrument auf welche anderen Instrumente hören muss, dann wird man das unmittelbar sehr viel besser nachvollziehen können (Rüdiger Schumacher, Köln, 22 July 2004).

[2]   Jedes Semester haben Studenten mindestens einen workshop über mehrere Wochenenden, wo es um Latin, und insbesondere Brasilianische Musik geht .... Das üben die hier stundenlang zusammen, und dann iregendwann fängt das an zu grooven .... Das schlägt sich positiv in der Rhythmusbelastbarkeit in anderen Bands nieder (Wolfgang Schmiedt, Rostock, 25 November 2003).

achievement, and instead emphasised the musical processes that led students towards cooperation (Figure III.1):

> [Musical] participation is a very important element ... for music making is more of a social activity .... New experiences are always a good thing because it also opens your eyes how different people do different things, and different kinds of musical structures and sounds, and different kinds of skills and discipline when they acquire their co-ordination and so on. (Hae-kyung Um, Belfast, 18 November 2003)

Figure III.1   Korean drumming workshop with Hae-kyung Um; Queen's University Belfast, 17 November 2004

Meanwhile, some ethnomusicologists advocated 'learning to perform' as a preparation for field research, which can also bring students numerous social advantages, such as giving them an understandable role as musical learners amongst the people studied (see also Baily, 2001:95). Rüdiger Schumacher suggested that 'it is an important preparation above all for the area of field research. Someone with basic skills in playing these instruments also has much quicker contact with the people, and far deeper contact with the people during field research' (Köln, 22

July 2004).[3] Performing world musics also enables students to understand music from new perspectives as 'it is really a kind of deepening ... of their experience through approaching the music from a different position' (*ibid.*).[4] At the same time, students can learn about the music 'from an anthropological point of view, so that gives them another dimension of understanding' (Hae-kyung Um, Belfast, 18 November 2003). Performing ethnomusicology also has the capacity to deepen students' respect for other music cultures, and the beauty of different timbres and the subtle or difficult complexities inherent in music ensemble structures. Enabling students truly to understand a non-Western other through its cultural expressions may indeed challenge any eurocentric musical stereotypes. Yet besides ensemble performance, ethnomusicologists also advocated displaying and demonstrating on musical instruments, or conducting simple hands-on activities during occasional workshops so as to present students with a further level of experience of music making in a non-Western tradition:

> Sometimes I demonstrate particular vocal techniques and show them ... the differences between female and male voice .... Also on *kayagŭm* ... I show them sometimes traditional and modern techniques .... Actually seeing it makes for very good communication .... when you can make your lecture – if you are a performer – as live as possible. (Hae-kyung Um, Belfast, 18 November 2003)

> I have showed them some instruments .... I think just to hold a physical object from another musical culture is a way of making it more real for them .... Students always appreciate it when they can see the actual instrument in front of them, and they can hear it being played ... by someone who can play the instrument .... Live performance by a visiting artist who was able to play music for them .... I often noticed that students become alive and just more interested. (Andrew Killick, Sheffield, 3 October 2003)

Whichever approach adopted by ethnomusicologists, performing ethnomusicology in its various forms frequently impacted on students' mindsets by connecting them on a positive, experiential level. Through performing ethnomusicology, students often acquired a sense of musical ownership, which generated more real and relevant musical experiences:

---

[3]   Insofern ist es eine wichtige Vorbereitung auch überhaupt für den Bereich der Feldforschung. Wenn jemand Grundzüge im Spiel dieser Instrumente hat, hat der auch einen viel schnelleren Kontakt zu den Leuten, sehr viel tieferen Kontakt zu den Leuten in der Feldforschung (Rüdiger Schumacher, Köln, 22 July 2004).

[4]   Das ist eigentlich eine Art von Vertiefung ... der Erfahrung durch eine Herangehensweise von einer anderen Position aus (Rüdiger Schumacher, Köln, 22 July 2004).

I think, students remember things better if they have actually done something in a practical way, rather than sitting and listening …. So I try to get students involved as much as possible, get them to do something practical, physical every time, and I think they just remember that better than as if they are just sitting and taking notes. (Andrew Killick, Sheffield, 12 November 2003)

I usually bring in some African drums and do hands-on workshops on African rhythms, which enable students to experience how cross-rhythms work … and they always enjoy doing that because they find that they are able to do that because it is not that complicated. (Caroline Bithell, Bangor, 29 October 2003)

Ethnomusicologists generally agreed that performing ethnomusicology is crucial in students' encounters with world musics. Even at universities with significant financial constraints, ethnomusicologists felt that 'I would find it absolutely splendiferous if we had a *gamelan* ensemble here … or whatever group …. But that is still music of the future' (Britta Sweers, Rostock, 25 November 2003).[5] At some UK universities, performing ethnomusicology has thus already become a subject for academic study in its own right:

It seems fairly logical to have performance at the heart of musical education …. I think increasingly we are going to see performance treated as study in its own right …. But we see the performance and the academic side as really being two sides of the coin. It doesn't make sense to have the one, and not the other. (Richard Widdess, SOAS, 12 November 2003)

Understanding Student Experiences during Performing Ethnomusicology

The chapters presented here will illustrate students' experiences during performing ethnomusicology, and how these impacted on students' attitudes and perspectives. This theme has already been addressed in Part II, and there is necessarily some overlap, as students will also be listening during performing ethnomusicology (see also Blacking, 1987:124). The discussions on performing ethnomusicology will be located along a continuum that includes students' discovering of world musics' material culture (Chapter 6), musical expression and form (Chapter 7), and cultural values (Chapter 9) so as to illustrate their experiences along this continuum, and the impact that these had on them musically and personally.[6]

---

5   Ich fände es absolut herrlich, wenn wir hier ein Gamelanorchester hätten … oder egal, was für welche Gruppierung …. Nur das ist noch Zukunftsmusik (Britta Sweers, Rostock, 25 November 2003).

6   I have derived the tripartite conceptualisation from a helical model by Boyce-Tillman (1996), which represents a framework for world music education of discovering (1) material culture; (2) expression; (3) form and (4) value.

It is important to note that the chapters will draw particularly on examples of performing ethnomusicology as they have been observed at universities in the UK. This is mostly due to the restrained frequency and length of my research visits to German universities, which in turn restricted opportunities for observing and participating in performance classes and/or ensembles.

Chapter 6 will discuss the ways in which students discovered musical instruments and became more actively involved during simple musical imitations and occasional world musics workshops, while encountering material culture and developing a broadened sound awareness of the music. This kind of musical engagement may be described as spontaneous, vivid and novel (Boyce-Tillman, 1996:59) during which students felt heightened levels of joy and excitement. Happiness, in particular, is one of the most important and frequent aspects of musical performance, which can make people feel good and result in a heightened state of musical arousal and excitement (Becker, 2001:144–5). The feeling of emotions in the form of pleasurable excitement was so pivotal to students that it deserves further attention in a subsequent chapter. Beforehand, however, Chapter 7 will discuss students' longer-term ensemble participation and learning to perform a musical instrument, during which students discovered musical expression and form. This resembled more structured and musically more meaningful performance participation, enabling students to recognise that sound is organised in some way, while considering artistic meaning and personal expressivity. This resulted in exploring expression, a process which begins with a personal and individual response to a particular piece of music and form, and which involved grasping the ways in which music becomes more organised, including music's phrase structure, rhythm and metre, and melodic gesture. Students often experienced a deeper-level understanding of the music's intricacies and particularities, and gained a deeper awareness of music-as-music. At the same time, the requirement of a final (and often formally assessed) performance led most students to feel emotions, yet these crystallised in form of performance anxiety.

The two emotions of enjoyment and anxiety were pivotal in students' musical experiences. At this point, an excursive chapter will be included that illustrates students' experiencing of enjoyment and anxiety.[7] Both kinds of emotions shared a somewhat dichotomous relationship, with enjoyment at the first level and anxiety at the second level of performing ethnomusicology. This will form the basis for a cross-institutional comparison examining other pivotal factors that impacted on students' emotional experiences. Chapter 9 will then move on to discuss the ways in which performance also concerned a more socially engaged, experiential ethnomusicology through music. The focus will be on performance as a social phenomenon, while illuminating the motivations and experiences of

---

[7] At the third level of performing ethnomusicology, students also experienced emotions, yet these seemed to be of a different kind as they were more inwardly directed. Their explanation is deemed outside the scope of this chapter.

students who utilised performing ethnomusicology for their ethnographic writings in order to make sense and understand their shared musical experiences. Such deeper-level musical and cognitive processes embraced students' logocentric processes of conceptualisation, reflection and analysis, and necessitated students' deep, self-reflexive and critical thinking in order to understand the values that people and societies hold about and express through their own music. Students learnt through performance and critical reflection how and why individuals and cultures value artistic products in often unique and differing ways. This kind of performing ethnomusicology enabled students to learn about music-as-culture and how and why music is a means for understanding society (Cook, 1999:213). This type of performing ethnomusicology also represents what ethnomusicologists themselves do and are professionally (Solís, 2004b:2), which may similarly lead students towards a deeper level of musical and cultural appreciation.

Throughout the chapters, it will be shown how students' attitudes and perspectives changed along the performance continuum. At its most basic level, discovering material culture (Chapter 6) resembled '*animation*' (John Baily, telephone interview, 7 June 2006) and led students towards experiencing heightened levels of enjoyment in the otherwise formal university environment. Meanwhile, more substantial participation in performing ethnomusicology (Chapter 7) led towards deeper insights into music-as-music, which also generated performance anxiety as a result of the Western performance paradigm. At the third level, performing ethnomusicology was used to enhance deeper understandings of music-as-culture (Chapter 9). This led students to gain not only musical insights but also to understand its makers better, resulting in deeply shared emotional experiences with the people whose music they studied and wished to understand.

Chapter 6
Performing Music, Discovering Material Culture

The differing kinds of performing ethnomusicology offered at universities obviously depended on ethnomusicologists' individual choices and were often marked by their sociocultural identities, research allegiances, personality characteristics, concepts and beliefs, institutional constraints, as well as their own learning experiences (see also Baily, 2001:94 for the latter). Thus not all ethnomusicologists at UK and German universities led world music ensembles. Yet most ethnomusicologists utilised performing ethnomusicology in form of seeing-hearing-trying musical instruments, and this occurred most typically during world music classes. Less frequent were occasional world music workshops, often led by invited guest musicians who either applied musical imitation or used real musical instruments. Such basic performing experiences enabled students to discover world musics' material culture and, with it, their infinite varieties of timbres, methods of sound production, tone quality, technology and construction, leading them towards a broadened sound awareness of world musics.

Seeing-Hearing-Trying Musical Instruments

As briefly mentioned, students frequently encountered the seeing-hearing-trying of musical instruments during their world music classes. At QUB, for example, students experienced demonstrations of Korean singing styles and *kayagŭm* playing techniques performed by Hae-kyung Um. Some students commented that this experience enabled them to gain a deeper understanding of the differences between classical male and female singing techniques, demonstrated in the form of chest and head voice. Other students felt that they grasped the difference between contemporary and traditional playing styles on the *kayagŭm*. The ethnomusicologist agreed that 'they really take it in because actually seeing it when someone is doing it seems to make for very good communication …. I think it works for every level … when you could activate lecture and your performance skills' (Hae-kyung Um, Belfast, 18 November 2003). At SOAS, students similarly experienced specialist musicians demonstrating musical instruments during a lecture on Thai classical music. Students paid particular attention to certain playing techniques, for example the Thai categorisation into *diid* (to pluck), *siid* (to bow), *tii* (to hit) and *paw* (to blow), which was demonstrated by the guest musicians on a range of Thai instruments (Figure 6.1). Most students commented after the lecture that it was 'useful and interesting to see real instruments ... as this brought the strange music culture alive' (informal group interview, SOAS, 10 November 2003). Indeed unknown and strange music cultures can become more real and relevant to students due to their visual experiences. Some students suggested that 'knowing what the instruments look like made it easier to understand how they are used in Thai music' (informal group interview, SOAS, 10 November 2003).

During a *mbira* workshop at Bangor University, students similarly found it to be important to be able to 'put a picture to the name ... [because] it was different than I imagined', whilst other students showed an interest in its construction and were astonished about 'the detail that went into making the instrument' (group discussion, Bangor, 6 March 2006). Seeing an instrument for real rather than in pictures enabled students better to relate to it. Yet whilst their visual participatory experiences allowed students to grasp the instrument's intricate characteristics, students also frequently emphasised hearing the instrument's sound. Live demonstrations by specialist musicians seemed particularly interesting. The students who participated in the *mbira* workshop commented that 'this is the main thing that sticks out in my mind .... It really helped with understanding how the instrument sounded ... [and it was] very interesting ... to hear the different effects created' (group discussion, Bangor, 6 March 2006). At Sheffield University, meanwhile, students emphasised the fact that they 'got to hear the sound for real, not just on a recording .... Also hearing her perform was great, better than hearing recordings alone' (group interview, Sheffield, 20 February 2004), while particularly referring to live demonstrations on the Chinese *guqin* and *guzheng*. Rebecca felt that 'the live demonstrations on these Chinese zithers were really good because I will not forget that .... You can appreciate it better .... They didn't do very much, not very complex stuff, but I liked it nevertheless because you could actually see and hear it' (Sheffield, 20 February 04).

Besides live demonstrations, students also experienced more active participation in form of actual sound production, even though some scholars may dismiss such activities as being superficial music-making and dabbling.[1] Yet the extent of active involvement was obviously determined by the musical instrument and style. In one instance, students learnt about Taiwanese *nanguan* music and particularly how traditional musicians learn to perform this music and the appropriate behaviours associated with its performance. Students experienced how to pass instruments politely, count and play the beat on woodblocks and sing the melody in a melismatic manner. During students' singing, the ethnomusicologist demonstrated the melody

---

[1] The 7th International Symposium entitled *The Local and the Global* on Cultural Diversity in Music Education (CDIME) held in Australia in November 2005 included a theme on 'Dabbling or Deepening', asking questions such as: 'With the increased interest over the past twenty years, has world music become a commodity that is best dealt with superficially: bang away on an African drum, improvise along the scale of an Indian raga? How is the balance between introductions to world music and profound immersion into other musical styles and idioms?' (CDIME, Call for Papers, 5 August 2004).

Figure 6.1   Koong Paphutsorn Wongratanapitak demonstrating Thai musical instruments, SOAS, September 2006

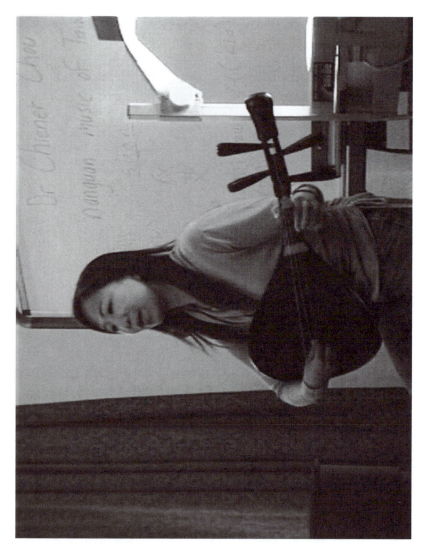

Figure 6.2   Chou Chiener demonstrating the Chinese *pipa*; University of Sheffield, 30 April 2004

Figure 6.3   Andrew Killick demonstrating the Korean *kayagŭm* in a lecture on East Asian music; University of Sheffield, 15 February 2004

on the *pipa* and emphasised that 'once you can sing this, it is easier to transfer the melody to the instruments' (Chou Chiener, Sheffield, 30 April 2004) (Figure 6.2). Students finally tried playing the melody on various instruments passed around the group, yet this activity was too difficult to accomplish so that students simply tried producing sounds on these instruments.

The extent to which students can acquire musical performance skills obviously depends on the music's intricacies and the construction and playing technique of the musical instruments. Some aerophones, such as the Japanese *shakuhachi* require rigorous instruction and practice before an actual sound can be produced. Unfretted chordophones, such as the Chinese *erhu* can challenge students' initial efforts to produce meaningful melodies. Meanwhile, some idiophones and membranophones may be constructed in such a way that students could more rapidly 'learn to play the rhythms that are used in the music and put them together. So students can experience more of the music. But you can do that only if you have got an instrument that students can make rapid progress with' (Andrew Killick, Sheffield, 7 May 2004). Whilst the instruments themselves clearly determined students' musical experiences during seeing-hearing-trying musical instruments, it also led them to express heightened interest in and awareness of the various world musics and instruments. Joanne commented that 'dabbling is a useful way of getting to grips with a strange instrument' (Sheffield, 20 February 2004). Experiencing actual sound production on a physical level also surprised many students about the difficulties in handling the instruments. Students commented that 'I didn't think it would be that hard to play .... I had no idea how difficult it can be .... The instruments were very different to my preconceptions' (group interview, Bangor, 6 March 2006). Students who participated in the Taiwanese lecture also suggested that:

> It helped me to relate to the instruments and to experience Taiwanese culture ....
> Instead of a theoretical experience, I have a practical one which has increased
> my understanding of this topic .... It was good to see the materials used, how
> the instruments are played and the sound they create .... It was brilliant to try
> out the instruments and to experience them first-hand .... It was very exciting to
> hold the instruments. This informed me better on the way the instruments work.
> (group discussion, Sheffield, 7 May 2004)

Students generally felt that seeing-hearing-trying musical instruments and watching live demonstrations enriched their musical encounters. I frequently heard students commenting that 'it was really helpful in gaining a better idea of the instrument, its construction and how it works [and] holding and trying the instrument was a wonderful experience! I really want to buy one and use it in compositions' (group discussion, Bangor, 6 March 2006). Students' experiences of world musics clearly involved visual, audio and kinaesthetic dimensions, as they engaged with the material culture at physical and cognitive level. Their experiences were more complete and meaningful, often instilling in students excitement and further interest in the music culture. Seeing and hearing the Hardanger fiddle, Sandra felt that 'if I hadn't had the experience of seeing and hearing it, it wouldn't have seemed relevant in the literature, and I would just have turned the page .... It's about getting exposure to things' (Belfast, 18 November 2003). For this reason, most ethnomusicologists advocated that (Figure 6.3):

> Effective teaching is always to have the instrument with you. To have a physical object to show people makes things much more real to students, especially when they learn about music from a distant part of the world. So the ideal thing is having an instrument there that you can play. I suppose the next best thing is having an instrument there that you can't play because at least you can show it, show what it looks like. (Andrew Killick, Sheffield, 17 October 2003)

Occasional World Musics Workshops

Students also discovered material culture during occasional workshops, of which there existed two types, namely workshops that imitated the music's material culture in the form of sing-along and play-along participation and workshops that utilised real music instruments. Even though the first kind of workshop utilised simple and easily learned musical imitations (see also Seeger, 2002:112), both kinds of workshop were musically more meaningful to students than dabbling on musical instruments, as workshops transmitted a complete (albeit often short) performance piece. This enabled students to experience deeper-level musical consciousness, whilst entering (albeit only to some extent) the stage of discovering musical expression and form.

Workshops Imitating Material Culture

At Goldsmiths College London, I participated in a lecture-workshop on Palestinian music led by Reem Kelani, a London-based singer from Palestine.[2] The sing-along participation induced positive and meaningful musical experiences in students through a state of embodied experiencing (see also Kisliuk and Gross, 2004). The session was informative and stimulating as the tutor blended formal instruction with practical demonstrations and active audience involvement. For example, Reem Kelani vocalised melody and rhythm, sang (through improvisation) classical Arabic poetry, and demonstrated the *shabbaabeh* flute and *daf* frame drum. Students were completely immersed in their musical experiences. The tutor also approached students in a non-patronising, enjoyable manner, which

---

[2]   I am very grateful to Reem Kelani for providing detailed comments on this chapter. The debut album *Sprinting Gazelle: Palestinian Songs from the Motherland and the Diaspora* (2006) provides an excellent insight into Reem Kelani's beautiful musical style (see also http://www.reemkelani.com/).

was visible in their smiling and laughing. The following vignette helps to evoke the overall picture of this session, which intentionally avoids analytical and interpretive discussions (see also LeCompte and Schensul, 1999b). The rich and thick descriptions help illustrating the ways in which students experienced musical participation that led them towards deeper and more complete musical experiences. Yet it must be emphasised that such an ethnographic 'impressionist's tale' (Van Maanen, 1988:101–24) is always shaped by the researcher's own biases and preconceptions. The vignette thus serves the purpose of providing subjective insights into the ways in which simple, in-class imitations were utilised as an effective means for enthusing students that led not only to heightened levels of participatory consciousness but also towards an awareness that extended beyond the level of music's sonic structure:

> While we sat on chairs in a half-circle, the tutor started by asking to put both feet firmly down on the floor and to think of them as our tonic centre, playing an extract of *Qur-ānic* chant and writing the words *maqam bayati* on the whiteboard.[3] She asked invitingly while smiling: 'I would like to know what you felt.' We replied: 'comforted …; it was very primal (?) …; it's very cosmic ….' A practical exercise followed during which we were asked to stand up and sing the same tonic pitch, on top of which the tutor improvised a melodic line, walking around the circle to hear each of us singing the tonic. Then she played a CD extract of a Christian hymn, suggesting: 'this uses melisma … and *'ourab* (vocal ornamentations) …. Any comments on this?' We replied: 'This seems to sound more Arabic', upon which she answered: 'Yes, exactly. It's Christian Arab. The recitation, NOT singing of the *Qur-ān* is called *tajweed* or *tarteel* … and *Qur-ānic* chanting is very close to Byzantine, also Greek chanting'.
>
> 'Now I am going to sing another example ….' The tutor's voice is not only beautiful; she also demonstrated very clearly how improvisation works, how to ornament a basic melodic line. She invited us to join in by humming the tonic. We then commented about our reactions to the singing: 'I kind of forgot the world around me and became totally lulled into the sound. I was really aware of the group of singers …', upon which the tutor replied: 'This is exactly the feeling and experience I hoped you'd have ….' We commented that: 'After a while I felt that your singing left my head somehow, as if it was disappearing …', upon which the tutor replied: 'Yes, I started singing in *maqam hijaz* and modulated to *sijah* and back to *hijaz*. This is called *qaflah*', meaning to return to the original *maqam* and 'closing' the musical sentence. We asked why she covered her ear while singing, which some of us had seen on a picture before. She did not answer this question, but instead encouraged us to try it ourselves

---

[3]   In the literature, there exist numerous ways for writing the word 'Quran'. Here, I will use Qur-ān, based on K. N. Davies', *The Qur-ān Recited* (The Garland Encyclopedia of World Music, Volume 6, The Middle East; 2002:157–63).

while singing a tone. It worked, of course, to our astonishment: 'Yes, I can hear my own voice much better when covering the ear ....'

'The third part in Arabic music besides the tonic, which you sang and the melodic mode, which I sang, are rhythmic patterns, also called *iqa* ...', writing on the whiteboard: *dum, tak, silence, tak, dum, silence, tak, silence*. 'This is *iqa maqsum*', inviting us to vocalise the rhythm. The tutor showed a *daf* frame-drum and further explained the two basic drumstrokes, dum and tak: 'Dum is produced by hitting the middle of the skin. Imitate the sound with your voice!' We reacted rather shyly, upon which she encouraged us to really feel the dum as coming from the chest. She started imitating a Western aria in a high falsetto voice, pulling a funny facial expression, to our enjoyment. 'Don't sing like this! Sing out of your chest, like that!', demonstrating the dum in a much breathier and deeper tone.

The tutor bubbled over with enthusiasm, which made it much easier for us to lose our inhibition. We now sang much louder, more confidently and ... much better! While we now chanted the rhythm loud and clearly, the tutor started improvising elaborate rhythms on the *daf*, walking around, smiling and laughing with us. Everybody was completely immersed in this experience and enjoyed themselves. One after the other of us proceeded in dance-like motion, getting literally into the groove. A following exercise increased the intensity of the musical experience even further: one half of us now hummed the tonic, while the others chanted the basic rhythm, over which the tutor improvised an elaborate rhythm on the *daf* and sang a melody based on a *qasida*. The tutor kept moving around the group, smiling and laughing at us, and resembling a performance-like appearance with facial expressions and opened arms, which reminded me of performances by Umm Kulthūm. She showed her experiencing of emotions through tensioning her body and facial expression. Her voice was fantastic. Our music-making was thrilling. We truly experienced the groove. Afterwards, I remembered that I had completely forgotten the world around me. After ten minutes the tutor moved her arms in an inviting motion to become quieter and to finally stop, looking at us with honest appreciation and astonishment.

After this enthralling exercise, we discussed our experiences and all confirmed a deep, emotional response, upon which the tutor explained the Arabic concept of *tarab*, an ecstatic emotional response by performers and listeners at the heart of much Spanish and Arabic musical performance. Somehow it was possible for the tutor to convey some extent of *tarab* to us in this workshop.

The tutor now imitated the *flamenco* style of singing and laughed full-heartedly about her poor attempt. She demonstrated the grabbing and ripping-off of clothes by performers when *tarab* or *duende* is being experienced, commenting that still today many *flamenco* singers pull their shirts .... Encouraging shouts from the audience, such as *Ole* originating in the Arab word *Allah* (meaning God) are used in praise of a good performance that is when *tarab* is being felt. The lively session ended and we continued talking, singing and playing long after the workshop had finished. (Fieldnotes, Goldsmiths, 13 February 2004)

Recreating the music by singing the drone and chanting the rhythms, while at the same time feeling the music's emotional content, clearly led students towards profound participatory experiences. The use of real musical instruments and imitations, together with the singer's melismatic, Arabic-sounding vocal delivery provided first-hand insights into the material culture so characteristic for Arabic music. Yet I also observed other workshops utilising simple sing-along musical imitations when students expressed concerns about the depth of their musical understanding. In a class on East Asian music, students experienced Korean music through vocally imitating its melody, rhythm and texture. Rebecca explained that:

> It was a bit silly really .... We did like Korean rhythms and sort of acted out the parts because he didn't have any of the instruments that we could play. So we were being the sounds and it was quite fun .... It was good to have more hands-on experience of it .... We just acted the instruments out. We were walking around in a circle saying things like *Ding, ding, dang, dang, dung* .... I really can't remember the sounds. But it was quite fun .... And then we sort of acted it out which was quite fun. I mean, it was just ... a good idea to do it .... Feeling it, being it, rather than listening all the time. But I don't think that I got that much out of it in reality. I don't know. (Rebecca, Sheffield, 20 February 2004)

Meanwhile, in a class on Ghanaian music, students learnt about rhythm through simple play-along imitations of the original percussion music. Yet learning to clap the rhythms of the bell and the rattle simultaneously (used to accompany an African children's rhyme) was too difficult for students. For this reason, the ethnomusicologist asked students to replace the African children's rhyme with an English equivalent that matched its rhythm and stress, alongside which students were asked to perform suitable jumping movements. Some students clearly enjoyed the active participation, such as Joanne who emphasised the fun and enjoyment experienced in this workshop. Some students, such as Rebecca, felt that they grasped the music's sonic structure. Yet other students like Melanie were more critical of this activity:

> Last week we were clapping the rhythms. We did that again this week and we talked about how the ... melody line comes over the top rhythm, and how the different percussion instruments have a different pitch as well. So, it makes it easier to differentiate between each of the lines. (Rebecca, Sheffield, 17 October 2003)

> That was really fun. I enjoyed that. Why? We jumped up and down. It's a bit more involved than being lectured at. So we learn more. He can tell you about rhythm, but until you are doing it yourself, it's not gonna make sense. (Joanne, Sheffield, 10 October 2003)

> I didn't really know what he wanted to bring out or to show us with that kind of thing; I am not sure. Maybe it's a kind of teaching method in Africa; that they teach people … just by … actually being involved. And then you feel the music … and can just pick up the music, rather than learning it very formally. (Melanie, Sheffield, 20 October 2003)

Students' responses remind us that their musical experiences are always individualistic and subjective, yet also highlight some of the problems that may arise when using simple imitations of world musics in the university classroom. There is obviously an inherent danger to transmit to students a perspective that world musics are simple (by Western standards) and therefore easy to imitate. It is thus crucial for ethnomusicologists to be critical about the ways in which simple imitation workshops can lead students more fully to understand material culture.

Workshops Using Musical Instruments

Besides imitative workshops, there were also workshops that utilised musical instruments, and these often generated in students heightened states of arousal and enjoyment. Reflecting on the *kora* workshop at the University of Sheffield (Figure 4.2), Joanne stated that:

> The *kora* workshop was amazing! … The *kora* workshop was so good because we were improvising and singing along. I just thought 'We need more of this!' It is really important to experience it musically …. The music makes more sense when we are actually practically involved as musicians. Just listening to the music, I won't remember half those tracks in a few months. (Joanne, Sheffield, 20 February 04)

During this workshop, students were not only engaged in the playing of the *kora* but also participated through singing and clapping. Joanne commented that 'when we were singing, I definitely felt much more connected to the music and understood the culture behind it better' (Sheffield, 20 February 2004). Some students clearly related better to the singing or engaged with the material culture, whilst others gained deeper insights into the operational features of the musical instrument. Edward comprehended some of the instrument's technical and operational characteristics, thus revealing a deeper understanding of the music's material culture:

> The instrument … is like tuned to F …. The alternating strings left and right to the bridge create the scale …. Is it pentatonic? I don't know. I'm not too sure …. It's just right-left-right-left-right-left …. At a certain point this changes … because of the bottom three strings on the right …. This workshop experience certainly helped me with my transcription project in what you can do with it and how to play. (Edward, Sheffield, 12 December 2003)

At Bangor University, meanwhile, students engaged in a *mbira* workshop during which they gained a sense of the complexities of the musical instrument and the form and texture of the music through their active participation in singing and playing. Students highlighted particularly the singing element by suggesting 'I can't believe he made us sing! … I particularly liked the singing element' (group discussion, Bangor, 6 March 2006). Students also compared their experience to multi-tasking, suggesting that *mbira* performance was difficult as the music was created in multiple parts. Indeed, even those world musics that do not seem particularly difficult can be challenging to students in the West. To one student, the performance experience 'made me see it's a hard instrument to play properly. To perform while singing and clapping showed how hard it can be to do both', while another student commented that 'I learnt that I can't triple-task' (group discussion, Bangor, 6 March 2006). Students clearly developed a deeper appreciation of the musical demands on the performer and the music's difficulties, as they found the musical performance more complex than initially expected. Another student commented similarly that 'it made me realise that *mbira* musicians have to be quite skilled to be able to perform the music well' (*ibid.*). This in turn provided a sense of accomplishment to those students who were able to make progress on the instrument. Students also claimed to have established a deeper understanding of the musical culture, giving one student 'a sense of being in a *mbira* celebration', whilst to another student, 'it was helpful for my understanding of *mbira* music and how it is used in parts of African culture' (*ibid.*). Similarly, another student felt that the workshop enabled a deeper understanding of how the multilayered music 'reflects African co-operative community life' (*ibid.*).

It is clear from the discussions that world music workshops enabled students to have deeper and more profound learning experiences into a music's material culture. Yet some ethnomusicologists somewhat discarded such workshops as 'in French, *animation*' (John Baily, telephone interview, 7 June 2006). Students often agreed that 'it would be good to have more world music workshops because more of this sort of learning would be beneficial' (group discussion, Bangor, 6 March 2006), and 'I wish we could have had longer with the *kora*!' (Joanne, Sheffield, 20 February 2004). There thus exists a clear need for longer-lasting, rather than occasional performance experiences, and this will be the focus of the subsequent chapter.

Chapter 7

Performing Music,
Discovering Expression and Form

More longitudinal, regular ensemble participation and learning to perform a musical instrument enabled students to discover musical expression and form. Musical expression, in particular, involved students' personal and individual response to a particular piece of music, whilst musical form was discovered when students understood that sound and pieces become more organised through phrase structure, rhythm and metre, and melodic gesture. Students also understood music-as-music more deeply due to the (frequent) requirement of a final performance for formal assessment. Yet whilst students had more goal-directed musical experiences, this also resulted in considerable performance anxiety. Nonetheless, during this type of performing ethnomusicology, students developed more advanced musical and technical skills over a limited, bounded period of time, allowing them to gain a more enriched and complete musical understanding. Longitudinal participation in *gamelan* ensembles, for example, occurred frequently across universities, in which the ethnomusicologist or ensemble teacher began by teaching basic pieces transcribed in cipher notation and moved on to practise longer, more complex pieces. Students often stated that such longer-lasting performance experiences were the most significant aspect of their musical study, as it helped them more fully to grasp and understand the music's structure and workings. Playing in the *gamelan* also allowed students to develop better oral–aural skills. Some York students who studied *The Music of Indonesia* commented that (Figure 4.1):

> The practical side, the playing, is the most significant aspect of this project to me ... not only learning about the different tuning systems, instruments, etc. but also experiencing that. (George, York, 17 May 2004)

> Every Monday afternoon when we are actually playing, that helps a lot in my understanding .... I think the best part is the playing. Without playing you don't grasp it completely, I think .... It's the best way to learn .... Playing is definitely the best way to help you understand it .... Musically, I feel that I have developed better aural skills .... Outside of music ... it sort of offers a view into other cultures ... which is interesting. (Stephanie, York, 17 May 2004)

Meanwhile, some students like Patrick at QUB participated in ensembles outside the university, and this longitudinal ensemble practice helped him to develop more confidence as an ensemble flautist. He described his experiences as non-patronising while being in the position of musical learner:

> I actually reached the level where I could play in a band, which I didn't know if I could do when I first started …. But it's not really out of reach. So the confidence is part of it, and the enjoyment, and as I say, it's a way of studying society in a non-patronising manner …. You are accepted as being an aspiring flute-player there and the fact is that you are not really as good as all the other people there and willing to learn from them. It's a much better situation to be in. (Patrick, Belfast, 19 November 2003)

Whether inside or outside the university setting, most students valued and appreciated such practical experiences. Some students even suggested that longitudinal performance practice created a certain intimacy between themselves and the music that may be impossible through a mere imagining of the music. Celine felt more complete and whole, as 'it felt like a part of yourself, rather than being distant to it' (Sheffield, 30 April 04), whilst Kathrin commented that:

> I tend to find playing music very important in any case, not only as part of this course. Then you get a totally different relationship to it. Then you don't just hear it and forget half of it anyway …. That may also be an incentive for the teacher …. You cannot just talk about it to schoolchildren either. Then you can also 'get into' it much more and understand the people better. I found it good when … last week … the Norwegian man was here, and we even danced – Norwegian dances – and his wife played this instrument live. This has a totally different effect. I believe that you never forget that, because these lectures indeed whoosh past [without any effect] relatively quickly again …. And so I find it equally important … that we 'go into' [the topic] properly and experience for ourselves what this really means. (Kathrin, Rostock, 24 November 03)[1]

Expressions that emphasise an 'intimacy with the music' or 'it felt part of yourself' or 'I got into the music' indicate a truly deeper engagement with and relationship to

---

[1]   Die Musik zu spielen würde ich auf jeden Fall sehr wichtig finden, auch als Teil dieses Kurses. Dann kriegt man einen ganz anderen Bezug dazu. Dann hört man das nicht nur und vergisst sowieso die Hälfte wieder … Das wär dann vielleicht auch noch mehr Anregung für den Lehrer … Den Schülern [Schulkinder] kann man das auch nicht einfach nur so erzählen. Dann kann man sich vielmehr auch hineinversetzen und die Völker auch besser verstehen. Das fand ich eben gut, als … letzte Woche … der Norweger hier war, und wir dann sogar getanzt haben – Norwegische Tänze – und seine Frau spielte dieses Instrument live. Das hat eine ganz andere Wirkung. Das vergisst man, glaub ich, nie, weil diese Vorlesungen doch relativ schnell wieder an einem vorbeirauschen … Und so find ich das genauso wichtig … dass man richtig auch reingeht, und das dann selber erfahren kann, wie das wirklich ist (Kathrin, Rostock, 24 November 03).

the music. Such experiences are often profound and deeply satisfying, particularly during the discovering of musical expression that follows the discovery of form. It is the personal and individual response to a particular piece of music that intensifies one's own musical understanding, leading from hearing and surface comprehending (during which form is discovered) towards deeper knowing. When such personal experiences are triggered by performing music, students often felt a sense of musical ownership that was unique to them and felt very special indeed.

Learning to Perform as a Research Technique in Ethnomusicology

One excellent example of performing ethnomusicology is John Baily's concept of learning to perform as a research technique in ethnomusicology, which can provide potential insights into musical structure and the methods and institutions for musical transmission (Baily, 2001:96). At Goldsmiths College in London, I encountered this same concern during my first round of research in 2003. Here, students on the MMus in Ethnomusicology selected music from a repertoire outside of their own primary music culture so as to learn to perform it (for the duration of up to one year), which culminated in a final performance at the end of their studies. This required students – without much guidance of the learning process itself – to discover and explore a music culture and to draw their own musical and cultural conclusions. According to the course description:

> The rationale for the performance exam is using 'learning to perform' as a research technique. It is not expected that the candidate should necessarily reach a particularly high standard, certainly not 'public concert' or equivalent .... The candidate must show some progress in performance as a result of a learning/research process, a matter to be explored in the performance viva. (MMus course description, Goldsmith College London, 2003/04)

During a personal conversation with John Baily, he explained that (Figure 7.1):

> There is the whole argument about as a performer, the kinds of insights you get into the music itself, you know, understanding it from the inside. In some ways, this is comparable to learning the language of the people with whom you are working, rather than always being on the outside, having to negotiate through translators .... Then there were the reasons that people can understand perhaps more readily what you are doing when ... actually to learn to perform, rather than do more abstract kind of research that they can't really understand ... because they don't have training in ethnomusicology .... Then there is the aspect of the *entrée* that it gives you into, let's just call it, scene, so being within the musician community, however big or small that may be .... It's a very good way of becoming a member of the community because in many such musician communities, there is a notion of learning and apprenticeship, and you are

readily slotted into a pre-established role. And the consequence of that is you get to hear about all sorts of things, about what's going on in the world of music, just through the fact that the people you are working with, hanging out with …, which in non-musician-circles people hardly talk about at all. (John Baily, telephone interview, 7 June 2006)

Figure 7.1   John Baily playing the *rubab*; 31 October 2001; photograph by
               Simon Turtle

In 2006, I conducted – with John Baily's generous support – a follow-up programme of research that included telephone and skype interviews with the ethnomusicologist and two MMus students. I also wished to talk to students who had completed the programme, and I was fortunate to be able to re-establish contact with Argibel whom I had met at Goldsmiths in 2003 and who was now living in the Basque country. During conversations with John Baily and students, I found that the main concern of learning to perform was to gain musical insights and to understand it as a research method:

> The student is encouraged to think of learning to perform as not just learning to perform, but as a way of doing research, something that, if they go on later, they will apply those ideas to their learning experience …. The other part is that they have to document this in a performance diary …. It is a document that supports the student's claim to have used learning to perform as a research technique … about how they have gone about it. (John Baily, telephone interview, 7 June 2006)

As indicated here, students also had to write reflexive accounts about their learning processes and present these during a viva that followed the formal performance. Performing ethnomusicology thus served as a training ground or preparation for ethnomusicological research and included instrumental and singing practice, and at times also dancing. Students selected all kinds of musics, including the Greek *bouzouki*, African and Afro-Caribbean dance, Uzbek *dutar*, Indian singing, Spanish *flamenco* guitar, Bluegrass guitar, African guitar, to name a few selected examples. Musical skills in these specialist genres or styles were learnt either through ensemble participation in a chosen community or during individual, private lessons with a native specialist. To provide a more specific example, Argibel who already possessed some experience playing Western drumkit learnt to perform on the Iranian single-headed, goblet-shaped drum *tombak* (Figure 7.2).[2] Lessons with a specialist teacher started in January 2004, culminating in a 30-minute performance in June 2004. At that time, Argibel revealed considerable concern about the strong performance element, as it counted one-third towards the total final mark. He also felt anxious about the forthcoming final performance and explained that:

> I try to prepare my performance …. I didn't know that performance was so important, so weighted. I mean, the third part of the whole assessment of the whole (MMus) programme is worth as [much as] a whole dissertation …. I was really surprised …. You really have to work hard for it! (Argibel, Goldsmith, 12 February 2004)

---

[2]   While the single-headed drum exists in various countries with different names (*darbukka, darabukka, dumbuk, dumbak),* in my writings, I will use the spelling *tombak* according to Argibel's suggestion.

Other Goldsmiths students even felt that 'I was terrified, absolutely terrified' (Jake, skype interview, 4 July 2006), and 'I was a bit nervous during the performance ... because you do want to perform well, you do want ... to show that you have learnt something, that you can achieve something on that instrument .... I did want to show that I could play' (Natasha, telephone interview, 10 July 2006). Such strong feelings about the final performance led most students to focus on the musical aspects of performing ethnomusicology. To Argibel, 'the cultural aspects were secondary' in learning to perform, which instead revolved around 'knowing more about the actual process of learning to perform, and the technical aspects' (skype interview, 3 June 2006). Jake similarly focused on mastering the instrument (here, the Gypsy mandolin) and emphasised that 'I really want to get a feel for the music and the workings of the instrument' (skype interview, 4 July 2006). Natasha, meanwhile, learnt to perform on the *sitar* and was 'very interested in the learning process itself ... to work my way around the *sitar*' (telephone interview, 10 July 2006). Anna, who immersed herself in the Indian community in London while participating in an Indian singing workshop, similarly reflected that:

> I don't know if I only understood the culture or meanings by singing or by socialising with my Indian friends because [giggles politely]. I am not sure if I am able to use this as a tool to learn something else from another culture .... For me ... I don't think it works for me. (Anna, Goldsmiths, 11 February 2004)

John Baily agreed that 'not all of our students engage with the community and its culture' (telephone interview, 7 June 2006). In a few instances, however, students also engaged with music-as-culture, yet 'it is usually the more exceptional ones who ... do kind of enter into the scene in some depth' (*ibid.*). Natasha, for instance 'noticed that the musicians are so disciplined, and there is such an emphasis on going away and practicing .... but in terms of background information about Indian culture itself, I did not learn that much' (telephone interview, 10 July 2006). The majority of Goldsmiths students thus focused on gaining musical skills and understanding whilst trying to develop technical competence on their chosen instrument. This will be further illustrated in the subsequent section by focusing specifically on how Argibel mastered the *tombak* while gaining a deep-level understanding of the music's intricacies.

Mastering the tombak, *discovering expression and form*

Argibel aimed at mastering the *tombak* and to learn about Iranian music. His initial experiences of the instrument were 'tough [as] it's quite hard to produce the actual sounds required .... It has a very complex finger technique, and you really have to make very precise movements'. The instrument's specific playing technique necessitated Argibel's dedicated and regular practice, whilst the first weeks were spent learning to play the basic drum strokes in order 'to try to reach the proper sound and also to make the fingers stronger because you have to play flicks with your fingers, which are quite painful at first' (skype interview, 3 June 2006) (Figure 7.2; note the intricate finger techniques used to perform on the *tombak*).[3] This same concern with developing technical competence was also evident in Argibel's reflexive learning diary. Providing one example, Argibel described his diary entry as follows:

Figure 7.2   Argibel practising the *tombak*; Bilbao (Basque country), June 2006

I'm having problems with this finger and this particular stroke, and I think if I move my wrist in a different way, it would be better, and I think my wrist is more relaxed now than before. And my forearm shouldn't move from the drum. I mean, it's pretty much like that. (Argibel, skype interview, 3 June 2006)

Before Argibel came close to discovering musical expression and form in Iranian music, he had to engage in the routinely practising of the instrument's basic playing technique. As this was a significant challenge, Argibel focused his efforts on improving the actual sound production on the *tombak*. The reflexive learning diary was pivotal in the learning process, leading Argibel critically to reflect on the skills and techniques required to master the instrument. The learning diary thus supported Argibel in focusing on music-as-music:

> For me, the most important thing was having that attitude of analysing everything I was doing. I was always practising with my notebook beside me. After each lesson, of course, I would take many notes. And then, while I was practising, I would also keep an eye on those notes. And I would take more notes certainly on what I was doing, not only the exercises that I was doing, but also how I was dealing with them, and how I was feeling about them, or what I could do. So I think that was really, really effective not only as a learning tool, or as a tool for research, but actually it was very effective to learn how to play the instrument much faster …. If I had done that with the drumkit, or with my first instrument, I think it would have been much more effective from the beginning. I think it forces you to have an attitude that you wouldn't otherwise have while you are learning to perform an instrument. (Argibel, skype interview, 3 June 2006)

The subsequent step involved the discovery of form. Argibel learnt how Iranian music is rhythmically organised, while 'combining the actual technique itself with a few basic rhythms'. In preparation to the performance, Argibel learnt to perform solo in order to demonstrate the acquisition of technical competence and knowledge of basic rhythms that were played 'in a row … starting with 6/4, then 4/4, 2/4, 6/8'. The learning process was shaped by an important landmark when Argibel learnt to play more complex rhythmical accompaniments to music performed on the Iranian *tar*, which also formed some of the repertoire in preparation to the final performance. This consisted of several compositions and songs in the *radif*, the traditional Persian repertoire. At this point, learning to perform on the *tombak* became more intense and rigorous and felt musically more complete. Learning to perform the compositions and songs in the *radif* also led Argibel to discover musical expression in Iranian music. Considering artistic meaning and expressivity, Argibel explained that:

> *Tombak* … belongs to that tradition … it's an accompanying instrument …. After all, what the instrument had to do was accompany the melodic instrument …. What I had to do was listen carefully to the main melodic instrument, and try to

evoke or express the same thing as the other instrument through my instrument. (Argibel, skype interview, 3 June 2006)

Discovering expression also meant having to internalise and assimilate the rhythmic patterns, enabling Argibel to feel the rhythms and to assume what rhythmical pattern fits the music. Argibel entered into a process of experiencing his own personal and individual response to the music in which musical discovery occurred not only at cognitive but also motor-sensory level and resulted in the ability to 'feel that you can express more with the instrument'. This led towards deeper familiarity with the musical tradition as a performer, as 'I played all these patterns, and they would just come out so naturally, so fluent. I don't know, I couldn't really think about them, they could come as reflex .... There was something like a motor-grammar that wasn't explicit' (Argibel, skype interview, 3 June 2006). Musical competence beyond mere technical skill also enabled the experiencing of a shared musical understanding with the *tar* player during the final performance, a state of musical involvement, which ethnomusicologists often aspire to achieve. Argibel described that:

> ... as Persian classical music is not fixed ... the songs were not going to be same as we had rehearsed .... We just looked at each other, and I accompanied him. The last song, for example, was much shorter than we had rehearsed .... We didn't have any problem to understand .... We weren't having any misunderstanding .... It was very nice! (Argibel, skype interview, 3 June 2006)

Learning to Perform: Exploring Music's Sonic Qualities

Learning to perform as a technique for research in ethnomusicology formed striking and profound experiences to most students. To Jake, this experience opened up possibilities for continued music making with Eastern European musicians in London. It was also the social aspect that led him to strive towards high levels of musical competence, as 'they [other musicians] were of such a high standard ... that the only way I would even be tolerated was ... to achieve some level of what they considered acceptable' (Jake, skype interview, 4 July 2006). To Natasha, such experiences opened up her perceptions of acquiring musical competence so useful for her own music teaching, whilst also continuing to play the Indian *sitar* together with other Indian musicians. According to Hae-kyung Um, learning to perform can also enable students to 'become musical insiders ... [because] their musical involvement was much, much greater' (Belfast, 18 November 2003). They can understand the music from the inside, comprehend it operationally, learn something about the music's ergonomics and the ways in which it reflects the human sensory-motor system, and apprehend something about the instrument's morphology (Baily, 2001). Students thus recognised that learning to perform is a useful research technique in ethnomusicology so as to develop deeper musical understandings:

The best part was the opportunity of doing this performance at the end, so that they give you the possibility to specialise in something and to spend one year to get deep into it. Because you kind of know that you only have one year and so you give everything. (Alexandra, Goldsmiths, 11 February 2004)

When you are trying to learn to play an instrument, you get so many insights, you wouldn't have otherwise. I mean, if I wanted to analyse rhythmic aspects in Persian music, or actually the rhythms in *tombak*, or a particular type of stroke or pattern in this rhythm, I think it would be impossible to do it properly without playing it. Then you actually see the difficulties, and the advantages, and the different characteristics of the process. (Argibel, skype interview, 3 June 2006)

In some instances, students also learnt about the ways in which a musical tradition would typically be passed down. Natasha, for example, learnt to perform on the *sitar* by imitating and memorising scales and musical passages demonstrated by her teacher during formal, individual lessons. She explained that 'I began with practising lots of technical exercises for about five months ... to know my way around the *sitar*', which was followed by learning just one *raga* and composition at the time. Natasha indeed felt that 'my teacher is quite traditional in the way he teaches, so there are very strict guidelines as to what you can do when' (telephone interview, 10 July 2006).

More generally, students' learning experiences seemed to be profound in developing in-depth understandings of an unknown type of music. Yet it is important to emphasise here that learning to perform as a research technique often focused students' attention towards the study of music-as-music. Some students, for instance, concentrated on the routinely practicing of technical exercises in order to acquire high-level musical competence. Some students even suggested that 'strangely enough, it was like learning any other [Western] instrument .... It was a long, slow process starting ... playing a line incredibly slowly and just slowly speeding it up' (Jake, skype interview, 4 July 2006). Jake followed a rather formulaic routine of constantly repeating more difficult musical parts with the help of a metronome. Such practicing of exercises resembled Western ways of acquiring musical and technical competence. Jake's pre-existing ideas surrounding musical progression through 'taking graded examinations on the piano' seemed further to contribute to his adapting of Western learning practices (*ibid.*). Yet from an ethnomusicological perspective, students may be guided more directly towards learning about both musical and cultural aspects of a music-cultural practice that is quite dissimilar to Western music. In doing so, students would not only gain in-depth knowledge about music's sonic structures but also insights into the contexts in which the music is made. A more nuanced pedagogical approach would thereby resonate more closely with contemporary ethnomusicology's concern with people making music. Nonetheless, from an educational standpoint, students' appropriation of Western methods during performing ethnomusicology is indeed desirable, as it enabled them to achieve advanced performance skills in a non-

Western musical style within a relatively short period of time. Learning about music-as-music through this type of performing ethnomusicology helped students to develop complex knowledge and deep-level understandings into the music's sonic qualities.

Chapter 8
Performing Music, Experiencing Emotion

The previous chapters have shown that musical experiences may be extremely pleasing to many students, specifically at the first performance level of discovering material culture. Returning to the *mbira* workshop mentioned earlier, students summarised their experiences as 'interesting, intriguing, informative, enjoyable, memorable, fascinating, excellent and horizon-widening' (group discussion, Bangor, 6 March 2006). Interacting with a living music culture, this simple workshop was enjoyable in the otherwise formal educational environment:

> It was fun to learn how to play the *mbira* …. It was amazing. I found it far more interesting than I expected …. I really enjoyed the workshop …. Awesome fun! … I really enjoyed playing the instrument …. I thoroughly enjoyed the workshop. Playing the *mbira* made my day! (group discussion, Bangor, 6 March 2006)

At Sheffield University, Joanne similarly commented on the *kora* workshop that:

> There are only three classes that I can clearly remember from my first year. The first was when a visiting musician demonstrated a *kora* and then developed the lesson from a class to a group of eager participants. There was a limited number of *koras*, so whilst some people were experimenting with a pattern demonstrated by the visitor, others were encouraged to clap and sing along in the style of the native people. This was very enjoyable, as it was both an extremely exciting and interesting lesson, and it helped to bring the class mates together as most of us had never spoken before. (Joanne, Sheffield, 20 September 2004)

Ethnomusicologists too were aware of students' enjoyment during these occasional performance workshops and thus wished to provide opportunities that are 'fun mostly …. I would like to teach students, not bore them silly!' (Neil Sorrell, York, 17 May 2004). Others similarly suggested that 'performing would be fun for most students and they would learn from it' (Andrew Killick, Sheffield, 12 November 2003), and that 'motivation comes predominantly from the fun-factor' (Wolfgang Schmiedt, Rostock, 25 November 2003).[1] Yet at the subsequent performance

---

[1]   Momentan werden die workshops auf Freiwilligenbasis angeboten. Studenten finden das manchmal schon ziemlich hart, bleiben aber mit Spaß und Eifer dabei. Die Motivation kommt hauptsächlich vom Spaßfaktor (Wolfgang Schmiedt, Rostock, 25 November 2003).

level during which students discovered expression and form, performing ethnomusicology seemed to result in feelings of anxiety. This was due to the final performance frequently encountered in such longitudinal performance practices. Formally assessing students' technical and musical accomplishment as performers, such final performances were modelled on the Western classical concert paradigm resembling formality, musical standards and talent. Argibel explained that:

> After all, you have a performance at the end of the year. It's open to the public, and I have to do it right! So it's very easy to fall in that, I don't know, in that fear of wanting to play very well, of focusing mostly on learning to play, right. I think we all did that at the end of the day .... You cannot avoid getting anxious or nervous about the performance, and try to make a good performance. Even though, as strictly speaking, the performance in itself wasn't that important. But at the end of the day, it really was the most important thing, or the central event. It was like a rite, so to speak. (Argibel, skype interview, 3 June 2006)

Jake similarly felt that 'it's not just performing .... It's about the audience, the crowd ... judging you .... My biggest concern was achieving quite a good standard, although that's not really essential in using music as a research technique' (skype interview, 4 July 2006). Such pressures led most students to prepare a performance of very high standard, even though the level of performance skills was apparently less significant in ethnomusicology. Yet while many students presented a good final performance, 'there have been failures as well .... Last year, we had ... a student playing the Basque pipe and tabor. Unfortunately ... half way through [the performance] she cracked up and left the stage' (John Baily, telephone interview, 7 June 2006). Performance anxiety indeed played a significant role in shaping students' experiences of performing ethnomusicology:

> Clearly, anybody is anxious about performance; it's part of the experience. You know, we call it stage fright ... We've got this [performance] coming up on Wednesday ... I expect I'll be ... told about a few nerves coming up. But I will just point out that I'm playing a concert on Friday, and I'm feeling pretty nervous too. (John Baily, telephone interview, 7 June 2006)

Music and Emotion

It is clear from the above discussions that the experiencing of enjoyment and anxiety at the differing levels of performing ethnomusicology appeared to be profound to students. Yet what are the causes of such emotional experiences? One view, notably by scholars from musicology, assumes that the feeling of emotions is a predominantly intellectual, 'higher' response to affections of the will, a stirring and modification of willing and not-willing (Budd, 1992:93). This view also advocates that music cannot only shape people's emotive experiences or induce emotions, but also represent human emotions. Scholars in this camp are thus often concerned with music's sonic structures and their meaning potential, while drawing heavily on semiotic theories from linguistics in order to derive general laws and principles about emotional responses to music. An alternative view claims that music expresses sociocultural processes (Cook and Dibben, 2001:60). Musical emotions are thus culturally conditioned (Becker, 2001:136). People in different cultures and contexts are believed to learn to associate particular emotions with different situations and to conceptualise them appropriately (Finnegan, 2003:183). Emotions are thus shaped by sociocultural and extra-musical factors. In my writings, this latter perspective is deemed particularly suitable to explain student experiences of both enjoyment and anxiety as it recognises the complex interaction between different shaping factors. Some of these factors will be illustrated here as they have impacted on student experiences of emotions during the first two levels of performing ethnomusicology.

The Simple – Difficult Dichotomy

Many ethnomusicologists felt a certain tension when introducing students to the exuberance of the world's musics whilst wishing to provide meaningful performance experiences with the limited musical equipment and time available at university. This tension was particularly pertinent when students expressed a dichotomous perception between simple versus difficult performing of ethnomusicology, namely simple-is-enjoyment versus difficult-is-serious. Music that was difficult to perform was thus often regarded as serious, professional music. By contrast, music that was easy to learn was often seen to be simple, whereby mistakes did not matter. The latter included occasional in-class demonstrations and music workshops, which appeared 'very light-hearted and enjoyable' (group discussion, Bangor, 6 March 2006). Such workshops emphasised musical process over product, generating more immediate and enjoyable musical experiences. Students frequently emphasised the informal, spontaneous and non-patronising atmosphere of such world music workshops, which seemed to provide a freedom of music-making students were previously unaware of (see also Keil, 1994a:55). Since most students wanted to feel they have made good progress with their technique, musicality, practising skills and confidence (see also Mills, 2002), occasional workshops also provided a sense of achievement quite quickly:

> He taught us in steps which was good in order to take in a lot of information in a short space of time. At the end of the session, I was playing and singing; the whole thing sounded amazing .... I was really surprised and pleased that we were able to learn a piece so quickly. It was brilliant and lots of fun! (group discussion, Bangor, 6 March 2006)

The Sheffield students compared this to amateur rather than professional music making, a differentiation often made in the West to connote musicians who simply play for enjoyment as opposed to those who work hard to achieve high musical standards:

> It was really good ... to play at that level. Well, it wasn't that hard, but ... it sounded good. You could get a tune out of it without too much trouble, if that makes sense. It sounded like something vaguely new .... It's sort of easy-going. It didn't matter too much, whether you played it wrong .... It's more like playing it for fun rather than being perfect. For us it was .... If it was a professional musician, you would want to play it right. (group discussion, Sheffield, 12 December 2003)

Some students even compared their musical encounters to childlike play, as 'I felt like a toddler with a new toy .... I was able to imagine what a child receiving the instrument for the first time would' (group discussion, Bangor, 6 March 2006). In such novice music making, students seemed to experience a kind of euphoria, inducing a childlike, untroubled and secure excitement (see also Keil, 1994a:76; Meyer, 1956 in Budd, 1992:171).[2] Most students thus quickly overcame any initial anxieties, as 'at first, I was quite nervous as I didn't know anything about *mbira* music. As the workshop went on I began to feel much more comfortable' (group discussion, Bangor, 6 March 2006).

Meanwhile, longitudinal performance practice was often seen as difficult and serious musical study, whilst the requirement of a final performance generated feelings of anxiety due to 'the academic environment of the university' (Jake, skype interview, 4 July 2006) and its associations with Western art music performance. Such performance practice was in some ways individualistic, self-centred and even perfectionist (see also Solís, 2004c:246), as students' main concern revolved around 'being of a certain standard ... to show what I can do ... and not to play the pieces wrong during the final performance' (Natasha, telephone interview, 10 July 2006). Yet whilst many students worked extremely hard to present a final performance of an excellent standard, they also felt anxious and even demotivated. Tina, an undergraduate anthropology student at QUB expressed apprehension about performing in the *gamelan* as she did not regard herself as a performer, and performing made her nervous. Having to perform a concert led to even further inhibition: 'I am not interested in performing it myself. I am just not good at it!' (Tina, Belfast, 17 November 2003). Negative self-perceptions on musical ability and talent can affect students' performance activities and academic work in general (Pitts, 2005:17). Such pressures surely impact on students' experiences at university:

---

2   While Keil relates in his discussions to Jazz, he also suggests that the same is true for world music (Keil, 1994:76). Meyer's discussions are equally interesting and relevant in this context, yet Meyer's differentiation between sophisticated and primitive music is less desirable in ethnomusicology.

It was the music, rather than the performance that I wanted to learn about ....
The lectures relate very much to my anthropology studies. I don't think that
the performance part relates as much to me, probably because I am just not
a natural performer because it makes me really nervous and I am not really
interested in it .... I would rather learn about and read up about it. (Tina, Belfast,
17 November 2003)

The New – Familiar Dichotomy

Besides perceptions of simple versus difficult performance in ethnomusicology,
students also communicated dichotomous perspectives between new musical
encounters and those musics they were already familiar with. For example, when
students encountered new, different musics during occasional workshops, they
often found themselves in an enjoyable state of musical discovery and exploration.
Familiarity, by contrast (typically occurring during longitudinal performing
ethnomusicology) somewhat denied students a sense of musical adventure due
to a state of musical normality at this subsequent performance level. Yet musical
encounters that were new and unfamiliar appeared far more exciting and enjoyable
to students. This occurred at the material, musical and personal level, whereby
students enjoyed 'to see authentic instruments [and] liked the fact that we actually
played something authentic, something different' (group discussion, Bangor, 6
March 2006). Joanne also commented on her enjoyment 'to clap and sing along
in the style of the native people' (Sheffield, 20 September 2004), whilst Stephanie
highlighted difference in the unusual performance setting: 'It feels to me quite
relaxed ... sitting on the floor' (York, 17 May 2004). Steven also, while learning to
play *kayagŭm*, described his experiences as more relaxed and different, as students
sat on the floor:

> My most poignant experience was the *kayagŭm* workshop .... First I was taken
> a bit aback, then I felt that it seems just so relaxed .... The ethnomusicologist
> came in, asked us to take off our shoes and sit down cross-legged on the floor.
> This was unusual .... There is almost like an honesty about it, a sort of down-
> to-earth nature and quality about it that took me aback. That then persisted, the
> down-to-earth feeling although it's surrounded by a huge amount of rules. But it
> doesn't seem so ... pansy. It's elitist to an extent but it's about who can play it,
> not who can listen to it .... Western music is a lot more inaccessible. The music
> itself excludes a lot of people who feel they do not really understand it .... East
> Asian music hasn't got the same weight of intellect behind it. (Steven, Sheffield,
> 30 April 04)

To Steven, the *kayagŭm* workshop indeed felt outside the norm of the formality and
conventions of musical study at university, which seemed to provide pleasurable
excitement. This was also true for Sian who learnt to play the Taiwanese *suona*
(a loud, oboe-type double-reed instrument), and to whom the music seemed more

exciting and intriguing the more different it sounded in terms of harmony and loudness:

> It was really good …. I liked playing … the loud things …. It actually sounded quite bad because they weren't in tune with each other …. It's not the easiest music to listen to. It's quite horrible to listen to, actually. But when you are playing it, you don't really notice …. It was really good last night. I really like it … because I was playing really hard …. You walk out and your ears are kind of ringing. You don't know when you are actually playing well. You are all playing. Because it sounds like we are playing out of tune …. So it's really fun. (Sian, Sheffield, 24 October 2003)

Whilst such harmonic and rhythmic discrepancies (by Western standards) seemed to create an excited state of enjoyment (see further Keil, 1994b:98), students also emphasised enjoyment at a personal level, specifically with teachers who seemed inspiring, stimulating and imaginative, without being intimidating. Students specifically enjoyed occasional workshops with guest musicians 'who have been quite enthusiastic …. We've had one from Cuba who I remember very clearly' (Emma, Durham, 27 October 2003). Students participating in the African workshops felt that 'he was very encouraging and positive about our performance …. He seemed to praise us after playing, even if it was wrong' (group discussion, Bangor, 6 March 2006), and 'he was really encouraging …. I was making so many mistakes, and he was "Oh, it's good!"' (Joanne, Sheffield, 12 December 2003). Others similarly suggested that:

> I found the teacher very good, friendly, interesting …. He made the workshop fun …. I liked his … passion for the music …. He seemed very adept and patient. He made the session very fun and informal …. He seemed to enjoy teaching us, and we responded. This came across in the workshop through knowledge and enthusiasm. (group discussion, Bangor, 6 March 2006)

> He was so enthusiastic, that was ace. He really got you into it as well … It was great. I would do that again, rather than sitting in the lecture …. He was awesome, wasn't he? He was just really enthusiastic about everything he had to say. (Graham, Sheffield, 12 December 2003)

During such workshops, authenticity also impacted on student experiences, an issue already discussed in Chapter 4. A native teacher embodied cultural difference, and students often imagined what his or her culture would be like, which seemed exciting. Students were also thrilled about guest teachers whom they often regarded as highly skilled, professional performers:

> He is very authentic obviously, which made the event really good …. It's good to have an actual *mbira* player from Zimbabwe …. He was obviously very

knowledgeable .... The *mbira* workshop gave me experience of meeting an African and being able to experience African culture. Experiencing this culture enabled me to see how *mbira* is played by natives rather than Westerners. (Leeroy, Bangor, 6 March 2006)

Such new encounters with guest musicians were clearly exciting and enjoyable. Yet during longitudinal performing of ethnomusicology, students seemed to take a more critical stance towards their more familiar teachers. Here, students preferred teaching that was well-focused with clear objectives and felt planned and purposeful. Enjoyment played a less pivotal role, as students instead focused on developing the knowledge and skills required for passing the final performance. At Goldsmiths, Teymoor, an accomplished Iranian *tar* player revealed considerable dissatisfaction with his instrumental teacher:

> I am not happy about my teacher because she does not put enough effort into teaching me. She is not ambitious in her ways .... I would expect to learn more .... So I expect when I go to the class you know, first of all you have to have enough time, at least an hour, to talk about the music because the piece itself is no problem. I can play it anyway because my fingers are ready. I practice on my right hand ... that's fine. I can play. My technique is much better than my teacher's herself .... But what I'm expecting is to learn about culture itself, the music itself, terminology .... Over here [in the West] we don't really have enough time to do that. Maybe we need more time, or I'm expecting too much; I don't know. But that's what I expect from this postgraduate performance programme, to learn about the culture, to learn more about the music, to learn about the philosophy of the music. (Teymoor, Goldsmiths, 12 February 2004)

With such concerns about the transmission style of native and guest teachers, students valued transmission methods that were clear and understandable to them. They also appreciated verbal explanations and conceptualisations, as it helped students to grasp musical expression and form and decreased their anxiety about the final performance. Stephanie particularly appreciated that 'our teacher is really stimulating with a nice balance between creativity and providing good explanations' (York, 17 May 2004) (Figure 4.1). Reflecting critically on their actual learning, students placed heightened emphasis on the instructor's ability as a musician and educator, whilst clear conceptualisations made students feel that they learnt something. Enjoyment seemed less significant. Interestingly, aural transmission methods also impacted on student experiences of emotions, as these differed to students' conventional music learning in form of routinely practicing of technical exercises.[3] Sandra described that 'gradually I have managed to move away from learning by music to largely learning by ear. And the way we were

---

[3]   In this statement, I particularly refer to the acquisition of musical skills in Western art music through repeated practising of musical exercises, including scales, arpeggios,

being taught the *gamelan* here and the Korean drumming …. Certainly, my experiences … were all by ear' (Belfast, 18 November 2003). Some students felt that such methods 'are a lot easier, you are not thinking. We just did it!', whilst others experienced these as a 'nice change' to the literate musical transmission in the West (group discussion, Bangor, 6 March 2006). Yet there were also students who felt anxious about adopting aural transmission methods:

> There is an ensemble of Andean music, so I went there two or three times, and I gave up because … I found it was quite difficult for me to follow because there is no notation; it's aurally transmitted. So I didn't have Western notation to help me, and I was always anxious to find where the note is, and I couldn't follow. (Shu, Goldsmiths, 13 February 2004)

Nonetheless, most students regarded aural transmission as an easier, more informal and enjoyable way of learning. Indeed, young musicians who learn their skills in oral/aural, informal ways often continue playing for enjoyment later in life (Green, 2002). This may be due to the social possibilities of aural musical learning: 'I really enjoyed that we didn't read notation. Instead of looking at the paper, we could look at each other and follow the instructor …. We sat in a circle and could see and listen to everyone in the group' (group discussion, Bangor, 6 March 2006). Aural learning allowed ensemble closeness, which was comforting and exciting, as 'it helped to bring the classmates together' (Joanne, Sheffield, 20 September). As indicated here, students' perceptions were also shaped by the ways in which performing ethnomusicology provided social as opposed to individualistic experiences. The latter was pertinent during longitudinal performance practice that culminated in a final performance and emphasised individuality and goal-directedness. In stark contrast to collaborative, communal processes of music making, such achievement-driven learning to perform can also generate a sense of competition among students (Koskoff, 1999:556). Students also often revealed feelings of embarrassment at the thought of peers or tutors regarding them as musically untalented. By contrast, occasional workshops allowed the forming of social bonds among students due to a collaborative and communicative quality not found in individual performance practice. The social dimensions were a result of students' rhythmic and melodic interaction, eye contact and co-ordinated singing and body movements (Finnegan, 2003:186). Such social involvement and contribution resulted in enjoyable excitement. The Bangor students described 'making music as a group [as] a fulfilling feeling of performing in an ensemble' (group discussion, Bangor, 6 March 2006). The Sheffield students felt that the *kora* workshop helped them to establish positive, bonding friendships with fellow students, as 'it was an excellent and effective way of bringing a class together'

---

and the like, which is also integral to graded examinations of, for example, the ABRSM (Associated Board of the Royal School of Music).

(Joanne, Sheffield, 20 February 2004). Perhaps most importantly, social bonds generated mutual trust and increased students' confidence in themselves:

> I hope to get more confidence in my performance abilities, and performing in a group with two people that I know and trust seems to be a good opportunity. (Joanne, Sheffield, 20 February 2004)

Clearly, emotional experiences played a significant role to students during performing ethnomusicology. As shown in this chapter, certain patterns existed across some student populations, expressed in the form of enjoyment and anxiety during different kinds of performing ethnomusicology. These were typically shaped by students' perceptions about musical simplicity and difficulty, familiarity and the lack thereof. Yet musical performance is also a deeply personal experience. This personal response to world musics, whilst playing and performing them, resembled perhaps one of the most profound and long-lasting experiences for students. Further research into this area of theory may thus bring other pivotal understandings into students' experiences whilst performing ethnomusicology.

Chapter 9

Performing Music, Discovering Value

Ethnomusicologists often wish to gain in-depth cultural understandings during ethnographic participant-observations of musical events and activities. The possibilities that ethnography affords are even further extended in musical performance. Here, performing ethnomusicology concerns a more socially engaged, experiential ethnography, involving participation in actual performance as a privileged means of access to embodied knowledge and fellow feeling, which can also lead to performative outcomes. This differs to the second level of performing ethnomusicology when musical expression and form was discovered. Here, students' immersion in actual performance provided potential insights into artistic structure and the methods and institutions for transmission and understanding. Participation in performance sensitised the student-researcher to aspects directly or indirectly related to a creative work and precipitated a sense of the style and aesthetics of a piece of music. At the third level of performing ethnomusicology, however, musical participant-observation can lead the student-researcher towards a kind of intrinsically cultural and imaginative experiencing. This form of performance starts with the researcher's own immersion as a performer whilst observing in preparation for writing about human experience in music. Students can experience a music culture directly and personally while immersing themselves in it as musicians and gaining a deeper understanding of the interrelationships between music and culture. Such performance participation leads students towards shared musical experiences and greatly enhances their understanding of music-as-culture and thus the values, people and societies hold about and express through their own music. Through collaboration with teachers, community members or musicians, students utilise vital skills in establishing and maintaining human relationships. The extent of students' musical insights thus depends heavily on the success with which they create and maintain effective social and musical interactions.

Performance Ethnography: Discovering Music-as-Culture

Performance in music is not only a tool for research, but a means for the writing of ethnographic texts, often referred to as performance ethnography (Kisliuk, 1997:41). Performance ethnography means students' direct participation in performance so as to write about people's rich and intertwined experiences through participating and observing, and experiencing for themselves people's engagement in music. Through performance and critical reflection, students are able to describe how and why individuals and cultures value artistic products in often unique and differing ways. However, the concern of this brief chapter will be students' self-reflexive accounts on their performance experiences and fellow feelings, rather than an analysis of their written ethnographies (the latter will be the focus of a subsequent chapter). This chapter will thus briefly illustrate the ways in which students learnt about the beliefs and values that people held and expressed through their own music. It will show how artistic understanding became closely tied to cultural understanding through the epistemological status of students' own artistic experiences.

It is important to note that performance ethnography was rarely utilised at undergraduate levels of study due to the requirement of students' longitudinal, intensive immersion in a music culture. Most undergraduate students instead conducted a fieldwork project that was based locally and completed in a relatively short timespan. Nonetheless, some undergraduate students, such as Rita, Helen, Violet and Tom who studied at Bangor University in 2006 (they were also my students) chose to do performance ethnography, which involved active musical participation in a chosen music culture at home, for instance the local folk club, the music department's jazz band or the local hip hop scene. More specifically, Rita joined a local brass band in order to participate in and observe live music making as a cornet player. She hoped to understand the perspectives of the brass band players and what their band participation meant to them musically and personally. Meanwhile, Helen participated as a singer in a cathedral choir and as an oboist in a Baptist church's worship band. She hoped to find out why people use particular musics in different churches and 'what the music means to the people … and why they feel that music helps them with their worship' (Bangor, 2 June 2006). Through performance ethnography, students sought an understanding of the role music plays in people's lives and what the music means to them. In their role as social actors, students placed themselves at the heart of their performance ethnographies. This also provided some students with a more understandable role and easier access:

> I myself, even in the short time I have attended the club have been very warmly welcomed in my capacity as an ethnomusicologist but more so as another valued regular attendee at the club as both a listener and a performer. (Violet, Bangor, 8 May 2006)

Students' concern with cultural understanding also led them towards a kind of deeper-level participation in their chosen music culture. Helen, for example, also worshipped when singing in the choir. This in-depth experience enabled her to draw on her own experiences of music and worship, and to understand other people's feelings when they worshipped:

> I could use my own experiences of how I felt when I was singing in the cathedral or playing in the Baptist church …. What I felt helped me to worship best … and

I understood that this happened to other people around me as well. I could see how it was helping them to worship. (Helen, Bangor, 2 June 2006)

Some students also felt that performance ethnography enabled them to 'see' aspects of a musical performance, including non-verbal and visual communication that would otherwise go unnoticed by observers. Tom who participated in a brass band 'noticed how many of the men make sexist remarks throughout the rehearsal' and gained an insider's view into issues important to the male players who he described as 'quite coarse and masculine' (Bangor, 8 May 2006). Meanwhile, during Helen's participation in the cathedral choir she grasped 'what the words mean to people, and what the music means to me' (Bangor, 2 June 2006). Helen indeed realised that singing helped people and herself more directly in their worship as the sung words conveyed the meanings more clearly:

> When I sang in the choir the music produced a response emotionally from me, perhaps more so than if I was just listening because I was thinking about the words more in order to convey the meaning to the congregation. I think that taking part in the music making does help me personally to focus on the meaning of the words of the music. But when I'm in the congregation it is easier for me to concentrate on the rest of the service, and use the music to enable me to think about my own faith. (Helen, Bangor, 2 June 2006)

Other students similarly understood the music culture more intuitively, as 'through performing at the club myself, I have discovered it is particularly conducive to relaxed performance as the audience are always supportive and encouraging with all performers' (Violet, Bangor, 8 May 2006). Rita equally felt that only as a performer could she gain specific insider's knowledge into a brass band culture and the experiences of the performers as it placed her 'first-hand at the receiving end'. For example, Rita gained a sense of the changing atmosphere from 'a distinctly high spirited aura that was consistent on a majority of the occasions' towards 'a more serious persona of the band as the competition approached' (Bangor, 3 June 2006). Providing another example, Rita explained that:

> ... they had this band tradition of playing their hymn tune 'Onward Christian Soldiers' to end the final rehearsal before the contest. I think, hadn't I have been in the band playing that with them, I wouldn't have shared that ... the really strong emotions, a sense of belonging, a sense of unity .... Very strong! (Rita, Bangor, 3 June 2006)

In that particular instance, the hymn itself, which Rita described as a quite arousing piece, triggered deeply emotional responses in all participants as it resembled tradition and a sense of community. Being part of the music culture, Rita experienced a strong sense of shared musical and personal identity. 'Being there' and 'sharing the atmosphere' enabled Rita directly to experience and understand the effect that the music had on people in shaping a strong group identity and community spirit. Through performance ethnography, students gained a deeper understanding of other people's perceptions and better relate to the musics and their makers so as to share their musical and cultural experiences at a very deep and personal level. This impacted on students personally who also began making connections between their research-related and life experiences. Helen now better understood 'how I felt when I'm in church' (Bangor, 2 June 2006). Her research-related experiences also intensified Helen's shared love for God. Students' longitudinal immersion in the chosen music culture also led towards friendships with other people who became increasingly vociferous in sharing personal experiences and feelings. This also allowed Rita to understand insiders' communication, as 'I did understand what some of the members meant when they said ... the band didn't gel with the piece 'cause they said it was technical, and it's not their sort of piece .... They preferred something more romantic, something more pictorial or programmatic .... I could empathise with that because it was a very technical piece' (Bangor, 3 June 2006). Reflecting on the trust gained in the band, Rita also recognised the consequence of age differences:

> Had I not been close to some of the younger participants, they wouldn't have said so much to me. Because they are young, they tend to be ... a bit quiet but because I knew them ... I just spoke to them informally. It was a very unstructured, conversational type of interview ... just like a normal conversation .... It helped me ... approaching them ... as a researcher .... I think I would have had a much colder reception had I not been part of the band. It would have been more difficult for me to approach them. (Rita, Bangor, 3 June 2006)

Such friendships also extended beyond students' projects: Rita's relationships with other brass band players became such an important part of her personal life that she continued playing in the brass band after completing the ethnographic project. Violet similarly revealed that 'I intend to return to the club regularly in the future ... [because] it has become an important part of my musical and social diaries' (Bangor, 8 May 2006). As a result of such personal relationships, many students highlighted a more equal and reciprocal, rather than one-way relationship, which made Rita more comfortable in her role as a researcher. Reciprocity and musical sharing seemed equally pivotal to Violet:

> Through the method of participant-observation, I have become involved in this sharing of music in many ways. I perform music and listen to others, thereby sharing the experience of performing, sharing the songs I play, and enjoying the music others share with me. Also on a more literal basis, others have shared lyrics and chords for songs with me. John, who was one of the first regulars I spoke to at the club, now regularly sends me emails with attachments of web pages containing lyrics and chords for songs he thinks I might enjoy. (Violet, Bangor, 8 May 2006)

Whilst participation in performance clearly triggered deeper and more meaningful cultural and musical understandings in students, they also had to engage in a process of critical reflection at the level of consciousness. Many students achieved this through logocentric processes of analysis and conceptualisation during the writing-up of their musical and cultural discoveries. This involved an inductive and bottom-up process of data analysis and interpretation so as to explain how people think, believe and behave. To this end, students needed to be more alert, which also helped them 'later to remember important issues in the rehearsal for further observations' (Rita, Bangor, 3 June 2006). The process of analysis thus already started during students' musical fieldwork and the making of fieldnotes. Rita explained that 'when you actually go back and write it up, just write up the event, you see it in a different light again. And then, when I come back to read my fieldnotes, I would see something different again' (*ibid.*). To Helen, this critical, self-reflexive process was crucial for her understanding:

> Doing this project ... helped me to analyse ... what I was performing and what it did mean to me because I had never actually stopped to think about it before. I think it did help me to think more clearly and more carefully about what I was doing .... It helped me to be more reflective because after I had performed, I thought back about what emotions I felt and what things I'd gone through, whereas before, I would have just done it ... and not thought about it. (Helen, Bangor, 2 June 2006)

More generally, performance ethnography meant students' direct participation in performance, which enabled them to grasp people's rich and intertwined experiences through participating and observing and experiencing for themselves people's engagement in a music culture. Students learnt to look at both the music and people's emotions and beliefs. Learning about a music culture more intuitively and deeply, this level of performing ethnomusicology helped students to understand what the music means to the people studied, for example 'how it helps them to worship God' (Helen, Bangor, 2 June 2006). Performance ethnography became a more privileged means of access to embodied knowledge and fellow feeling. It sensitised students to aspects directly or indirectly related to a music-cultural practice and thus a kind of intrinsically musical and imaginative experiencing (Blacking, 1973:54; Cooley, 1997). Students' understanding of musical practices became closely tied to cultural understanding through their own performance experiences. It enabled students to write about how and why individuals and cultures value artistic products in often unique and differing ways. It also allowed them to learn about the values, which people hold and express through music.

Rethinking Performing Ethnomusicology?

As shown throughout Part III of the book, musical performance occupies a crucial position in the transmission of ethnomusicological knowledge at universities. Located along a continuum that included students' discovering of world musics' material culture (Chapter 6), musical expression and form (Chapter 7) and cultural values (Chapter 9), specific emphasis has been placed on student experiences to better assess the ways in which performing ethnomusicology at universities led students towards changes of attitude and perspective. Overall, these changed along the performance continuum: from *animation* and enjoyment towards deeper insights into music-as-music combined with performance anxiety, finally reaching deeper understandings of music-as-culture. The latter type of performing ethnomusicology (performance ethnography), more specifically, was a suitable means for students to gain a better understanding of people making music. Students became musical and cultural insiders, whilst studying and understanding people making music. Participation in performance ethnography helped students to learn about ethnomusicology's most significant concern with studying a given music-cultural practice whilst discarding the difference between self and others.

By comparison, the first type of performing ethnomusicology during which students observed demonstrations and had basic participatory performance experiences enabled them to discover real material culture. It was specifically their visual participatory experiences, together with the hearing of the instrument's sounds that allowed students to grasp the intricate characteristics of the most diverse musical instruments. Occasional workshops were thus of educational value for enabling students to experience deeper-level musical consciousness, whilst entering (albeit only to some extent) the stage of discovering musical expression and form. Particularly noteworthy here were occasional workshops with specialist musicians who enabled students to experience more complex musical structures and performance techniques. Whilst the chapter has shown that demonstrations and workshops are pivotal in bringing strange musics alive to students, this type of performing ethnomusicology has also seen some criticism for dislocating music cultures outside of their true contexts and for being conservative in orientation (Averill, 2004:108). The entertaining nature of these educational activities may thus be seen as *animation* that can even reinforce eurocentric notions of simplicity, exotic otherness and authenticity, which resonates with a recent warning about the trivialising and exoticising of cultural traditions at universities (Averill, 2004:108). Such critiques thereby raise the question of whether performing ethnomusicology at universities is not ethnomusicological enough. Ethnomusicologists may thus be more alert about challenging potential essentialisms constructed in such a performing of ethnomusicology at universities.

Meanwhile, more longitudinal, regular ensemble participation and learning to perform a musical instrument enabled students to discover musical expression and form. Here, students understood music-as-music more deeply due to the (frequent) requirement of a final performance for formal assessment, which also resulted in considerable performance anxiety. Nonetheless, students' learning experiences seemed to be profound in developing in-depth understandings of an unknown type of music, allowing them to gain a more enriched and complete musical understanding of a given music-cultural practice. Whilst this type of performing ethnomusicology also resonated to some extent with the Western performance paradigm (as shown in the chapter, many students appropriated Western modes of acquiring musical competence during learning to perform a musical instrument that may traditionally be transmitted in entirely different ways), students' appropriation of Western methods was indeed desirable, enabling students to achieve advanced performance skills in a non-Western musical style within a relatively short timespan. From an educational standpoint, learning about music-as-music through performing ethnomusicology helped students to develop complex knowledge and deep-level understandings into the music's sonic qualities. Yet a concern with music-as-music alone during performing ethnomusicology may also be critiqued for reinforcing a perception that music is abstract and even detached from its cultural context (see Locke, 2004:180), raising yet again the question as to how ethnomusicological the performing of ethnomusicology is at universities. Ethnomusicologists may therefore guide students more directly towards learning about both musical and cultural aspects of a given music-cultural practice. In doing so, students would not only gain in-depth knowledge about music's sonic structures but also insights into the contexts in which the music is made. A more nuanced pedagogical approach would thereby resonate more closely with contemporary ethnomusicology's concern with people making music.

PART IV
Constructing Ethnomusicology

Constructing ethnomusicology is perhaps the most challenging and artistic stage in the transmission of ethnomusicological knowledge at universities. It is a product of creativity, a special kind of intellectual ability and personality. It may be associated with the exploration of new sounds and the relationships between them. Indeed, some ethnomusicologists strive to encourage creativity in students through musical composition as the ultimate goal in their ethnomusicological endeavours (see also Hughes, 2004). Necessitating originality and imagination, sounds are explored and experimented with in the classroom, while producing something that is new. At the Hochschule für Theater und Musik in Rostock, popular music students learnt to use 'MIDI for songwriting projects in popular music in order to enhance their creativity' (Wolfgang Schmiedt, Rostock, 25 November 2003).[1] Yet at most universities, composing world musics outside their original sociocultural contexts seemed to be rare. While studies in composition exist that may also allow students to focus on world musics, in reality, no university has yet offered a separate framework for accredited composition in ethnomusicology. Composition in ethnomusicology remains little explored, and in their roles as educators, ethnomusicologists often refrain from teaching musical composition. They rather focus on an older repertoire reflecting recognised aspects of tradition. Nonetheless, creativity may be aspired to and achieved by students through actively engaging in musical activities other than musical composition, namely creative transcription, ethnographic writing and ethnographic filmmaking. The chapters contained in this part will thus focus on students' experiences during the constructing of a musical transcription (Chapter 10), the creative composing of ethnomusicological texts (Chapter 11) and ethnomusicological uses of film and video (Chapter 12). The concept of creativity is thus seen here as a kind of symbolic creativity (Toynbee, 2003:102), which dispels the idea that musical creation must be entirely or mostly new in order for it to be termed creative (Sanger and Kippen, 1987:14).

Discussions on students' experiences of musical transcription will inform the part's first chapter, which regards transcription as a kind of constructing ethnomusicology, the constructing of a graphic map to melodic and rhythmic components of the music. Musical transcription is also understood here as a culturally constructed process, as students actively negotiated their choices for the

---

[1]   Die Studenten hier lernen Songwriting von populärer Musik mit Hilfe von MIDI, um die Kreativität zu fördern (Wolfgang Schmiedt, Rostock, 25 November 2003).

process of transcribing and for making it meaningful to the reader. The advantages of transcription as an educational tool are obvious. Necessitating students' careful listening and intellectual internalisation while being placed inside the music and its sonic structures, the constructing of a transcription enabled students to activate several channels simultaneously, involving skills and knowledge, imagination and reflection. Transcription may also be a tool for research that can lead students towards deeper cultural experiences and perhaps even emic perspectives towards the music culture whose music is being transcribed. Creativity may also be aspired to by students during the composing of ethnomusicological texts, which will form the basis for the subsequent chapter. Equally regarded as being socially and culturally constructed, writing ethnomusicology also reflects the ethnomusicological canon, and thus the ways in which ethnomusicology constructs and disciplines music. Focusing on ethnography as a method of research and way of writing, students typically embarked on fieldwork projects during which they engaged in participatory observation and interviewing. Posing significant challenges, writing ethnomusicology led students towards active and deep engagement with musics and their makers, experiences that often seemed exciting and interesting, yet also new and challenging. More generally, writing ethnomusicology enabled students culturally to construct very unique and individual, yet profound, multidimensional knowledge and thus emic understandings about a music culture.

Another means that sparked creativity in students was visual ethnography, and specifically ethnomusicological filmmaking. Ethnomusicological film was deemed not only more stimulating and accessible, but particularly suitable for communicating experience so pivotal in contemporary ethnomusicology research and writing. This form of constructing ethnomusicology enabled students to mediate their fieldwork experiences through an even more creative treatment of actuality than ethnographic writing. This creative freedom for exploring both the aesthetic and functional aspects of a given music-cultural practice triggered deeply gratifying experiences in students. The emphasis beyond curriculum also led students to become politically and globally more aware. Their increased global consciousness impacted in powerful ways upon students' perspectives, leading many to develop more democratic attitudes. While the constructing of a musical transcription, ethnographic text and ethnographic film are indeed suitable for generating creativity in the formal university context, such transmission methods should also discard eurocentrism. Transcription, ethnographic text and film would thereby reflect students' more emic stance towards the music culture studied. Many ethnomusicologists already transmit this same concern to their students, although in some instances, specifically during the constructing of transcription, some students seemed to maintain some of their eurocentric preconceptions. This will be the concern of the closing section, which discusses the problems surrounding processes of appropriation and representation of world musics in the constructing of ethnomusicology.

Chapter 10

Transcribing Music: Exploring Musical Structures, or Reinforcing Eurocentrism?

The transmission of ethnomusicology at universities frequently involved students in constructing a musical transcription. Yet in writing down musics that are very different to students' own Western art music culture, ethnomusicologists were less concerned with the constructing of a Western musical score, but instead 'an approach to doing transcription. I'm not looking for the small details …. I'm more concerned with how they thought about it, and especially thought about the problems of notating music that doesn't readily conform to Western notation' (Andrew Killick, Sheffield, 28 November 2003). A musical transcription project thus aimed at challenging eurocentric musical views. It hopefully led students to think from an emic musical perspective, whilst focusing on those musical aspects deemed important to the people whose musics are being transcribed. Transcription was thus seen as a research tool enabling both musical and cultural understandings. It was deemed particularly useful when it enabled students to draw conclusions about musics as reflector and generator of social meaning. Neil Sorrell advocated that:

> Transcription is really a shortcut for the things you really want to know whether they have understood …. You want them to demonstrate a direct relationship to the music …. If you understand what's going on in the music, then you can show that you have understood it. Transcription does that …. If you are asked to transcribe what you hear, you can only do it if you have understood it during the course. Do I actually transcribe everything I hear? No, you are actually transcribing the essentials …. It's a way of demonstrating an understanding … and to be able to do that, you don't only have to hear it, but understand what belongs where, even if you don't hear it. It just shows so much about basic grasp of all the important things …. It is a demonstration that they had a one-to-one confrontation with the actual music. (Neil Sorrell, York, 17 May 2004)

Hae-kyung Um agreed that 'I would use a score as a kind of map to show certain aspects of this music …. So the transcription itself is just a tool to lead us to a bigger picture and understanding' (Belfast, 18 November 2003). Transcription necessitated students' more complete musical and cultural understanding to capture the most important musical elements of a particular music culture. This in turn required students' musical knowledge and understanding from the perspective of the people whose music they transcribed. A musical transcription thus enhanced students' listening to music in particularly emic ways. Such learning also involved researching the social, cultural and political context in which the music is embedded, leading students towards deeper levels of musical and cultural insight. Neil Sorrell concluded that:

> With *gamelan* ... if you transcribe, you can only do it if you understood the things in the course ... You are actually transcribing the essentials in that particular way .... It just shows so much the basic grasp of all these things .... [It is] a demonstration that they had some confrontation with the actual music .... You may not understand the social dynamics of the music; you may not have anything like emic perception. On the other hand, transcription, in many ways, you are getting towards that, you have to start listening in a different way, in a Javanese way. (Neil Sorrell, York, 17 May 2004)

Some students showed an understanding of these principles. At QUB, Sandra pointed out that recognising the melody in Irish traditional music requires an understanding of stereotypical embellishments, as 'it's very ornamented .... Sometimes I try to hear the tune behind the ornaments, and I can't .... I have seen the tunes written out, and it's useless because what the person is singing can diverge so much. You have to understand really what's going on before it does make sense' (Belfast, 18 November 2003). Meanwhile, George at the University of York had to research into the tuning, rhythm and melodic structure of *gamelan* music, explaining that 'I start by reading about the possible tunings first and decide which tuning is used in the piece. Then I try to decide where the gong is coming in, and again, I get a good idea from reading about *gamelan* music in books. Then I try to work out the shape of the melody' (York, 17 May 2004). Gaining a more complete understanding behind the music, students gradually learnt to differentiate between essential and less essential elements in musics' sonic structures. Some Sheffield students even understood that this approach reflects what ethnomusicologists do, as 'although it seems quite daunting, it is good for us because it's doing what ethnomusicology is' (Rebecca, Sheffield, 31 October 2003), and 'with a transcription you actually do what people in the world of ethnomusicology actually do. It's a useful practical skill' (Graham, Sheffield, 19 December 2003).

Yet whilst some students grasped the importance of an emic perspective to the constructing of a transcription, most students actually relied on strategies and approaches that felt familiar and safe to them, specifically those from classical musicology. Andrew Killick agreed that 'most of them were more interested in the details of the musical sound' (Sheffield, 7 May 2004). Students' concern with music as sound represents a rather eurocentric approach to the constructing of a musical transcription, and this was evident in four ways: (a) while ethnomusicologists encouraged transcriptions of world musics that were significantly different, students returned to 'easy' musical examples that sounded familiar (by Western standards); (b) while ethnomusicologists transmitted to students a bottom-up strategy to constructing a transcription, students instead adapted a top-down approach; (c) while ethnomusicologists encouraged the use of non-Western or innovative notation, students instead relied on familiar Western staff notation; (d) while ethnomusicologists encouraged students to construct the transcription aurally, most students instead utilised Western tools (e.g. musical instruments, technologies) designed to facilitate the composing and playing of Western music. In the following sections, I will illustrate students' experiences of constructing a musical transcription according to this four-partite conceptualisation, also taking into account ethnomusicologists' formal methods for instruction. These matters will be explored with specific reference to the experiences of undergraduate students. Indeed, transcription projects occurred most frequently at undergraduate level (*Grund-* or *Hauptstudium* in Germany), whilst at postgraduate level, students were allowed to decide for themselves whether to transcribe music as part of a written dissertation. Viktor, for example, omitted musical transcriptions in both his *Magister-* and *Doktorarbeit*, as he 'prefers approaches from social and cultural anthropology' (telephone interview, 5 July 2006).[1] This chapter will thus focus on the experiences of a small group of my own former undergraduate students at Bangor University in 2005/2006.

Seeking Familiarity in a Musical Transcription

In earlier chapters, I already highlighted the fact that world musics often resembled difference, leading students to feel uncertain or even anxious when approaching such strange musics. The constructing of a musical transcription often generated similar experiences, as most students found transcriptions of the world's musics 'quite daunting and frightening' (group interview, Sheffield, 17 October 2003), 'quite hard actually' (Anna, Goldsmiths, 11 February 2004) and 'complicated; interesting but hard' (Joanne, Sheffield, 20 February 2004). Others similarly commented that 'it was so painful …. I lost confidence in transcription' (Shu, Goldsmiths, 13 February 2004), and 'even though I read music, I found the transcription very, very difficult and quite confusing …. I find it quite challenging!' (Xavier, Goldsmiths, 12 February 2004). Andrew Killick explained one possible reason for this, namely that 'in most cases, students transcribed music that was quite different to any music that they would perform or know how to write or analyse, as in Western music' (Sheffield, 7 May 2004). Yet in reality, most students selected a musical example for transcription that 'is the easiest to transcribe' (Melanie, Sheffield, 20 October 2003). Such an easy musical example often consisted of melody and accompaniment, similar to the construction of much Western music. Among the Sheffield students, the musical examples chosen for their transcription projects reflected Western conventions, notably a clear melody

---

[1] Nein, also ich mache keine Transkriptionen, hab ich auch nicht in meiner Magisterarbeit gemacht, weil ich eher von der sozialen und culturellen Anthropologie an die Sache herangehe (Viktor, telephone interview, 5 July 2006).

consisting of tones and semitones (rather than microtones), harmony and chords and a clearly distinguishable rhythm (without syncopation) and time signature (in triple or duple time). For example, Rebecca selected a track with Persian *ney* to the accompanying sound of the player's humming voice, whilst Sian chose an Irish folk song with banjo in the accompaniment. Graham selected a *flamenco* piece featuring vocals and accompanying guitar. Meanwhile, Samantha at Bangor University selected a musical example of Andean flute music that resembled familiarity to Western musics and featured melody, harmony and rhythm:

> I listened to lots of CDs in the Archive and chose a track that was the easiest, well … or that would suit what I had in mind to do …. Yeah, but I wanted to choose an example that I thought would be fairly easy, and not something that would be too daunting, but I didn't just want to do something that had just one single-line melody … something in the middle …. It was fairly easy; it wasn't in some wacky key or something like that. (Samantha, Bangor, 25 May 2006)

Criteria for selection thus revolved around clarity, as Samantha's musical example had clearly audible lines and distinguishable musical instruments. There also seemed to be a strong emphasis on music that featured a clear melody, while avoiding rhythmically complex examples:

> I am really bad at rhythm. So I knew I'd have so much trouble if I chose something with drum rhythms …. I deliberately avoided that, so I chose something melodic. Although the piece I chose did have a beat to it and I actually notated that but … it wasn't in any strange rhythms that I couldn't notate. (Samantha, Bangor, 25 May 2006)

Kevin similarly applied such criteria, while selecting a Hungarian folk tune entitled *Khosid Wedding Dances* in order to construct a musical transcription (Example 10.1). This fast dance tune featured a fiddle playing the melody to the accompaniment of other stringed instruments, such as viola and double bass. The folk tune clearly reflects a Western musical construction with a melody below which lower-pitched instruments provide simple harmony and rhythm in duple time. The double bass itself provided the rhythmic framework while playing a continuous drone on the tonic and related notes in the same key. Interestingly, in his transcription Kevin chose to feature the melodic line played by the fiddle, while omitting the accompanying stringed instruments.

Kevin selected this musical example because 'this would be the easiest to transcribe …. Rhythm-wise, I suppose … less syncopated … but more melodic'. An easy musical example seemed to depend on rhythm and how easy it is to 'count the beats in my head and write the pulse up. I would think it would be easy because pitch is just a matter of time …. You can just find that out by pressing the keys into the right note'. Kevin thus selected *Khosid Wedding Dances* as 'there wasn't much difficulty in the rhythm … and it is quite repetitive as well' (Bangor, 25 May

2006). The discussions make clear that while some ethnomusicologists encouraged transcriptions of world musics that were new and different, students returned to 'easy' musical examples that sounded familiar to them by Western standards.

Example 10.1   Student transcription of *Khosid Wedding Dances*; University of Wales, Bangor, 15 October 2005 (reproduced from original).

...Cont.

Applying a Top-down Approach to a Musical Transcription

In approaching a musical transcription, some ethnomusicologists encouraged students to apply a bottom-up strategy. Such a strategy may also be described as an inductive approach, allowing the musical analysis and transcription to emerge from the music itself without being hampered by preconceived musical ideas. In this approach, the individual parts of the music are specified in detail and then linked together to form larger components, which are in turn linked until a complete musical transcription is formed. In a course on Indonesian *gamelan* at the University of York, students learnt to use the bottom-up strategy to construct a cipher notation that would facilitate the new, different musical characteristics. Step-by-step, students learnt to identify the rhythm, tuning, the texture of new musical instruments, the overall musical form and structure and musical development (e.g. modulations). Students first learnt to identify unfamiliar musical elements, such as the beat and rhythm underlying the composition:

> First work out what the beat is …. It almost becomes a process of diminution. Try to hear the gong, which might give a clue that it is an 8-bar or 16-bar phrase. (Neil Sorrell, York, 6 May 2004)

Subsequently, students were instructed to identify the tuning of either *pelog* or *slendro*, recognisable in the inclusion or exclusion of semitones:

> What's the tuning? You can hear five tones but this does not tell you really. The relevant question is whether the tune used any semitones …. Without would be *slendro*; with semitones *pelog*. (*ibid.*)

Students then learnt how to single out individual instruments, particularly those of key relevance to the overall texture of *gamelan* music in providing clues regarding the tempo of the piece:

> It's important to know what *kempong* and *pelong* are and label them in your transcription properly …. It's about the sound of each instrument! … So, first get the tuning and then the character of the piece, the sense of tempo! (*ibid.*)

Deconstructing a piece of *gamelan* music into its elements through such an inductive approach, the ethnomusicologist subsequently instructed students to recognise the *gendhing* (two sections in a *balungan,* the skeleton melody).[2] Listening to the *rebab* (a spike-fiddle, also the melodic leader of the ensemble),

---

[2] Music is not notated in a score for all the instruments, so a transcription generally shows the *balungan*, or melody. Other parts can be notated but this can be difficult to read; it is often easier to learn how to derive one part and use one's own shorthand notation for reminders.

students were required to transcribe the melody and ornamentations, but also to listen to clues to changes (e.g. modulations) in the performance (Figure 4.1). Students were also encouraged to count and compare phrases with each other (for repetition), to sing along with or perform the music and to sketch a contour line or graphic score. Through this bottom-up strategy, students learnt how the individual parts in *gamelan* music are fitted together and constructed as a whole. Stephanie clearly understood this approach:

> I listen to the whole piece as much as possible to get it into the head .... I try to derive the framework from listening to the whole piece. Then I concentrate on one line each time, and write down the bare bones .... Then I listen to the individual instruments and what type of instruments. (Stephanie, York, 17 May 2004)

This bottom-up strategy to constructing a musical transcription clearly discards eurocentric perspectives by enabling students to derive the transcription from the music itself. Yet whilst some students grasped this approach, most students adopted a top-down strategy by trying to appropriate world musics into their Western musical views. In the top-down approach, an overview of the music is formulated first, which typically occurred in the form of Western staff notation. Each stave was then refined until the entire transcription was detailed enough to represent the musical example. Samantha, for example, fitted the example of Andean flute music into Western four-part harmony notation, featuring the flute (melody) on the first stave, *charango* chords (harmony) in the second stave, and rattle and bongo drums (rhythm) in the bottom two staves. During the actual constructing of the transcription, Samantha began by transcribing the melodic line played by the flute, followed by defining its note values. She then identified the accompanying *charango* chords and rhythm in relation to the melody, clearly placing the latter at the heart of the music. Samantha finally listened to the piece as a whole to illuminate the phrasing, and 'find how it all interrelates and how it all works together (Bangor, 25 May 2006). Familiarity with the Western notation system clearly shaped Samantha's considerations, which involved 'putting it … into Western music score because … that is the easiest way to do it' (*ibid.*). The process as a whole involved the initial separating and breaking down of the musical example into Western musical elements, followed by reassembling these and checking the accuracy of the complete transcription. Applying such a top-down approach to a musical transcription, students reconstructed the world's musics from a eurocentric perspective, evident in their adapting of Western musical conventions, for example the separating out of Western musical elements (melody, harmony, rhythm) and the use of the Western notation system.

Adapting Musical Literacy to a Musical Transcription

The previous discussions have shown that most students found a musical transcription project daunting. Students in the West have indeed become used to Western ways of writing music, which in turn seemed to make them reliant on it. Yet ethnomusicologists often encouraged students to utilise different, non-Western notation systems, or to invent new ways of writing musics. A more nuanced ethnomusicological approach to musical transcription often facilitated musical elements that are unusual in Western musics, such as microtones, asymmetrical metres, polyrhythm or heterophonic textures. For example, the York students learnt to read different *gamelan balungan* in cipher notation, whereby the melody was written in numbers (1=C; 2=D; 3=E; 4=F; 5=G; 6=A; 7=B) with octaves being distinguished by placing a dot below (indicating that the tone rings one octave below) or above the number (indicating that the tone rings one octave above). Sharps and flats were typically omitted as the relative pitch of sound is used. Students also learnt that rhythm can be indicated by means of lines below the numbers concerned: no line indicates a crochet; a single line indicates quavers; a double line indicates semiquavers. Longer sounding tones were indicated by adding short lines, such as 1 – for a minim, 1 – – for a dotted minim, and 1 – – – for a semibreve. Most ethnomusicologists advocated alternative ways of writing musics and stressed alternative means of musical notation. This included (besides cipher notation) circular transcriptions, graphical representations and drawings as well as 'native' notations. Some students grasped that the tools for their musical transcriptions would be inevitably different and individual. Samantha remembered that 'we can try it ourselves. It didn't necessarily have to be Western' (Bangor, 25 May 2006). Some of the Sheffield students similarly understood that:

> The first thing I thought I'd do is to go about it in the classical sense of writing it out. But then he said that you don't have to do that at all. You have to write it out how it best suits it, and it could be in any strange way. So we have got quite a bit of freedom. (Joanne, Sheffield, 31 October 2003)

> We discussed how my example is different when transcribed than that of the other two people .... It's very difficult to transcribe. I think it's different for everybody. (Rebecca, Sheffield, 31 October 2003)

As a result, some students invented new and alternative ways of constructing a transcription of world music. These more innovative methods were indeed also suitable to students without knowledge in Western notation. To Anna at Goldsmiths College, this resembled an enjoyable experience: 'I really like the transcriptions. Yesterday we transcribed three Inuit songs .... I don't know how to use the Western notation system, so I had to use a system I could create in order to transcribe what is most important' (Goldsmiths, 11 February 2004). Yet whilst many students adopted innovative notation, most students relied on the use of familiar Western staff notation. Rebecca remembered:

> I have chosen a piece ... for ... Persian *ney* .... I have done about half of the transcription, working it out on keyboard .... It's a bit strange .... It is slightly sharper than our tones .... I think I will have to make a note or so to make it as close as possible to normal, Western notation .... I just tried to get it as close as possible to Western notation. (Rebecca, Sheffield, 24 October 2003)

Thus not all students made use of alternative notation systems and instead tended to rely on Western conventions. Even at the University of York where the ethnomusicologist introduced students to a more thorough ethnomusicological approach to musical transcription, some students completed the transcription in Western musical notation. My Bangor students similarly relied on the Western notation system, yet also utilised some inventions and innovations. Delyth, for example, transcribed a Latin American music track entitled *Camino al Sol* (Road to the Sun) featuring nature sounds, such as birdsong and sounds of birds flying, Latin guitar and panpipes and other instruments, such as rainsticks, rattles and tom-toms (Example 10.2). Highlighting the invention of alternative means for transcribing nature sounds and the more specific notation of pitches of birdsong, Delyth reflected that:

> I found it hard but also interesting to figure how to write out the bird whistles, rattles and rainsticks in a conventional stave. Maybe another notation system may be better to show these sounds more accurately. (Delyth, in-class presentation, Bangor, 15 October 2005)

Particularly at the start of the music, which features birdsong and rainsticks and occasionally an 'oriental' guitar, Delyth used rather innovative ways to indicate the occurrence of nature sounds to establish the general feel of the music. Only towards the end of the piece did Delyth transcribe the pitch of birdsong in more detail. Delyth commented on the difficulties in finding a steady pulse to determine the time signature or identifying the tonality of the musical example to establish the key signature. She indicated this by omitting bar lines and adding the Latin expression *ad lib* at the beginning. Reflecting on the use of Western notation more generally, Delyth emphasised that she found Western staff notation inadequate, particularly for transcribing 'the twiddly bits' (in-class presentation, Bangor, 15 October 2005). Other students found it similarly difficult to accurately transcribe pitch, melody and rhythm as these often differed to the Western diatonic concept or the duple and triple time signatures typical in much Western musics. Janet, for example, transcribed a Buddhist chant from Sri Lanka and experienced particular problems with the non-conventional pitches and intervals in the melodic line (Example 10.3). Noteworthy is the invention of signs and symbols added to Western notes to indicate pitches smaller than those in Western music, as well as the omission of rhythm to accommodate the free-flowing, unmetred atmosphere of the chanting. The transcription shows Janet's attempts to appropriate the non-Western pitches into Western staff notation, reflected in the invention of additional signs, symbols and lines (the wavy lines and symbols represent trills and vibrato) while assigning a diatonic concept to the music. In reflection, Janet explained that:

> The notes and intervals are not simple tone or semitone values, although I have identified them as being so as these are the smallest values I know to write ….
> I used chromatic patterns of notes as these are the smallest intervals used in Western music. However the intervals on the recording are smaller. (Janet, in-class presentation, Bangor, 15 October 2005)

Example 10.2   Student transcription of *Camino al Sol* (Road to the Sun); University of Wales, Bangor, 15 October 2005 (reproduced from original)

Example 10.3   Student transcription of Buddhist chanting; University of Wales,
                  Bangor, 15 October 2005 (reproduced from original). Sri Lanka,
                  Buddhist Chant II Various Rituals; this track features *Nampada*
                  or *vitadra-aradhana*, praise of Buddhist *viharas*.

The music is typically free-flowing. To Janet, the piece thus lacked structure or organisation, which she indicated by omitting time signature and bar lines. Yet Janet also made some attempts at identifying an underlying metre by using semiquavers, quavers, crotchets and semibreves, whilst acknowledging that 'it is only a rough sketch of the rhythm. To indicate the long-held note, I used a semibreve. With no time signature it is very hard to determine the true length of the notes'. As usual when writing music in Western notation, Janet also considered symbols for indicating rests in composing the transcription, yet found it difficult to determine whether 'the quick scratches of breath at times ... are rests' (*ibid.*).

Samantha also relied on familiar Western notation because 'that was the only thing I really knew, and this was the first thing that came to my mind.' (Bangor, 25 May 2006) Yet in hindsight, Samantha also reflected on the possibility and necessity of inventing new symbols and signs: 'It wasn't until I actually did it that I realised I could put my own kind of thing to it' (*ibid.*). This included the use of wavy lines across *charango* chords to indicate its unique *rasguado* playing technique. During our conversation, Samantha also mentioned the seminar during which students presented the transcriptions to their classmates. This experience enabled her to gain insights into the various possible ways in which to construct a musical transcription. For example, Delyth's transcription (Example 10.2) opened Samantha's mind to the ways in which world musics could be transcribed. The seminar thus served as a useful stimulus to further develop transcription skills. Thus, 'it would have been really good to probably have done, like once we'd opened our minds to it, once we'd seen what everyone else had done, perhaps have gone away and done another one, something that was quite contrasting to what we had already done' (Bangor, 25 May 2006).

More generally, most students utilised familiar Western notation when constructing a musical transcription of world musics, while focusing on the melody in relation to an underlying harmony and rhythm. Yet the Western notation system posed significant challenges for transcribing musical elements of non-Western musics, and students found that 'the most difficult problem was in transcribing the subtle rhythmic nuances and embellishments' (Babette, Bangor, 15 October 2005), and 'to transcribe the fiddle's upward glissandos' (Kevin, Bangor, 25 May 2006). Some students thus realised that their approach reflects a rather etic perspective to a music culture, which may put into question its autonomy and sovereignty. Samantha, for example, showed heightened self-criticism towards constructing a musical transcription from eurocentric perspectives:

> The only drawback was that I did think about it in a Westernised way, and I do think that was a drawback .... I should have just taken it for what it was and just tried to transcribe as it was. But I didn't really know how to do that at the time, you know, so the only way I thought I could do it is to put it into the Westernised way .... I didn't really know how ethnomusicologists would have approached this, and that would have probably changed the way I have done my transcription .... So the only way I thought I really could do it was through the Westernised

way. Yeah, it would definitely be useful to go through an ethnomusicologist's way to transcribe the music, definitely! … It would have been really interesting to find out how they would do it. (Samantha, Bangor, 25 May 2006)

Utilising Western Tools for a Musical Transcription

It is clear thus far that a more thorough ethnomusicological approach to musical transcription would adopt an emic perspective. To this end, ethnomusicologists often encouraged students to construct the transcription aurally. However, most students commented that 'I find the transcription tricky because I can't pick up things by ear very well' (Christopher, Sheffield, 20 November 2003), and 'the aural part I find very hard because I am not very good at it anyway …. Sometimes it is quite difficult if you are just listening …. Transcriptions can be quite hard, to start off' (George and Stephanie, York, 17 May 2004). Students thus often utilised tools to support their transcription projects. For example, the York students used the actual instruments of *gamelan* to check the accuracy of their musical transcriptions. Neil Sorrell encouraged students to do so by suggesting that 'when you have written an approximate *balungan*, check whether you can play each part on the *gamelan*. Play your transcription! The best way to do this is live' (York, 6 May 2004). Students' actual experiencing of *gamelan* was indeed significant, as it enabled them more fully to grasp and understand the music's structure and workings and to develop better aural skills. Stephanie commented that 'when we are actually playing, that helps a lot in my understanding …. Playing is definitely the best way to help you understand it' (York, 17 May 2004). The advantages of checking a musical transcription through performing it on the actual instruments are obvious, as many world musics are likely to feature musical conventions that fall outside the Western norm. The use of instruments from the music culture can accommodate the tones, pitches and melodies that do not readily 'fit' into the Western notation system. The use of the actual instruments thus enabled students to construct a musical transcription from an emic perspective deemed of such importance in ethnomusicology. In reality, however, not all universities possessed the musical instruments needed to check musical transcriptions in the style of non-Western musics. In such instances, students utilised tools that were designed to facilitate the composing and playing of Western music, including their own Western instruments so as to check their transcription for accuracy:

I play the piano …. Yeah, I tried to work it out manually on the keyboard …. I have listened to them and tried to play them on the keyboard, and then put it on the computer. (Kevin, Bangor, 25 May 2006)

The only way I really got around the transcription was to listen to it and trying to play it back on the piano and trying to find the pitch of it …. I listened to it and tried to play it back, and then write it down. (Samantha, Bangor, 25 May 2006)

The piano was most often used to assist students in the constructing of a musical transcription, enabling them to convert unusual sounds into familiar notation and check it for accuracy. This was also evident in Kevin's approach used for transcribing *Khosid Wedding Dances* (Example 10.1), whilst utilising more innovative tools, including a keyboard (Creative Prodikeys) and software (Cakewalk Sonar) that enabled Kevin to play the music into the computer and listen to it at a slower tempo:

> I put it into the computer, you know, from the mini disc …. I slowed it down … to hear the pitches and everything. Then I just got a manuscript paper out and, each beat, just worked through it …. The technique is very useful … Yeah … it was quite quick … fast. It's a great tool. So you can keep the pitch the same and slow it down, you don't need to worry about that. (Kevin, Bangor, 25 May 2006)

With specific focus placed on the melody, listening repeatedly to the slowed down track enabled Kevin accurately to determine its beats and pitches:

> I usually start with the rhythm …. It is so slow that I can take each beat to work out the rhythm first, and then do the pitch next while playing along on the keyboard …. I wasn't entering the notes the first time though …. I wrote them down like that … by hand …. I go through it starting with bar 1 …. I use notation like this … and the first thing I did is identify the pulse, and that is usually 4/4, and then I split the bar into four like that, and then, the rhythm would be my first thing, you know just crosses …. Then I go back and do the pitch. (Kevin, Bangor, 25 May 2006)

Kevin's focus on the fiddle's melodic line led him to disregard other musical features, including rhythmic cycles or phrasing. He explained that 'the accompaniment was quite basic' (Bangor, 25 May 2006) and thus perhaps not an interesting consideration. The transcription thus omitted the music's other salient features so typical in Gypsy wedding music. For example, a closer analysis of *Khosid Wedding Dances* reveals that the fiddle features frequent upward glissandos characteristic of gypsy fiddle playing, which lends the music its joyful and uplifting feel. Under the fiddle's continuous melodic line, the accompanying viola alternates rhythmically with the double bass (while the higher pitched viola emphasises the off-beats, the double bass accents the main beats, providing a solid rhythmic foundation for the dancers), which is equally uplifting. Another characteristic in the recording is the resemblance to rondo form, whereby the folk tune continuously alternates two sections, each lasting four bars in a different (albeit related) key signature. Typically accompanying couple or circle dances, the two alternating sections indicate to the dancers a swap between dance partners or to change the circle's dancing direction. Focusing on aspects that are more salient to a particular music culture may have better shown Kevin's more complete understanding of this music culture. Instead, the use of tools facilitated a Western reading of an unknown music and reflects more eurocentric perspectives towards an understanding of world musics.

More generally, this chapter has shown that students often relied on their existing knowledge when constructing a musical transcription. They focused on musical examples that appeared familiar (by Western standards) and adopted a top-down approach in order to appropriate world musics (with the help of tools) to the familiar Western notation system. Rightly so did students rely on and extend their existing knowledge, specifically from an educational perspective. Yet from an ethnomusicological standpoint, problems may arise from an application of eurocentric cultural values. The transmission of musical transcription in ethnomusicology classes may thus also facilitate critical reflection and interrogation. Students may be encouraged by ethnomusicologists to think about why and how to construct a musical transcription. A more thorough ethnomusicological perspective that discards eurocentrism would lead students towards a more nuanced understanding of world musics through musical transcription.

Chapter 11
Composing Ethnography:
Strategies, Impact and Change

Ethnomusicologists generally believe that one of the best ways to understand other people and their musics is through exposure. To do so, they focus on ethnography as a method of research and style of writing. The ethnographic process corresponds to deep-level learning that enables the ethnographer to transfer newly gained knowledge into a broader awareness of musics' place in both other cultures and her own. It is a highly individualistic and subjective process, as the ethnographic text draws heavily on the researcher's experience-based position inside a music culture. To this end, the ethnographer writes herself into the ethnography, entering a process of actively recomposing the self. Ethnography's social dimension is equally significant, as it depends on social cooperation and interaction. Composing ethnography thus has the capacity to generate a deeper understanding of the values people hold about their music. This chapter will illustrate the ways in which composing ethnography enabled students to construct unique and multifaceted knowledge about a music culture. Yet what does ethnography mean in the context of university education?

At universities, students often encountered the conduct of an original fieldwork project so as to study and understand the musical experiences and perspectives of a particular group of people (see also Krüger, 2008). For the duration of the project, the student-researcher was the primary tool for data collection, using methods of cultural and musical participant-observation and open-ended interviewing whilst becoming a cultural and musical insider. Discovering and exploring a music culture during fieldwork was at the heart of students' projects. Composing ethnography thus offered hands-on, in-depth experiences with musics and their makers in the otherwise formal university environment. Depending on their level of study, however, undergraduate students typically conducted an ethnographic research project that was based locally and in an urban environment, and that could be completed within a relatively short timespan (e.g. one semester). Ethnographic projects at postgraduate level were very different, as students frequently focused on remote communities while seeking full-time immersion over a long period of time (at least one year) into the community or culture studied. Such long-term research often enabled students to become much more involved in the culture as insiders and to gain deeper insights and understandings than might be possible over shorter timespans.

In exploring students' experiences of composing ethnography, I worked with a small group of my own undergraduate students at Bangor University in 2006, including Lilly, Les and Colette. Lilly studied the experiences of music students (herself included) and composed an ethnographic report about the culture of Bangor's music department. Meanwhile, Les focused on Philippine popular music, particularly OPM (Original Philippino Music), whilst writing about what the music means to younger people of the Philippines. Colette's project differed due to its virtual dimension. Focusing on international singer Tom Jones, Colette composed ethnography about a virtual fan club and the role that Tom Jones plays to his fans. At postgraduate level, I explored the experiences of Corinna and Linda at the University of Sheffield during the second phase of my research in 2006. Corinna conducted ethnographic research into music's role played to people from diasporic communities in the UK (e.g. refugees). Linda, meanwhile, composed ethnography about *The Folk Viola in England* that was concerned with 'making some historical record' (Linda, Sheffield, 24 May 2006). Through long-term immersion into their chosen music culture, all students showed heightened appreciation towards the people studied. Yet the extent to which students had in-depth understandings of their ethnographic encounters depended on the strategies adopted for the composing of their ethnographies. Whilst these were shaped by the quality of their analyses and interpretations, combined with other influencing factors, outlining these strategies and impacting factors will be the concern of the following section.

Strategies for Composing Ethnography

The composing of ethnography required students to construct a written portrait of their chosen music culture, which they approached via analysis and interpretation, a series of stages in which a whole phenomenon is dissected and then reassembled to make the phenomenon meaningful to others. More specifically, data analysis meant to reduce and crunch data into a more manageable form, whilst interpretation meant to go beyond the results so as to make them meaningful. The steps of analysis and interpretation were typically recursive. Viktor who conducted 'fieldwork in Berlin ... into specific culture groups ... among them also a group from Ghana' for doctoral studies at the Hochschule für Musik und Theater Hannover (Viktor, telephone interview, 5 July 2006)[1] felt that both analysis and interpretation 'somehow happen automatically ... and together' (Viktor, telephone interview, 5

---

[1]   Ich hab meinen Magister in Köln gemacht ... und meine Magisterarbeit über die kolonialistischen Räpresentationen von afrikanischen Kulturvölkern geschrieben .... Das war mehr ne Literaturstudie .... zum Beispiel ... das afrikanische Festival, dass im Zoo stattfand ..... Dann hab ich in Hannover meine Doktorarbeit als Teil eines größeren Projektes angefangen .... Dafür hab ich Feldarbeit in Berlin gemacht ... in spezifischen Kulturgruppen ... unter anderem auch einer Gruppe von Ghana. Darauf hab ich mich dann mehr spezialisiert und bin auch deshalb jetzt in Ghana (Viktor, telephone interview, 5 July 2006).

July 2006).[2] Yet in their strategies, there existed a significant difference between undergraduate and postgraduate students: undergraduate students usually gained perspectives that enabled them to 'see', while postgraduates often developed deeper understandings, a kind of deeper-level knowing. This resulted from the differing extents to which students engaged with their ethnographic data: undergraduate students often remained at a basic, analytical level, while postgraduates moved beyond basic analysis so as to draw out deeper meanings of their ethnographic results.

The Analysis of Ethnographic Data

Ethnographic data analysis often began as soon as students entered the field whilst writing down fieldnotes from participant-observation and transcriptions of interviews. Les, for example, 'would make notes within 24 hours ... and think about the aspects' after he inscribed his observations and informal conversations with performers in a Videoke bar in the Philippines (Bangor, 25 May 2006). To many students, making fieldnotes was specifically useful to 'aid in creating questions that I haven't asked already' (Roger, Sheffield, 8 December 2003). Most students then coded the data into categories so as to make the data more manageable. Les, again, coded his data collection according to the categories 'radio, TV, karaoke/ videoke, malls, CDs and bands'. He thus identified simple, descriptive words and wrote them next to the transcribed interview passages or fieldnotes. Highlighting through colour-coding similar sections was also commonly used. This also enabled students to identify the relationships among sections and derive themes so pertinent in ethnographic writing. Interestingly, how such themes emerge is often unclear (LeCompte and Schensul, 1999b:45), and students similarly described the process as being intuitive. Les approached this by grouping the items 'radio', 'TV' and 'CDs' under the theme 'mass media', while 'karaoke/videoke', 'malls' and 'bands' formed the theme 'live performances'. Meanwhile, Colette analysed the online messages in a similar manner, which 'prompted what I ended up writing about' (Bangor, 25 May 2006), so that the derived themes included the happy family atmosphere; the use of fun and humour; the fans' identity; the role of the message board; and the role of the media. These themes informed the structure of Les's and Colette's ethnographies by forming the basis of headings and subheadings, allowing for their ethnographies to become more organised. This was challenging, and students often commented that the process was 'also quite confusing ... [and] felt like all-over-the-place' (Les, Bangor, 25 May 2006).

Yet how exactly did students approach the composing of ethnography? There seemed to exist a range of useful strategies. For example, students focused on specific research questions so as to concentrate on the most important issues: 'The

---

[2] Ich sehe die Analyse und Interpretation nicht als getrennt .... In meiner Erfahrung laufen beide gleich, und irgendwie automatisch ab (Viktor, telephone interview, 5 July 2006).

points I focused on in my ethnography came from my research questions. So I asked what was people's initial influence on becoming a music student, and the next step was to ask about other influences .... And so I was just concentrating on these research questions, and also saying what I went through, and then just backing it up by saying how other people agreed to it' (Lilly, Bangor, 25 May 2006). Linda's ethnography was similarly shaped by predetermined research questions that she had derived from her 'own experience before I started, because they were things I wanted to find out about' (Linda, Sheffield, 24 May 2006). Instead of paper-based analysis, Linda utilised the computer by cutting and pasting interview excerpts directly into the thesis and organising them into some kind of overall structure:

> So a lot of the process of the writing involved cut and paste .... It was a question of pulling out the themes from all the interview material. *[How did you do that?]* By reading it, and putting them together in a file in a sort-of completely jumbled-up, random order, and then trying to make the most sense ... on the computer. But then again, you've got to arrange them in a way that it makes logical sense to a reader, you know, and develop some sort of argument. It's quite hard. (Linda, Sheffield, 24 May 2006)

Students also often utilised standard narrative form by structuring the ethnography chronologically from the earliest events to the most recent, whilst bringing into focus their own experiences of the music culture. Michael, who conducted doctoral research into Ghanaian communities in the German *Ruhrgebiet* (area around Düsseldorf), commented that 'I have tried to build a structure ... starting at the beginning .... Firstly, I write what Africa means to me ... then I introduce the network, how I got to know the people ... the first contacts .... Then comes my first ... conceptual part in which I illustrate the history of immigration in Germany during the last 120 years .... The rest depends on what I'll find out .... But roughly speaking, it will be chronological' (Michael, telephone interview, 8 July 2006).[3] Linda similarly tried to 'make it coherent' by constructing 'a story ... with a beginning, a middle and an end' (Linda, Sheffield, 24 May 2006), and Les similarly composed ethnography in a chronological order by dividing 'all the key subjects into a ... logical structure':

---

[3] Ich bin jetzt bei Seite vierzig immerhin .... Im Grunde ... hab ich versucht, ne Gliederung aufzustellen ... und vorne angefangen .... Erstmal schreib ich was für mich Afrika ist ... dann bau ich langsam mein Netzwerk auf, wie ich zu den Leuten gekommen bin ... die ersten Begegnungen .... Dann kommt mein erster mehr oder weniger wissenschaftlicher Teil, wo ich die Immigrationsgeschichten in Deutschland während der letzten 120 Jahre darstelle ... und das misch ich eben ... mit meiner eigenen Kindheit ... und meinen eigenen Ausländererfahrungen .... Danach ... hängt das von den Einzelheiten ab .... Allerdings in der groben Geschichte wird das schon chronologisch (Michael, telephone interview, 8 July 2006).

I sort of implemented, linked it all together ... as if I had done it on a daily basis ... even though I did it over a space of four weeks. The end result made it look ... as if it is like a diary-type of project, which is what ... a fieldwork project should sort of resemble. (Les, Bangor, 25 May 2006)

Students also often used a strategy that involved the description of social events. Les's ethnography included a description of an event when 'people sit around the TV watching these programmes ... and music performances ... with famous artists on there' (Les, Bangor, 25 May 2006). Colette also used descriptions of an event when American fans attended a Tom Jones concert in the UK whilst depicting the light-hearted, humorous atmosphere:

> One of the ladies that I was speaking to, she comes from America, when the ... concert happened, a group of them came over to come to the ... concert, and from the airport they had a coach ... to the concert and back to the airport .... We shared our experiences on the board .... This woman got lost in the woodland area of the park ... and was walking pretty slowly, and the coach driver wanted to leave without her because he couldn't wait any longer, but she couldn't walk any faster because she needed a walking cane, and the driver couldn't understand .... Then the others were saying, you know, laughing at 'you had too much champagne and hoped that Tom would find you in the forest'. (Colette, Bangor, 25 May 2006)

Another useful strategy involved the creating of descriptive summaries of organisational structures, observations and interviews, which often formed considerable chunks in students' ethnographies. Lilly composed her ethnography using descriptive summaries of observations, since 'it needed to be ... descriptive; it was kind of like a story because, you know, it is a story of your research ... the time you've spent looking at people .... It was a bit more like a narrative story, rather than sort of another type of essay where you'd be analysing someone's music. It isn't factual .... It was more, "Oh, I also found out this"' (Lilly, Bangor, 25 May 2005). Some students also utilised visual frameworks. Linda approached this with the aid of mind-maps, which she prepared on 'many, large sheets of paper covered in spider-diagrams with lots and lots of connections. You couldn't make any ... logical sense of the data; there were about five different ways of ordering the data, none of which was particularly better than the other .... I pulled it out in themes' (Linda, Sheffield, 24 May 2006). More generally, students composed their ethnographies by organising and describing collected data and assembling the data into coherent, descriptive stories. Most students felt that 'it naturally made sense .... Once I started writing ... it fell into place really well' (Lilly, Bangor, 25 May 2006), and that it was 'such good fun, yeah, that was the best bit. It really was!' (Linda, Sheffield, 24 May 2006). Yet whilst the composing of ethnography into organised stories seemed logical and simple, the subsequent interpretation of these stories posed greater challenges to most students.

The Interpretation of Ethnographic Data

The interpretation of data meant to make the stories meaningful by going beyond the results and placing them into their broader context. This required students to highlight the significance of the findings and explain what conclusions may be gained from the results, which necessitated a deeper-level understanding of the music culture and original and creative thinking. This often involved cyclic, repeated analysis so as to move away from a descriptive and towards an interpretative writing style. Each reading generated new interpretations, which shifted the conceptual framework within which the results were organised and explained. Lilly used an interesting strategy that involved the presenting of contrasting emic and etic perspectives: 'I have friends who aren't musicians … and I got their perspective of music students' who they often perceived as different to the norm. This enabled Lilly to 'understand what we are like … and look through their eyes' (Lilly, Bangor, 25 May 2006). Lilly then contrasted this etic perspective to music students' emic perceptions (herself included) of themselves. This led her towards interpretations about music students' otherness and the existence of a strong sense of identity and community among them. Other strategies included the abstracting of current themes in ethnomusicological discourse, which necessitated considerations of the audience, as both Linda and Corinna interpreted the data with an ethnomusicological readership in mind. This involved an anthropological take on ethnography as a method of research and way of writing.

The interpretation of data revealed to be challenging, as it required students to take leaps beyond the data and set the results in a broader context. Most students found it hard to draw their own conclusions. They frequently highlighted that the process 'was just such a struggle … getting in a flow of writing …. It just never ever happened …. It feels … up in the air and all your ideas turned on their heads …. I hadn't a clue of what I was doing, and I didn't know what I was supposed to be thinking about it …. I don't think it did become easier! No, it didn't! That was just light relief to get to the end!' (Linda, Sheffield, 24 May 2006) Linda's inner hurdles seemed difficult to overcome:

> … that sort of feeling that you're sitting there and you've got a mountain of words to put together, and everything you're writing is complete rubbish, and it has no style, no flair, and it's all repetitive and boring, and you can't say what you think, and then you try to say it and it doesn't fit together, and then you read your chapter, and you haven't said what you said you were going to say at the beginning, and all that stuff …. Horrible process! (Linda, Sheffield, 24 May 2006)

Postgraduates generally agreed that 'I don't know how to write ethnography …. It's quite hard!' (Roger, Sheffield, 8 December 2003). Corinna agreed that the writing up is 'very, very hard' and necessitated time and patience:

Actually when it comes to writing, you need to have spare time in your hand. You need a whole morning where you might not write anything. But you are already thinking about it … and eventually you are fit by the afternoon. So it's very hard … you need a lot of time. But it doesn't mean you're going to produce a lot. You just need to have this frame of mind, this space for it. And then also, it's slow; it's very slow. You question yourself, every time I question myself many times …. You write and think this is great and I'm working to hundred percent. But then eventually that stops … and you think, o my god, what now? Because it's slow, it's really slow. Three or four years, it's a hell of a long time for me to finish a task …. It's very difficult for me not to have an end result always nearby. (Corinna, telephone interview, 21 May 2006)

It is interesting to note that undergraduate students commented less negatively on the writing process as postgraduate students. This is due to the fact that undergraduate students often remained at a descriptive, analytical level of writing and were less likely to engage with the interpretation of data. Undergraduate students thus revealed a heightened sense of enjoyment during the composing of their more descriptive ethnographies. Les commented that 'I found writing my essay really easy, and I did not have any difficulties' (Les, Bangor, 25 May 2006), as undergraduates 'merely scratched the surface' (Lilly, Bangor, 25 May 2006). Undergraduate students also enjoyed the fact that they were given 'the chance to do fairly independent study' (*ibid.*) in the otherwise prescriptive musical environment. Composing ethnography thus 'provided some light relief [and] made a nice change from normal essay subjects in Western classical music' (*ibid.*). Some students particularly valued the experiential portion of the ethnographic process, commenting that 'I really enjoyed the practical and social aspect of conducting fieldwork' [and] 'conducting the fieldwork was immensely enjoyable and a very valuable experience' (group discussion, Manchester, 9 May 2005). Students found it enjoyable that 'this research is a lot different than sitting in the library at a pile of books' (Colette, Bangor, 25 May 2006). They valued the more active, first-hand approach to learning, which seemed more 'real and concrete' (*ibid.*) and developed in students a sense of musical ownership. Colette further explained that 'the subject became very close to me, which made it more interesting' (*ibid.*). Les similarly felt that 'it's a lot easier for me to talk about something like OPM music because firstly, I'm interested in it, and secondly, it's a kind of music that makes sense to me, you know, popular music' (Les, Bangor, 25 May 2006). Lilly similarly enjoyed the fact that she could make her own choices and take responsibility for her own learning:

I think it was the fact that it was completely what you were doing …. I think it was the fact that … you were doing it all yourself. It was your work. It was your findings …. I really liked the fact that it was all about what I was doing, what I was finding out …. I think it's a sense of achievement in the end that you can go … I did that research, no-one else did it for me. Yeah, I think that's what I liked most about it, the fact that it was my own work …. That's what I liked about it, it's the freedom, and that it was my work. (Lilly, Bangor, 25 May 2006)

Factors Impacting on the Composing of Ethnography

While the previous section highlighted the various strategies used by students to compose their ethnographies, there also existed numerous factors that impacted on these strategies. These influencing factors included ethnomusicological discourse; ethical issues; research supervision; and examinations. Each factor will be further discussed in the following section.

Ethnomusicological Discourse

The most influential factor in students' writing of ethnography was the ethnomusicological literature that they encountered during their studies. Corinna felt that 'the way I carried out the research … was probably very much modelled by the books I read … like *Shadows in the Field* [Barz and Cooley, ed. 1997]' (Corinna, telephone interview, 21 May 2006). Lilly, meanwhile, 'found Titon's chapter on fieldwork [Titon, ed. 2002:447–74] and Myers' introduction [Myers, ed. 1992a:23–49) quite useful' (Lilly, Bangor, 25 May 2006). Ethnomusicological discourse also helped students to develop and shape the explanation of their results. Some commented that 'the literature has influenced my ideas … specifically poststructuralist theories' (Viktor, telephone interview, 5 July 2006),[4] while others reflected on the ways in which ethnomusicological discourse 'moved across disciplinary boundaries … into gender, feminism and other things …. I'm finding so much to help me … to making shape of my dissertation' (Jane, Newcastle, 16 March 2004). Certain texts, such as Clayton *et al.* (2003) were particularly useful in generating codes, themes and lines of thinking. Ethnomusicological texts were also useful in modelling a particular writing style. Viktor commented that 'literature is quite important to develop my own writing style. For me, that is probably most important, and the flow of the writing' (Viktor, telephone interview, 5 July 2006).[5] Michael similarly felt that 'reading, to be totally honest, only influences me when I think about writing … and how to do that well' (Michael, telephone interview, 8 July 2006).[6] Rüdiger Schumacher agreed that active engagement in the reading

---

[4]   Ja also, Literatur im allgemeinen hat Ideen herausgebracht, und mein Denken beeinflusst …. Insbesondere poststrukturelle Theorien (Viktor, telephone interview, 5 July 2006).

[5]   Also Literatur ist schon wichtig für mich, einen eigenen Schreibstil zu entwickeln. Das ist für mich wahrscheinlich am wichtigsten, und der Lesefluss (Viktor, telephone interview, 5 July 2006).

[6]   Das Lesen, um ganz ehrlich zu sein, beeinflusst mich nur, wenn ich mir Gedanken mache über's Schreiben … und wie man sowas gut macht (Michael, telephone interview,

of texts helps students to develop writing skills that are appropriate and attractive for the discipline:

> Reading is necessary .... Even when later the majority of students work in journalism, then it is especially necessary. One can basically just write in an appropriate style, an attractive style, when one has read a lot, that means when one has absorbed the language, and knows varied and rich ways of expression, and that is only possible through reading. (Rüdiger Schumacher, Köln, 22 July 2004)[7]

Students across universities understood that 'the more you read the better you write ... at the end' (Alexandra, Goldsmiths, 12 February 2004), and 'the readings have helped very much ... to write up my research' (Roger, Sheffield, 8 December 2003). Yet not all writing styles appeared revealing. Some ethnomusicological writings were perceived as difficult, as these were 'more self-analytical and self-thoughtful, and self-conscious and self-destructed ... [which] is not quite as open to an innocent reader' (Jonathan Stock, Sheffield, 6 October 2003). Yet more descriptive writing styles appeared more understandable:

> I quite enjoyed ... reading about folk dance and the Hardanger ... which wasn't factual .... It was more a story about the journey to a concert, and I thought that's really bizarre ... but really interesting ... as opposed to dates and facts. (Adrian, Durham, 27 October 2003)

Many students imitated the latter descriptive style for composing their ethnography as they were able to 'understand what the author means, so they learn from his example' (Jonathan Stock, Sheffield, 13 October 2003). Viktor preferred the writing style of Johannes Fabian (2002) and hoped to adopt a similarly 'interpretative and hermeneutic style' in the composing of his *Doktorarbeit*.[8] Linda sought to imitate the 'approachable and creative writing style' by Paul Berliner (1994). Meanwhile, some students felt that ethnomusicological texts helped them better to understand

---

8 July 2006).

[7]   Lesen ist notwendig ..., selbst wenn nachher ein Großteil der Studenten tätig sind im journalistischen Bereich, gerade dann ist es wichtig. Man kann im Grunde genommen nur in einem vernünftigen Stil schreiben, attraktiv schreiben, wenn man auch viel gelesen hat, d.h. wenn man Sprache in sich aufgenommen hat, und vielfältige und reiche Ausdrucksmöglichkeiten kennt, und das geht nur durch das Lesen (Rüdiger Schumacher, Köln, 22 July 2004).

[8]   Ich find Johannes Fabian ganz gut ... und zwar sein Buch *Im Tropenfieber: Wissenschaft und Wahn in der Erforschung Zentralafrikas*. Das gibt es auch auf English und heißt *Out of Our Minds: Reason and Madness in the Exploration of Central Africa...* Ich versuche auch so zu schreiben ... in einem interpretativen, hermeneutischen Stil (Viktor, telephone interview, 5 July 2006).

their own research identity, scope and methods. Corinna described this as follows: 'By reading books ... you identify yourself. ... You define yourself by agreeing or disagreeing with them. You sort of find what you really think, what you agree with, what you are doing .... In every book, you search for what you are doing, what you think' (Corinna, telephone interview, 21 May 2006). Colette, meanwhile, felt that the literature helped to locate her research within ethnomusicology, particularly since her ethnography had a virtual dimension. Reading an article by Bruno Nettl (1980), Colette understood that ethnomusicology also encompasses music cultures 'at home', and that:

> it means different things to different people. It could mean going ... to a village in Africa, or it could mean ... a culture in your own town that is a little bit foreign to you .... It's not just about going to Africa, going to a village and staying there for a year .... Culture is anywhere in the world .... That was influential for me because it summed up the actual feeling that I had been getting when I did my own research .... I could understand where he was coming from .... I could understand his point of view. (Colette, Bangor, 25 May 2006)

Ethical Considerations

The composing of ethnography was also often shaped by ethical considerations, a particularly pertinent issue in research that involves human beings. Most students were concerned with sensitivity, respect and integrity towards the people studied. Viktor felt that 'ethics are more a question of general standpoint ... and attitude towards people .... I treat people in the field just like I would treat people normally ... most of all open and honest' (Viktor, telephone interview, 5 July 2006).[9] There also existed more specific strategies, for example gaining consent, permission and approval about students' presence as researchers. Colette, for instance, posted a consent letter to the message board, upon which she 'got massive responses saying things like "yeah, yeah. We don't mind. How long do you need us lab-rats for?" So they welcomed this; it wasn't a problem' (Colette, Bangor, 25 May 2006). These positive responses shaped Colette's ethnography, as they formed the basis for the introduction in order to convey the humorous atmosphere of this music culture.

Students' ethical considerations also often involved respecting the rights to privacy, confidentiality or anonymity of the people studied. Some students thus excluded informants from their writings, specifically when professional and personal relationships became blurred. Viktor even discontinued research into the experiences of informants with whom he developed closer friendships. Corinna felt that 'it is a matter of boundary, isn't it? You can't avoid people liking you, and

---

⁹ Ethik ist für mich mehr eine Frage von allgemeiner Einstellung gegenüber den Leuten ... eine Sache von Attitüde .... Also ich behandel die in der Feldforschung genauso wie ich mit denen normalerweise auch umgehen würde ... hauptsächlich offen und ehrlich (Viktor, telephone interview, 5 July 2006).

you liking people. But that's not why you went there in the first place' (Corinna, telephone interview, 21 May 2006). Such considerations also impacted on the ways in which participants' voices were referenced. Some students felt it important that 'people's commentary will remain anonymous' (Viktor, telephone interview, 5 July 2006).[10] Other students used participants' real names, as in Michael's writings who wished to convey a sense of 'knowing my informants, and that my informants got to know myself', yet also ensured that participants were aware about the scope and purpose of his research (Michael, telephone interview, 8 July 2006).[11] Another important ethical issue shaping students' composing of ethnography involved the sharing of the final report with participants so as to gain feedback. Some students explained that 'I showed the information to the people, and they can say what they think about it' (Roger, Sheffield, 8 December 2003), and 'I simply show it to them and ask whether I can write that, because there do exist some drug stories' (Michael, telephone interview, 8 July 2006).[12] At times, participants' feedback led to changes in students' writings. Reciprocity was also an important ethical issue that impacted on students' composing of ethnography. Colette, for instance, felt she was giving something back to the fanclub when she watched the UK-based programme *The Jonathan Ross Show* and reported it back to the message board, as the American fans could not receive the programme. This experience informed one section of her ethnography in which she described the ways in which fans gossiped about the programme.

The Feedback from Supervisors

Feedback from supervisors also impacted on the processes of analysis and interpretation, and thus the composing of ethnography. During regular tutorials, students discussed written drafts, ideas and methods for continued research. It is interesting to note that whilst tutorials were more regulated at UK universities, German students were supervised more occasionally and informally. Viktor, for example, commented that 'he offers more general advice .... He helps me more generally to make my way .... When I have a problem ... he somehow

---

[10]   In meiner Doktorarbeit werden die Kommentare von den Leuten anonym gelassen. Ich sehe das auch nicht als so wichtig, weil ich ja nur allgemeine Eindrücke wiedergeben möchte .... Also das macht in der Regel nichts aus, ob das nun der oder der gesagt hat (Viktor, telephone interview, 5 July 2006).

[11]   So ist ja auch meine ganze Forschung angelegt, sonst würd ich einfach mit nem Mikrofon bewaffnet durch's Ruhrgebiet ziehen .... Meine Forschung ist aber explizit dafür, dass meine Informanten mich kennenlernen, und dass ich meine Informanten kennenlerne (Michael, telephone interview, 8 July 2006).

[12]   Wenn's wirklich mal eng wird, dann frag ich den einfach, ob ich das schreiben darf, weil es gibt da paar Drogengeschichten (Michael, telephone interview, 8 July 2006).

helps intuitively' (Viktor, telephone interview, 5 July 2006).[13] Michael similarly received more generic advice and support and described his overall experience of the doctoral process as 'little institutionalised' (Michael, telephone interview, 8 July 2006).[14] Nonetheless, the supervisor's role seemed to revolve around reading drafts of composed ethnography and to comment on its quality and rigour. At a basic level, the supervisor's feedback related to students' standard of written English. This often led students to feel exposed and vulnerable: 'This was a painful time, the beginning of the writing and the showing for the first time' (Corinna, telephone interview, 21 May 2006). At a more conceptual level, supervisors often pushed students' thinking beyond mere results so as to gain a deeper understanding of the music culture studied. Supervisors also provided critical and constructive feedback for students to develop clarity of thought and to derive the conceptual explanations. The constant questioning of the meanings behind presented data often led students to constantly recompose their ethnographies.

Jonathan Stock, the supervisor of Linda, Corinna, Roger and myself, frequently commented on the following aspects of our writing: the correct spelling of names; the use of certain words in order to convey meaning more effectively; the cutting of unnecessary terms; the effective use of quotations; further explanations to convey an argument; questions about used terms; grammar and punctuation; and questioning of the actual content. Such deep-level feedback was indeed crucial for editing the writings, revisiting the literature, rethinking arguments and the constructing of knowledge. Roger praised this approach for 'giving me … a lot of interesting ideas … always pointing me into a relevant direction … [and] suggesting areas I haven't thought of' (Roger, Sheffield, 8 December 2003). Yet rather than being prescriptive towards students' foci, supervisors often instead highlighted what not to compose in the ethnographic portrait. This allowed a certain freedom, responsibility and autonomy in the composing process.

Formal Examination

Formal examinations were yet another shaping factor in students' ethnographies, specifically at postgraduate level. Yet the impact of a viva on students' composing of ethnography was more pertinent in the UK due to possible amendments to a thesis, whereas German students merely receive a final result. For example, in

---

[13]   Ja, also ich hab ne sehr persönliche Beziehung zu [Professor] …. Die Beratung ist eher allgemein, also nicht so im Detail …. Ich finde dass Grammatik und Rechtschreibung von jemand anderen als dem Betreuer korrigiert werden kann …. Er hilft mir mehr im allgemeinen, meinen persönlichen Weg zu finden … und wenn ich ein Problem hab oder nicht weiterkomme, dann hilft er irgendwie intuitiv, da wieder rauszukommen (Viktor, telephone interview, 5 July 2006).

[14]   Wenn wir in Hannover sind, dann schlafen wir halt bei ihm, und es wird n'bisschen erzählt, was es neues gibt …. Es ist aber wenig institutionalisiert (Michael, telephone interview, 8 July 2006).

order to be awarded the degree of MMus, Corinna had to make corrections that required further research and more substantial conceptualisations. I also found that the upgrade examination from MPhil to PhD at UK universities resulted most frequently in recommendations, which are intended to broaden students' understanding, skills and knowledge. Meanwhile, during her viva for PhD, Linda's examiners recommended minor amendments to the thesis in form of a revisited literature review. She further explained that 'I had to read ... seven books in a short space of time' (Linda, Sheffield, 24 May 2006). Reading such relevant literature obviously shaped Linda's critical analysis and interpretation of results, which in turn impacted on her (re)composing of ethnography.

Recomposing the Self

The composing of ethnography required students to engage in critical self-reflexivity. This process may also be regarded as recomposing the self, as ethnography impacted on a deeply personal level: 'It has become part of my life' (Viktor, telephone interview, 5 July 2006).[15] Ethnography also impacted on a personal level, as participants 'have simply become my friends .... It has also been a very intensive experience, since I have spent very much time by myself' (Michael, telephone interview, 8 July 2006).[16] In reflecting on their experiences, students often saw their own behaviours, values and concepts reflected in people's reactions. This led students towards deeper understandings of themselves, yet in distinct and individual ways. Ethnography thus often transformed students' attitudes and perspectives through a process of recomposing the self. Lilly became musically more confident during the ethnographic research through her growing awareness of the myths surrounding musical talent. She developed heightened self-awareness within the Western music department, as ethnography enabled her 'to step out of myself ... and understand myself a little bit better'. Feeling increasing confidence as a musician, Lilly commented that:

> I think that made me relax a bit more ... to think that people may say one thing to make themselves look good in front of other people. But we are all secretly sat there going 'oh, oh' and are worried about our status as performers and musicians .... It relaxed me a lot as I realised that other people felt the same way as I do .... I'm much more at ease now in the community, I think .... I didn't expect it; I

---

[15] Die Feldforschung und Doktorarbeit hat mich schon aus sehr persönlicher Ebene beeinflusst .... Es ist ein Teil meines Lebens geworden (Viktor, telephone interview, 5 July 2006).

[16] Ein großer Einfluss vor allem, dass die Leute in der Band auch einfach meine Freunde geworden sind .... Es war auch eine sehr intensive Erfahrung, zumal man auch sehr viel Zeit mit sich selbst verbracht hatte (Michael, telephone interview, 8 July 2006).

> didn't think it would affect me at all …. I really think I'm a lot more comfortable
> now I know what people's feelings are. (Lilly, Bangor, 25 May 2006)

Meanwhile, Les's experience of being a researcher seemed most significant, as it lent him prestige and status. He vigorously remembered people's interest in him 'when saying … "I'm a researcher". That was a new experience for me because I have never done that kind of thing before', which made him 'feel a little bit more special'. This seemed appealing to Les as 'you do get slightly special preferential treatment because … you are a researcher …. So it does make it a little bit easier when you try to make that approach … as if I was important!' [laughing] (Les, Bangor, 25 May 2006). During Colette's research, she developed considerable empathy and tolerance towards the fans of Tom Jones, specifically in the light of the media's frequent attacks against them. She genuinely recognised the values and beliefs that the fans hold about the music and found that 'at the end of the day, they are just normal' even though initially she thought 'they were all bonkers' (Colette, Bangor, 25 May 2006). While Colette found the fans' attitudes amusing at times, composing ethnography enabled her to realise that the people are indeed 'unique and individual'. Gaining a deeper understanding of the fans' love and loyalty to Tom led towards a heightened appreciation and tolerance for the fans, reflecting a change in Colette's attitudes and perspectives towards the people she wished to understand.

Postgraduate students also commented on processes of personal change through the self-reflexive portion of the ethnographic process, which led them to understand and recompose the self. Corinna experienced a transformation towards becoming a more autonomous person:

> I think it changed me in the sense that I had to do it myself. Before that … I
> always had … teachers teaching me, and I would do whatever tasks they would
> ask me to do …. The Masters was all very different because I had to do it myself;
> I had to push it myself. Although there is a supervisor, there isn't… the lesson
> every week… and an essay by the end of the month. It wasn't like that. So it
> changed the way I studied. It changed the way I looked at perhaps books, and
> even myself as perhaps having lots of motivation for myself. (Corinna, telephone
> interview, 21 May 2006)

Independence and self-directedness in the composing of ethnography necessitated students' creativity, as 'it's not something that is set for you …. You've got to invent yourself and invent the things you do all the time for it to work …. I had to find ways all the time … and make a lot of decisions'. This made Corinna 'think and stress and feel in a way that otherwise would just be normal'. Pushing beyond intellectual comfort zones clearly transformed Corinna's sense of self:

> I get all subjective …. I sometimes get completely tangled with thoughts, and I
> can't be practical anymore, which is very hard because I am a practical person.

I've become all this thoughtful being, which I wasn't before, if that makes sense. And ... it gets me fucked sometimes because things become too complicated, or they become not clear anymore .... On a personal level, I'm getting to know myself, which is very difficult .... The PhD is something very hard, and if you go through difficulties, you get to know yourself .... There are different ways of getting to know yourself, and going through hard times is one of them. (Corinna, telephone interview, 21 May 2006)

Linda similarly felt that the ethnographic process transformed herself. As a musician, Linda improved technical skills and mastery and also felt a stronger sense of belonging to the folk music culture:

... as a musician, it's made me an awful lot better, and it ... made it very much easier for me to understand and work with other musicians because ... I was very ... worried about going and asking for advice, particularly because of not having had training, or whatever. So I feel much easier about that now, and also, I feel I understand more about how other musicians work because I have talked to and interviewed quite a lot of people, so again, getting some insight. So it's made me better as a musician technically, but it's also made me better as a musician in terms of working as part of a team with other musicians, which is really nice. And it's made me feel more confident, and at the same time more sort of humble. (Linda, Sheffield, 24 May 2006)

At an intellectual level, composing ethnography led Linda towards developing a more critical stance:

A lot of the thinking ... gets turned upside down for a long period of time. And everything that you ... take for granted about the area that you're researching gets a question mark attached to it, and all of a sudden, you feel like, everything you have thought and done for years is all like sort of quicksand, which is quite disturbing. But I think it's a good process to go through ... because it teaches you not to take anything for granted, but it can also make you like chronically indecisive .... It just feels like you go on a sort of ride in your head... and then you end up sort of where you started off from, but different. (Linda, Sheffield, 24 May 2006)

To Linda, composing ethnography also impacted in a third significant way, namely by gaining the title Doctor of Philosophy. She proudly summarised that:

I'm really pleased I did it! ... I was absolutely determined I was gonna finish! ... But I did question why, and whether there was any point lots of times. No, after I had finished, I was pleased, very pleased I have done it! (Linda, Sheffield, 24 May 2006)

Chapter 12
Mediating Fieldwork Experience: Ethnomusicological Uses of Film and Video

Ethnomusicologists frequently suggest that the essence of ethnographic fieldwork today is centred on experience (Barz and Cooley, 2008:4). They believe that participatory participant-observation during fieldwork enhances deeper understandings of a given music-cultural practice. They study, document, record and write about their fieldwork experiences so as to make unknown music-cultural practices accessible to academic audiences. Yet whilst ethnographic writing for representing a music culture is widely accepted in ethnomusicology, less attention seems to be paid to visual ethnography as a means to mediate fieldwork experience. Visual ethnography is a specific kind of ethnography that makes use of a range of different visual methods and media, including photography, film, art and drawing, and the new media/hypermedia (see also Lange, 2001; Titon, 2008:35–6). Ethnomusicologists have long used audiovisual means in their research and writing, yet these audiovisual means are often seen as supportive of fieldwork, rather than as an ethnographic recording method for research, also evident in manuals or guides to ethnomusicological field research (examples include Fargion, 2001; Myers, 1992a; Post *et al.*, 1994; Stock, 2004). Thus whilst audiovisual recording is a useful means for making a permanent record of observations and gaining feedback from participants by playing back recorded episodes, constructing visual ethnography is still often tangential to mediating fieldwork experience in ethnomusicology.

The differing emphasis on writing and film is also reflected in the formal transmission of ethnomusicology at universities. Here, I found that ethnomusicologists frequently sought out various visual media to bring music cultures alive in the university classroom. Yet little attention was paid to constructing ethnomusicological film so as to allow students to mediate their own fieldwork experiences in audiovisual ways. This is the concern of this chapter with its specific focus on ethnomusicological uses of film and video in formal ethnomusicology education. It begins with discussions on the use of film and video in the university classroom. The second part will then illustrate the experiences of one student who engaged in ethnomusicological film making. The chapter will close with an assessment of the impact of ethnomusicological uses of film and video on students' attitudes and perspectives towards world music cultures. In exploring these matters, I will draw on the voices of ethnomusicologists and students from research conducted at four universities in 2008. Noteworthy to mention is the fact that there currently exists no academic discourse on the ethnomusicological uses of film and video in university education. Whilst educational literature often focuses on the usefulness of film and video in the classroom more generally (Champoux, 1999; Karppinen, 2005) and music education more specifically (Christopherson, 1972; Geringer, 1996), there is a significant gap in literature that focuses on the use of film and video in the transmission of ethnomusicology. This chapter is thereby a much needed contribution on this topic.

Film and Video in the Transmission of Ethnomusicology

Many ethnomusicologists utilised film and video in the transmission of world musics at universities. This included professional documentaries, such as David Fanshawe's *Musical Mariner: A Pacific Journey* and performance videos, such as the *JVC/Smithsonian Folkways Video Anthology of Music and Dance*. The latter were particularly useful for demonstrating playing and vocal techniques from different cultures, yet due to the absence of narrative, such videos were often regarded to have less educational value than documentaries that combined sound with words and images. Meanwhile, educational videos, such as *Khyal: Classical Singing of North India* by Martin Clayton and Veena Sahasrabuddhe (Open University) were deemed useful as an introduction to a particular musical genre or style. Some ethnomusicologists also utilised their own field recordings, yet this depended on the ethnomusicologist's research context. Henry Stobart, for instance, has since 2007 been involved with local musicians in the filming and production of DVDs and VCDs of indigenous Andean music, and these films are frequently used in formal university classes. The use of internet resources also varied across universities. Laudan Nooshin (Figure 12.1) and Henry Stobart fully embraced the new technologies during their classes, whilst Caroline Bithell frequently recommended internet resources as an extra-curricular means for stimulating students' interest. In some instances, ethnomusicologists also used anthropological and ethnographic films, which were useful for showing students 'about their way of life ... and that the music we're going to listen to on CD is taking place in this context' (Caroline Bithell, Manchester, 12 November 2008). Ethnomusicological uses of film and video in university education are clearly varied and multifaceted. Yet what specific pedagogical strategies are employed by ethnomusicologists in their use of film and video in world musics classes?

Pedagogical Strategies

Whilst no formal pedagogical framework exists about the use of film and video in ethnomusicology education, I did observe some common trends across universities. For example, film and video were most commonly integrated into a more holistic learning model that also involved students in reading, listening, discussing and watching (besides other activities). An integrated pedagogical approach meant the

Figure 12.1 Laudan Nooshin leading a class in ethnomusicology; City University London, January 2009

use of shorter sections or snippets of a film or video in formal classes, supported
by explanations, listening, reading and discussions. This enabled students to 'start
to piece together bits of the jigsaw' (Caroline Bithell, Manchester, 12 November
2008). Jess found the integrated learning approach particularly useful:

> What I like about Caroline's lectures ... is that she puts extra context in .... So
> before I watch it I'm prepared; I've got context in my head .... I think that's quite
> important. Afterwards, when she ties it in and then carries on, I find that really
> interesting .... I think it works well to show a bit of the film. (Jess, Manchester,
> 12 November 2008)

To most ethnomusicologists, shorter film sections were also used as a form of
primary evidence for their argumentation. Students understood that 'a musicologist
will refer to publications; that's his evidence .... An ethnomusicologist ... refers to
the actual people themselves' (Joseph, RHUL, 20 October 2008). Film and video
thus played a considerable role in validating and authenticating music cultures
from around the world, commenting that 'it definitely validates .... Video is like
evidence' (Jane, RHUL, 20 October 2008).

     Another (albeit rarer) pedagogical strategy was to show students a film or
video in its entire length, which was particularly suitable when there were less
time constraints. One pedagogical rationale for utilising a full-length film emerged
from formal assessment. Caroline Bithell, for example, 'set an essay and some
seminar questions on that topic [and] took two quotes from documentaries that
I knew they had watched for an exam ... and asked ... "What does he mean by
this?"' (Manchester, 12 November 2008). Longer video excerpts were also useful
'to really go into detail and ... get the overall picture of what's going on' (Miku,
RHUL, 20 October 2008). After watching longer or full-length documentaries,
ethnomusicologists often 'get students to discuss some of the issues' (Laudan
Nooshin, City, 18 December 2008), which students found important in order 'to
deconstruct the context of the video ... and to understand the broader content ... of
what you have just seen' (Jane, RHUL, 20 October 2008). Other ethnomusicologists
'tend not to have a lot of discussions immediately after a film, partly because ...
I like to leave them in that mood .... the impression that it has made on them'
(Caroline Bithell, Manchester, 12 November 2008). For example, showing to
students David Fanshawe's documentary was 'just to get them excited and happy'
(*ibid.*), specifically during the very first week of a world music module, which also
balanced what might have appeared 'a somewhat dry and possibly overwhelming
introduction to ethnomusicology as a discipline' (*ibid.*). Even without discussions
such whole-length documentaries had profound impacts on students. Jess, for
example, remembered that 'seeing him ... made him real and it made the whole
piece more real and I could see the dancers dancing, whereas before I had just
heard them on the recording .... So that was a big thing visually ... that really
brought some life to it' (Manchester, 12 November 2008).

Interestingly, ethnomusicologists often regarded film and video as a self-sufficient academic study tool whilst encouraging their students to 'treat the films ... like any other text, and take notes and reference it ... in your bibliography' (Caroline Bithell, Manchester, 12 November 2008). Some students followed this recommendation, commenting that 'I do then go back to the library and watch them ... I then make notes .... So I do re-visit the films. I certainly do because I'm quite a visual learner and I try to immerse myself completely' (Jess, Manchester, 12 November 2008). Yet when it came to essay writing, even Jess admitted that 'I didn't always use them as a text .... I might use books in the essay more than a film' (*ibid.*). Other students like Holly similarly admitted that 'I haven't really used them to write an essay .... I can't really be bothered, which is really bad' (Manchester, 12 November 2008), whilst Joseph felt that 'it is very easy just to watch it and take it all in and maybe not writing anything about it' (RHUL, 20 October 2008). Meanwhile, Jane's attitude was that 'keen students like me would occasionally watch them ... [and] take notes in preparation for an essay' (RHUL, 20 October 2008). One possible reason for certain students not regarding film and video as an academic study source may be that 'it's a bit like being in the cinema' (Caroline Bithell, Manchester, 12 November 2008). Miku agreed that 'you sort of enjoy and sit back and enjoy' (RHUL, 20 October 2008), whilst Emma and Holly found that 'I'm being entertained' and 'it makes you much more relaxed ... [because] the thought of ... watching a film doesn't make me think of doing work' (Manchester, 12 November 2008). Students seemingly gave film and video less credibility than written academic discourse, an attitude that reflects a common dichotomy in the West, which differentiates between work/serious versus leisure/enjoyable. What is enjoyable cannot be serious work, so that some students regarded watching film and video as less suitable for serious academic study.

Clearly, commonalities exist in the pedagogical uses of film and video in ethnomusicology education. Yet why do ethnomusicologists utilise film and video in the transmission of ethnomusicology? This is the concern of the following section, which will illustrate how and to what extent film has the capacity to mediate fieldwork experiences.

Mediating Fieldwork Experience

> Without being there you can't get the full experience, and the next best thing is ... a video. (Emma, Manchester, 12 November 2008)

> Experiencing it! When you experience it, I think you learn a lot better! (Holly, Manchester, 12 November 2008)

The opening section of this chapter emphasised the experiential portion of the ethnographic process during which ethnomusicologists study and seek to understand music in its cultural context. This requires them to pay attention not only to musical sounds but also to the visual dimension of a given music-cultural practice. They observe in detail the people, location, space, movement, choreography and performer-audience interaction during musical performances and situations. The emotional aspect of the music too is central to a deeper understanding of people making music. Ethnomusicologists thus often use film and video for capturing and studying the audio, visual, motional and emotional aspects of a musical performance (Stock, 2004:27). In formal ethnomusicology education, there exists a similar concern with using film and video to enable students to experience music in its context. Ethnomusicologists frequently suggested that 'I want to bring things to life by letting them see … the context, the country, the background, the situation in which music happens' (Caroline Bithell, Manchester, 12 November 2008). Students found it useful to see these music-cultural practices visually because 'without being there you can't get the full experience, and the next best thing is … a video' (Emma, Manchester, 12 November 2008) and 'you actually get the whole experience' (Holly, Manchester, 12 November 2008).

Henry Stobart specifically felt that seeing the context in which people make music was 'incredibly important to understanding music there [in the Andes]' (RHUL, 20 October 2008). Students like Rachel agreed that 'it comes to life so much …. It makes the culture and music more real, and it gives you an understanding of how to place the music in context' (RHUL, 20 October 2008). Jane similarly commented that 'it's impossible to imagine what some of those cultures are like' (RHUL, 20 October 2008), whilst Joseph added that 'you get a sense of almost as if we were travelling there ourselves; we can see it; we can hear it; see the dancing; see what the people do; listen to the music … experiencing it' (RHUL, 20 October 2008). Another useful dimension of film and video was 'music's connection with physical movement, the fact of music not just being sound, but dance and music being the part of the same thing' (Laudan Nooshin, City, 18 December 2008). Jess agreed that 'it was really helpful to just be able to visualise that … because so much of it is caught up with dance and with movement and performance' (Manchester, 12 November 2008). Clearly, the visual aspect of film and video seemed of central importance to ethnomusicologists because:

> It's … teaching students about … music as part of a *whole*, not just detached sounds …. The visual aspect is, I suppose, as close as we can get to actually taking them there …. So I use film and video to give them an added dimension …. It's a way of taking students … on a journey, so it makes that culture more immediate, more intense. It intensifies the experience of experiencing music in its context, whatever that context may be. (Laudan Nooshin, City, 18 December 2008)

Coming closer to experiencing music in its cultural context also meant gaining emic perspectives into people's concepts and beliefs. Henry Stobart, for instance, found that film and video helped to 'communicate ... the whole concept of fiesta ... [as] a multi-sensory experience' (RHUL, 20 October 2008), whereby students learnt that local Andean people often value 'their experience of the quality of the beer. That's the most important thing as far as they are concerned .... It doesn't downplay the music; it just says it's one ingredient within a much broader event' (*ibid.*). Caroline Bithell, meanwhile, prioritised a concern with 'living musicians ... [who] speak for themselves' (Manchester, 12 November 2008), allowing students:

> ... to experience feeling, imagining what it's like to be someone else; imagining what it's like to be in someone else's skin .... I want them to see people because people are so central to what we're about as ethnomusicologists .... To see those people and relate to them, I think, really helps them to understand the music .... So seeing it on video is making it embodied .... You are looking at people, and you're getting a sense of their lives, you're getting a sense of the hardship of their lives, or you're getting a sense of them having fun. You're getting a sense of them as a character. (Caroline Bithell, Manchester, 12 November 2008)

The impact of students' deeper emic understandings is noteworthy. Holly, for example, felt that 'it makes what we're studying more real [because] you can actually hear the musicians ... talk about their music and talk about the situation they are in' (Manchester, 12 November 2008). Jess further added that:

> I have a whole picture of his life now .... There is a face there; there is a personality there .... As soon as I had a face, he was a person, not just a name on the page ... It doesn't feel like a subject now that I'm studying ... as if they're something to be put under a microscope .... It feels like people that I'm observing .... I find that film has given me a link, a more direct link to the people, the people I'm watching literally, the people I'm studying, the people whose music I listen to. They feel like real people to me. And so it stops being a subject, and it becomes ... a really big part of my life. (Jess, Manchester, 12 November 2008)

Ethnomusicological Filmmaking

In discussions on ethnomusicological uses of film and video in formal university education, it is also pivotal to consider the use of audiovisual media as an ethnographic recording method for research, analysis and representation of a given music-cultural practice. I found that amongst some ethnomusicologists, ethnographic filmmaking is deemed particularly suitable for exploring the interplay of the aesthetic and functional in musical performance. Often called ethnomusicological film, ethnomusicologists seek to render their musical engagement and music-cultural encounter with different peoples, cultures and places in the world. Ethnomusicological film is concerned with depictions of reality. The aim is documentation, rather than fiction, and thus reporting, not inventing, whatever is in the world. It is used to exhibit the facts of a situation in a given music culture. Ethnomusicological film may also encourage viewers to come to a particular conclusion about the world or some parts of it. John Baily defined ethnomusicological filmmaking as 'the creative treatment of actuality' (Goldsmiths, 13 November 2008). At Goldsmiths College London, the constructing of ethnomusicological film, which is also one of John Baily's specialisms, was particularly well integrated in ethnomusicology education. It is interesting to note that no other university has yet similarly formalised ethnomusicological filmmaking in the ethnomusicology curriculum.

Formal education in ethnographic filmmaking, combined with an appropriate training in the use of technical equipment was crucial for students to construct ethnomusicological films for mediating their own fieldwork experiences. In exploring these matters at Goldsmiths College, I worked with three postgraduate students, Tom, Val and Patrick who studied on two research methods courses, which provided the necessary fieldwork training. Students then applied their newly gained knowledge in real settings during the conduct of a small-scale research project whilst engaging – over a longer period of time – with a given music culture. The availability of digital editing facilities and digital cameras meant that rather than presenting their fieldwork results in a 5,000 word ethnographic essay, students had the choice to mediate their fieldwork experiences by making an ethnomusicological film, which had to be accompanied by a 3,000 word reflexive study guide. Tom had the initial idea of making a portrait film about a female London-based fiddler who is leading a Gypsy quartet 'to see what is her relationship with this gypsy music and how does she view it; does she really think it's authentic or not' (Goldsmiths, 13 November 2008). Val also had plans for making a portrait film, specifically on a Bangladeshi woman in London and 'how she feels about singing, and how she feels about her community, and … that she wants to sing, but she's got to get through this barrier of not being able to perform … in front of men' (Goldsmiths, 13 November 2008).

According to John Baily, many Goldsmiths students have in the past presented films that 'were really quite remarkable' (Goldsmiths, 13 November 2008), even though students received only limited training. This included two formal sessions offered by the university's media services in camera usage and video editing. The research methods module itself was led by John Baily, during which students learnt about 'the history of documentary film, anthropological film, ethnomusicological film with opportunities for them [students] to report back on their fieldwork' (Goldsmiths, 13 November 2008). The first sessions intended to introduce students to the differences between direct and observational cinema. Here, Tom remembered watching examples of older silence and sound films whilst discussing the synchronising of sound with image and critiquing earlier eurocentric examples of ethnographic film. Students also viewed a range of observational films, including films by John Baily and Hugo Zemp, which Val found particularly valuable because these films showed 'the musician as a human being, not like a thing or an insect, and ... the relationship between the filmmaker and musician ... rather than hiding it' (Goldsmiths, 13 November 2008). Meanwhile, John Baily's film *Amir* (1985):

> ... was the most helpful because you see he's actually talking about his experiences ... about the interpersonal relations ... about the process of getting the shots ... [and] the interpersonal relations of the family .... That was very interesting, and talking about how these ... relationships work over the span of many years ....
> It's interesting ... listening to him talk about ... the challenging part [which] is not doing the film; it's negotiating all these other extra filmographic-type things.
> (Tom, Goldsmiths, 13 November 2008)

Patrick agreed. *Amir* (1985) 'was really fascinating' and understood that 'the focus really is ... on the social and cultural context' (Goldsmiths, 13 November 2008). These earlier sessions were followed with classes on 'video editing and the editing process, and the kinds of positions the editor takes' (John Baily, Goldsmiths, 13 November 2008). Subsequent sessions were used to discuss a range of other documentaries, including world music programmes that were broadcast on British television. The final session provided opportunities for students to report back on their fieldwork projects. More generally, students at Goldsmiths learnt that ethnomusicological films should adhere to the documentary, non-fiction (realist) style and reflect the filmmaker's experiences in the naturalistic setting depicted in film. Yet at the same time, the films 'are meant to have some creative flair to them' (John Baily, Goldsmiths, 13 November 2008). Thus instead of a set of prescriptive principles, students were allowed considerable creative freedom in constructing their ethnomusicological films:

> I don't think we have a problem of whether it's ethnographic or not .... What I like to see, what we're looking for is a mixture between performance – we would expect to have a considerable amount of performance – ... and a structure ....
> We would also expect to have quite a lot of ... conversation with the filmmaker.
> (John Baily, Goldsmiths, 13 November 2008)

Ethnomusicological filmmaking 'is a very creative work, and that's why I like doing it myself' (*ibid.*). Val agreed that 'it's more creative .... That's why I want to do it because there's more creativity in it' (Goldsmiths, 13 November 2008).

Constructing Ethnomusicological Film

In the first semester of the academic year 2008, John Baily opened the research methods module with a film by Fiorella, a former postgraduate student at Goldsmiths College London. John Baily wanted to show Fiorella's film because it is 'a very good model for them to follow' (Goldsmiths, 13 November 2008). Tom remembered watching the film and explained to me that 'this film is … very much a study of somebody … of a person …. I would define it more of a, at least in a film-sense, it's a portrait film …. Visually [it is] painting a picture' (Goldsmiths, 13 November 2008). In my quest to understand the motivations and approaches by students who had already made a film, I was keen to meet Fiorella to find out about her personal experiences of filmmaking. I also wanted to see her ethnomusicological film. I was very fortunate that John Baily helped in arranging a meeting with Fiorella during which I could explore her motivations and perspectives. When we met, Fiorella opened by saying that 'ethnomusicologists almost always record and write, and they'd share their experience through writing more than a video or film' (Goldsmiths, 13 November 2008). I fully agreed. It is perhaps for this reason that Fiorella wanted to do 'something completely different … to tell a story that people could read by watching' (*ibid.*).

The idea for the film emerged during Fiorella's fieldwork into Mongolian overtone singing, which began in November 2007 whilst learning to perform *khoomii* from a London-based teacher named Michael Ormiston. To the Peruvian-born student, *khoomii* was 'something that I did never before …. I chose the furthest thing that I could ever imagine … for my performance' (*ibid.*). Ethnographic film seemed particularly suitable for a deeper representation of this music-cultural practice. Fiorella specifically wanted to 'let the person … be very natural, and let the story develop itself; not look for anything in particular; talk about what you're seeing … use different techniques … and … then talking to me while I'm filming …. So it will be very very natural …. It's the story that tells itself.' (*ibid.*) As in Tom's example earlier, Fiorella found that the film *Amir* (1985) was the main source of inspiration:

> I was impressed because *Amir* (1985), for example, is such a nice film and it's so natural and you feel so involved, not only by the music but the character, by the context …. I watched *Amir* I don't know how many times to not only get the impression, but to see how he [John Baily] did things …. *Amir* was very sentimental …. A portrait film. Very powerful! (Fiorella, Goldsmiths, 13 November 2008)

Fiorella made a portrait film entitled *Sound Transformations: Michael Ormiston* (2008),[1] which is a representation of a foreign culture bearer who learnt to perform Mongolian throat singing while researching the tradition in Mongolia (Montero Diaz, 2008a:1). The film also intends to depict a journey through Michael Ormiston's sound transformation through *khoomii*. Filming began in January and continued until summer 2008, during which Fiorella recorded 'everything that has to do with Michael, everything …. I didn't have any specific idea; I just

---

[1]   Interestingly, Michael Ormiston also has a website entitled Sound Transformations; see http://www.sound-transformations.btinternet.co.uk/.

filmed everything' (Fiorella, Goldsmiths, 13 November 2008). This included *khoomii* lessons 'not only with Michael and myself but with other groups and their experiences ... so I just prepped the camera and drank tea with them and they told me things about their lives and their perceptions of this music' (*ibid.*). Other important ingredients of her ethnomusicological film included depictions of performances and interviews: 'There are two or three sessions where Michael Ormiston is giving his concerts ... in church ... and then in his home where he is talking about his background, his experiences how he came to learn [*khoomii*]' (John Baily, Goldsmiths, 13 November 2008). The filmed concerts depict Michael Ormiston in performance with Candida Valentino, 'singing Mongolian overtones but at the same time us[ing] electronic equipment to do loops. He was singing *khoomii* in the church, which was amazing!' (Fiorella, Goldsmiths, 13 November 2008).

This concern with openness in the initial stage of ethnomusicological filmmaking resonates closely with ethnographic research more generally, which typically begins with broad and descriptive ideas and questions, whereby the focus often evolves from a desire to explore and discover people's (rather than the researcher's) perspectives about a given music-cultural practice. In Fiorella's film, the focus emerged directly from her involvement in *khoomii* singing: 'That's the reason I chose *khoomii* because I was researching *khoomii*, because I was singing *khoomii*' (*ibid.*). As in ethnographic research, the open-ended purpose of ethnographic filmmaking obviously meant that Fiorella collected a vast amount of filmed footage and handwritten notes, which necessitated editing.

Editing

Editing may be compared to the analytical stages in ethnographic writing, which aims to reduce collected data to a more manageable form so as to tell a story about the people studied (Krüger, 2008:111). It involves dissecting a whole phenomenon, and then reassembling it in such a way to make the phenomenon understandable to others. Fiorella reflected that 'I had around thirty hours, and in the end I had to cut it to thirty minutes' (Goldsmiths, 13 November 2008). I found it particularly interesting that Fiorella compared film editing to musical composition: 'When you edit it, you grab this and that .... I do it in music with computers; it's the same thing: you cut, you paste, you listen, you kind of piece together the music, and then think "oh no, another instrument". [In film editing] it's the same thing: you cut, you paste, you watch, and then you say "well maybe I can put this". It's the same thing! So in the end, I felt I composed a song' (Fiorella, Goldsmiths, 13 November 2008). Fiorella explained that the software iMovie used for film editing is very similar to the software Pro Tools used for musical composition. For example, both types of software display multiple audio/video tracks at the bottom of the screen, 'and then you grab the footage at the bottom ... and you put in the film, and then you manipulate that with the effects that are right' (*ibid.*).

Initial ideas for editing often occurred with students' first encounters during fieldwork. Having already worked with Michael, Fiorella's initial aim was to 'dig a little bit into Michael's experience as a Brit but at the same time a culture-bearer of Mongolia' (*ibid.*). Editing also required a process of selecting particularly meaningful parts in the filmed footage, yet this also meant to exclude others. Fiorella particularly remembered 'a very nice footage of showing pictures; we're talking and he just grabs pictures and starts telling me about Mongolia [and] his teachers .... It was a very emotional moment. It would have been very nice to put it in the film but it was too long' (*ibid.*). Ethical considerations played another pivotal role in excluding certain parts of the footage:

> I was very aware ... which things I could show and which things ... I couldn't show, for example, when they confront each other, Candida and Michael, when they were kind of upset with each other .... But I filmed everything... but I knew I couldn't put that; I knew I couldn't discuss that but for my knowledge at least it was very valuable to see what happened between them .... That allowed me to ask in different ways... and I managed to get answers from Michael ... because of that discussion. (Fiorella, Goldsmiths, 13 November 2008)

Yet what specific strategies can be used to manage the vast collection of filmed footage? Fiorella's approach was to code her raw footage and looking for recurrent themes, a process that closely resonates with ethnographic analysis (Krüger, 2008:111). How these codes emerge and what causes them to emerge is often unclear, which Fiorella achieved by thinking of short names or words that described a particular passage, and then looking for interesting issues or recurrent themes:

> I would look at all the footage, and I would write exactly what things are in that image. So in the end I had like a mini-book with a lot of things that I filmed. So I said, alright, which are the things that impact me the most, and which are the things that I think people would learn, not only how *khoomii* sounds but what happened with Michael in all these thirty hours. And then, in all these thirty hours, I discover that there was one word always repeated in every single context, which was transformation .... So then I had to ask [him] 'What about transformation?'... 'How does this transform you?' And he was so vulnerable because of all that happened in his life. (Fiorella, Goldsmiths, 13 November 2008)

Every viewing and coding revealed new and interesting insights and caused ideas to change continuously so that in the end Fiorella 'decided to call the film *Sound Transformations* because I focused more and more on how this Mongolian *khoomii* changed Michael's life .... He left so many things for *khoomii* [which] was a very intense experience' (*ibid.*). At the same time, the initial focus on Michael Ormiston shifted so as also to include footage on Candida Valentino because Fiorella built a relationship with both characters during the time of her research:

> In the beginning, it was only going to be a film about Michael but I met Candida and I talked to her … and she felt it, she believed so strongly [in sound healing] that I had to portray her …. And it was also very nice to see that a woman was singing in a style that is only for men …. I had to put her in the film because she's also part of Michael's transformation! (Fiorella, Goldsmiths, 13 November 2008)

The editing process was thus recursive and open-ended, which began with a set of connected ideas that underwent continuous redefinition until Fiorella's ideas were finalised and presented in the final film. John Baily generally found that the editing process helps students to understand that filmmaking is not just about filming, yet requires critical reflections 'where you're constantly saying "I should have done this; I shouldn't have done that!" … Editing is a fairly laborious and time-consuming process' (Goldsmiths, 13 November 2008). Editing requires flexibility and open-mindedness, as students' understanding may change throughout the editing. Fiorella reflected on the editing process as a whole:

> I spent every day, yes, whole days, weekends sometimes …. I grabbed the bus I was editing; I went somewhere I was editing, so I didn't have a pause …. I edit everything and watch it from the beginning to the end, but then I said 'no no, that's not what I want to say!', so I grab paper and pen and said 'this is going here, this is going here, this is going here'. I had it on paper and then I did it on the computer. But I watch it again and I know … something was off balance …. So I had to cut a little bit more …. I had a plan, but then the plan changes every single day. (Fiorella, Goldsmiths, 13 November 2008)

I also wanted to know from Fiorella at which point she felt a sense of completion. Fiorella provided an answer typical amongst ethnographers: 'Oh, that's difficult to answer cause I don't think you can ever be happy with it … but there's a moment when you should let go!' (*ibid.*)' Not happy with her answer, I probed further:

> I think I was happy because it touched me. Like at the end, for example, I just watched it and I felt touched by the film and I understood. And at the end when I felt happy for the first time, I remember I tended to cry when I watched it, and I said 'oh wow!' … because I finally expressed what I wanted to …. I said 'yes' and I felt good …. I felt touched by it, so I said 'well, maybe now's the time'. (Fiorella, Goldsmiths, 13 November 2008)

Structuring

The previous discussions make clear that ethnomusicological film is based upon a similar framework as writing ethnographic reports, whereby extracted themes serve as the basis for the film's storyline (Baily, 1989; Baumann, 1989). In some ethnomusicological films, the filmmaker tells a story of gradual discovery and exploration, which he/she achieves through the sequential ordering of events. In

Amir (1985), for example, the story unfolds in chronological order of the actual events, while long, continuous shots explore one-by-one different aspects of the scene. John Baily reflected that 'it's not meant to be a chaotic collection of things; it has a structure' (Goldsmiths, 13 November 2008). Yet Fiorella's film is based on an alternative structure, which grew out of the themes that emerged during the filming and editing, and 'illustrates a possible structure quite well' (John Baily, Goldsmiths, 13 November 2008). Fiorella's aim was to generate 'a progressive feeling of empathy towards the main character by gradually revealing layers of his musical-personal life ... [and] take viewers on a progressive journey into Michael Ormiston's life, music and feelings' (Montero Diaz, 2008a:3). The structure is thus not based on the chronological order of events. Instead, it explores the main character's different engagement with music as 'performer, multi-instrumentalist, teacher, experimentalist, sound transformer, partner and duo with Candida Valentino' (ibid.).

The film is structured in three larger parts, which may be represented as A–B–A'. Each part contains a small number of sections whose beginnings are indicated by inter-titles. The inter-titles are used to provide a sense of rhythm throughout the film: 'Inter-titles make you breathe a little bit, prepare, because you know something else is coming, and the music that I put in there is indicating what is going to happen .... It marks how fast or how slow it's going' (Fiorella, Goldsmiths, 13 November 2008). There are eight inter-titles in total, each underpinned by a different piece of music that conveys the essence of the section that follows. In the first section, for instance, Fiorella used a medley of traditional Mongolian songs performed on jew's harp because 'I wanted something neutral and calm in order to build a climax' (Montero Diaz, 2008a:8).

The film opens with a profile shot of Michael alone in his home singing *khoomii*, leading into a collage of shots that depict Michael in his various roles as teacher, performer, multi-instrumentalist, experimentalist, instrument collector and friend, which is enhanced by Fiorella's voice-over commentary. The opening also mirrors the ending of the film: 'I started everything with the end ... where he's talking about his transformation, which is a very powerful moment .... So I put in the beginning when he says "this thing has made my heart start beating again", he says something like that, and "this music just woke me up" .... It's kind of the end because it's ... before he actually says "I'm a completely new man" (*ibid.*). Moving into the main part of the film, the first inter-title *About the learning process* announces the section in which Michael narrates how he learnt *khoomii*. As the film progresses, Fiorella also introduced Candida and linked her with the Mongolian singing style of *kharhiraa*, 'the style that she excels at and that means a lot to her as a sound healer and performer' (Montero Diaz, 2008a:10). The film as a whole is intended to build up tension by 'reach[ing] the critical part, the climax in a way .... It builds up, and then it goes on a little bit because you see Michael vulnerable showing pictures of his teachers' (*ibid.*). The final section entitled *Sound Transformation*, which is also the ending of the film, is intended to convey 'a series of revelations ... when [Michael] experienced something extraordinarily powerful through music … which, as he says, "woke him up" and transformed him' (Montero Diaz, 2008a:16).

Interestingly, Fiorella showed draft versions of the film to friends. Their feedback and comments led to changes in the structure of the film, 'such as including more music sections, adding more footage of Candida performing *khargiraa* and including inter-titles to guide viewers more' (Montero Diaz, 2008a:6). Fiorella found particularly valuable that her friends prioritised different aspects of the film 'because of their different interests …. It reached them in different ways' (Fiorella, Goldsmiths, 13 November 2008). For example, some friends who were musicians 'were very much into the music narrative … and they felt the rhythm and they felt what I was trying to do .. The musicians felt it, the others didn't' (*ibid.*). Fiorella also watched the final version of the film with Michael and a group of his friends: 'It was like the premiere of the documentary and they were all into *khoomii*; they knew what this was about …. So we did watch it, and it was very nice … the feel was very nice …. I asked Michael "are you happy with this; is that what you feel you wanted to say when you talked to me?", and he'd say … "It's perfect!", that's what he said … He said "no, don't change anything!"' (Fiorella, Goldsmiths, 13 November 2008). This experience surely helped Fiorella to feel a sense of completion and ethical contentment with the ethnomusicological film.

Reflecting

As mentioned earlier, students were required to write a reflexive study guide accompanying the ethnomusicological film. John Baily explained that the study guide 'is meant to talk about the film and to put in all the information that doesn't go in the film …. [It is] informative about both the general background and the contextual background, and also takes you scene by scene through the film' (Goldsmiths, 13 November 2008). Fiorella used the study guide for *Amir* (1985) as a model for her own study guide, even though 'it's like ten thousand words' (Fiorella, Goldsmiths, 13 November 2008). In her own study guide, Fiorella reflected on the technical aspects of filming, for example 'how did you film with which equipment [and] what did I see in that moment … and why my choices are the way they are; why did I choose this music' (*ibid.*). The following is an extract from Fiorella's study guide that explains the reasons for some of her choices:

> I deliberately omit his role as sound healer, using the term sound transformer instead, because he is quite reluctant to accept a sound healer's role. He states that in Mongolia *khoomii* singers do not use throat singing for meditation or healing, it is in Western countries that vibrations, harmonics and oriental sounds are used for relaxation and healing. Even though he organizes relaxation workshops with Candida, where he performs on gongs, singing bowls and does throat singing, he does not see himself as a sound healer, just as a sound guide, someone who through sound helps others find inner peace, he feels that this is every musician's duty, whatever their genre. (Montero Diaz, 2008a:7)

The excerpt clearly conveys a sense of Fiorella's ethical concerns with issues surrounding representation and power so pertinent in ethnography. Fiorella considered, for example, 'how to represent something they don't want ... and look[ed] for ways to portray Michael's opinion and Candidar's opinion [and] leave it to you [the viewer] to say what is happening' (Fiorella, Goldsmiths, 13 November 2008). Fiorella understood that extra care is to be taken when working with people and 'to tell the story and not something else' (*ibid.*). She understood that ethnomusicologists must be particularly concerned with people's experiences, rights and interests, which required open-mindedness so as not to let her own preconceived ideas shape and influence the filmmaking:

> Because it was an ethnographic work for real, I had to go there, I had to talk to people, I had to talk to Michael, I had to talk to the audience, I had to talk with myself .... When you have the camera and you believe something, then you film that and you have to be careful with that. You have to be careful ... with your own thoughts, so just have to open them. (*ibid.*)

Fiorella's ethical concerns also meant not to interfere with the characters during the filming. She remembered a passage when Michael looked deliberately into the camera, yet did not feel appropriate to instruct him to behave otherwise: 'Who am I to say "hey you! Have a natural conversation with me!"? (*ibid.*). The study guide thus served a particularly useful role as a reflexive critique of Fiorella's filmmaking experiences.

Being a 'fly in the soup'

Ethnomusicological filmmaking is also based on the idea that 'no film is free of the filmmaker' (Val, Goldsmiths, 13 November 2008). Students were thus expected to include conversations between themselves as filmmakers and the people studied, whilst making themselves noticeable. John Baily often compared the filmmaker's presence to being a 'fly in the soup':[2] the filmmaker is not invisible, yet non-intrusive, and reflexively available in the film, which allows for the production process to be transparent to the viewer. The filmmaker also narrates his/her personal experiences without dramatisation, interpretation or value judgements, whilst nonetheless being personal and subjective. In reflection on John Baily's *Amir* (1985), Fiorella found that 'he's there [and] you feel he's part of everything .... He is part of the story. But I don't know if I'm going to be able to be there and people are going to feel that, you know, that I'm [not] part of the story' (Fiorella, Goldsmiths, 13 November 2008). Thus in her own film, Fiorella 'has cut herself out as far as she could, which I didn't think was necessary; there could have been more of her presence. In the film you hear her once or twice and then she adds a bit

---

[2]   For example, I heard John Baily using this metaphor during his paper presentation at the Annual Conference of the British Forum for Ethnomusicology at the University of Cardiff in April 2008.

of voiceover now and then to point out her comments. So she's not pretending that she's not there; she is there, and she's getting the people to explain, to talk about their own work' (John Baily, Goldsmiths, 13 November 2008). Fiorella's choice to exclude herself from the footage was deliberate:

> I even thought about not featuring my voice .... I didn't want to be there; I didn't want to direct anything. There is only one part in the film ... where ... you can hear my voice .... I just left it there because I felt it was so spontaneous .... They were performing together ... and they didn't mention the fact that they were a couple .... So after this beautiful interaction between them, I had to ask "what does it feel to perform as a couple?" That's the only time you hear my voice because I didn't want to be there. I just wanted to be a spectator, someone that watches instead of someone that directs or leads. (Fiorella, Goldsmiths, 13 November 2008)

Fiorella clearly had ethical issues about including herself in the footage. As expressed above, Fiorella did not want to be part of the story, not having achieved a certain insider status that would legitimise her presence in the music-cultural practice. The deliberate exscription of the filmmaker from the film reflects Fiorella's ethical and moral stance as an ethnomusicologist.

The Value of Ethnomusicological Uses of Film and Video

Most students, whether they watched or made film, agreed that film and video is a stimulating and accessible learning tool because 'it creates a ... new dynamic in the lecture' (Joseph, RHUL, 20 October 2008) and makes music-cultural practice 'more vivid' (Emma, Manchester, 12 November 2008). Fiorella particularly stressed the accessibility of film and video. To her, ethnomusicological film appeared less intimidating than academic writing; it is a means to engage people with a topic that they might otherwise not read about; it can reach people. This was of central importance because 'as an ethnomusicologist I really want people to listen to what I'm saying' (Goldsmiths, 13 November 2008):

> Using film as a research technique is a fascinating tool to elicit information in a narrative-visual way .... It is an excellent way to gather information and disseminate knowledge .... [Given the] versatility and power of the 'audio-visual world' .... I think through films we are better placed to communicate than on paper, it is an ethnographic instrument that appeals to people of all backgrounds, academic or not, who both enjoy and learn from it. (Montero Diaz, 2008a:16–17)

Students across universities also regarded film and video as an excellent means to provide insights into a given music-cultural practice because 'you are getting the whole ... context .... You are getting the visual context ... otherwise it's just auditory .... It's a way of communicating the experience ... without being there!' (Tom, Goldsmiths, 13 November 2008). Val similarly felt that film and video 'tells you so much about the music and the musicians .... It is the way it can bring something to life really .... You can write about music, but that's never the same as hearing music' (Goldsmiths, 13 November 2008). Film was also often regarded as an excellent research tool, which allowed students to keep a record of a given music-cultural practice and to review it repeatedly for study purposes. Val specifically felt that 'when you review a film of the actual performance ... you can be looking at it more closely ... close-up on the instruments so I could see what they were doing .... I can learn from the recordings just hearing it over again' (Goldsmiths, 13 November 2008).

Yet film and video also impacted *beyond* the educational context. I heard ethnomusicologists suggesting that film and video opened and transformed students in often powerful ways. Caroline Bithell remembered that 'sometimes I've shown films and then the quietest girls told me that they'd booked a trip to Cuba. So I think it does inspire them ... to travel or to go out looking at new things' (Manchester, 12 November 2008). Holly, for example, commented that 'it's made me want to go travelling more and really experience that more' (Manchester, 12 November 2008), whilst Jess reflected that 'through watching films ... I've started going to films I'd never have gone to; I've watched more world cinema .... I've become so much more open-minded' (Jess, Manchester, 12 November 2008). The emotional impact of film and video was also frequently mentioned, whereby Holly, for example, reflected that 'sometimes I see things that really make me think, upset me a little bit' (Manchester, 12 November 2008). Film and video had the potential to touch students at a deeply emotional level. Caroline Bithell suggested that students' emotional responses to film and video were often triggered by experiencing reality as it exists elsewhere in the world, and this led many students towards a more global consciousness whilst questioning their own lives:

> Quite often there are students who ... come to my course and have these windows – partly through the films – into other worlds and start to question what the world is about. They start to worry about ethics and where the world is going ... and suddenly start feeling that there is a meaning and a mission and a fight, if you like, that they can be part of .... I think it's good for people. It's taking people outside the box ... out of their comfort zone .... I think that's part of what I think education is about ... to help people to find a place in the world and in their own lives where they feel there is a balance, and there is a meaning, and they can have a bit more courage. Again, it's a very human thing really not just to teach people to play the violin; you're actually helping them to find their way in the world and answer some pretty deep questions about why they are here sometimes. (Carline Bithell, Manchester, 12 November 2008)

The emphasis beyond curriculum led students to become politically and globally more aware. They often developed more democratic attitudes. Holly developed a strong sense of equality between all people, as 'actually it's not very much different to how we live; just the values and the morals .... They do like eating and talking and doing things [which] are actually exactly the same as to what we do' (Manchester, 12 November 2008). Holly also felt that such an education can lead to activism: 'I guess that some people ... might actually do something about it ... maybe organise a fundraising event or something .... Some people actually would probably go and do it ... [because] people become really affected by it' (*ibid.*). Experiencing the world through the eyes of a film maker led students towards greater appreciation of other people and their music. The democratising of students' attitudes and perspectives is an issue that has already been explored in Chapter 5 where I suggested that it was specifically the anthropological study of music that impacted on some students' attitudes and perspectives. Film and video clearly enhanced this aspect of study. During the process of filmmaking, Fiorella entered a process of 'researching beyond the film', which led her to 'learn about myself ... and my role and everything I'm learning' (Fiorella, Goldsmiths, 13 November 2008). Emma, Holly and Rachel, meanwhile, who watched film and video remembered that:

> World music did not interest me at all ... partly because I didn't understand it .... Then when I came to Manchester ... I think partly it was the anthropological and sociological side of it that excited me .... It made me appreciate people more and their cultures .... It makes me feel slightly less self-absorbed ... out of my English bubble .... Video and film ... opens your mind slightly ... and ... opens you up slightly, makes you less rooted in yourself. (Emma, Manchester, 12 November 2008)

> I'm not really politically aware at all .... Doing the world music ... I get a better understanding of the world .... It makes me want to go and watch the news as well .... The other day ... the news were on and because I could relate to it I watched it, and then I carried on ... watch[ing] ... whatever else came on. It just gives me a bit more of an interest of what's going on in the world. And it seems quite easy to ... just be in a little bubble that you never leave .... So I think actually watching the videos really helps me take more of an interest in what's happening in the world .... It's something that I wouldn't know about unless I'd been watching videos in class. (Holly, Manchester, 12 November 2008)

> I think it's good for people to realise that not everywhere is like England, and that, just because their culture is different and therefore their music is different, doesn't make it any less musical, that it's any less than what we do. It's just different. (Rachel, RHUL, 20 October 2008)

Mediating reality as it exists in the world through film and video thus led students to view their own culture within the world in a different light. Heightened awareness meant that students showed greater tolerance towards other people and their musics. They felt more closely connected with people. They no longer distinguished between us and them. Students discarded the dichotomy between self and others.

Constructing Ethnomusicology

In Part IV, I have discussed the ways in which students engaged in the constructing of ethnomusicology in form of transcribing world musics, composing ethnography and mediating fieldwork experience through film and video. As in the previous chapters, I was particularly interested in the ways in which transmitting ethnomusicology transformed students' attitudes and perspectives. I found that musical transcription often reflected a process of appropriation of world musics, even though ethnomusicologists often wished to transmit world musics as autonomous musical styles. Students instead retreated into familiar and safe territory by appropriating world musics into the Western classical paradigm by using musical examples that resembled Western musical conventions, and by applying a top-down approach in fitting world musics into Western staff notation. From an educational perspective, students rightly built upon existing knowledge and skills. Yet from an ethnomusicological viewpoint, students' appropriation of world musics into a Western concept of transcription is problematic as it undermines the autonomy and sovereignty of music cultures not from the West. Students would instead be better equipped when learning about the differences in methodology and musical style so that a true appreciation of people and their musics can be developed. Students should be guided to understand possible ways through which transcription can convey emic social and cultural meanings and perspectives. Through such an education, students may indeed be more culturally aware and tolerant. Meanwhile, the composing of ethnography and mediating of fieldwork experience through film and video seemed to resonate more closely with ethnomusicology's scope and concerns. Watching, experiencing and constructing representations of people and their musics was a profoundly gratifying experience. Students developed a sense of care and responsibility towards the people studied. Ethical considerations added a further level of compassion towards all people. Composing ethnography and mediating fieldwork experience through film and video also led towards students' personal transformations, as it impacted on students' attitude and perspective towards self and others. Such a transmission of ethnomusicology is an excellent means by which ethnomusicologists can truly impact on students' educational, musical and personal lives.

Modelling Ethnomusicology Pedagogy

Some ethnomusicologists and music educators have proposed to model music education on the basis of universal musicality and to question dominant elitist concepts in musical learning in the West (Blacking, 1973). They believe that at the heart of music education can be an universalist attitude towards all musics (Blacking, 1987:126) and thus a culture of tolerance (see further Oehrle, 1996). This view also resonates with more postmodern perspectives that celebrate multiplicity of position and perspective, and promote an inclusive and democratic stance towards all musics and their makers. Ethnomusicology as a discipline itself has been shaped by such debates on musical canon, postmodernism, globalisation and multiculturalism. These have profoundly transformed a sense of what music is and how it should be understood (Auner, 2002). Postmodern concepts had similar anti-canonic implications in music education.[1] This democratisation of music education also resonates with more recent developments in education studies, which point beyond curriculum and compliance, and towards the autonomous, thinking student (McGettrick, 2005:5–7). Music education should thus no longer be about imparting knowledge but also about preparing students for life, and to instil in them compassion and care for others. Such a music education involves discarding prejudice and recognising cultural difference. The ultimate goal of music education is thus personal and social transformation (Blacking, 1987:131). This view is at the heart of the epilogue, which will propose a model for ethnomusicology pedagogy that promotes in students a globally, contemporary and democratic sense of world musics and their makers.

First, however, I wish to illustrate the rationale behind a model for ethnomusicology pedagogy, rather than for a framework that illustrates prescriptive ideas towards ethnomusicology pedagogy and thus a blueprint of how ethnomusicology shall be transmitted to students at universities. The model presented here will portray the transmission of ethnomusicology as reflected in the actual concepts held by ethnomusicologists. This concern also resonates with the general trend in ethnomusicology away from detached objectivity and towards problems of conceptualisations seen from within a culture. The model is thus suited to represent emic perspectives to the transmission of ethnomusicology at

---

[1] Yet in the late 1990s, the ubiquity of its concept has led to debates about the applicability of postmodernism in the creative music classroom (Pitts, 2000b:111; Stanbridge, 2003:107). Only recently has the term postmodernism been readmitted to music education, whereby music education is currently in a stage of post-postmodernism (Fautley, 2004:346).

universities. Yet why do we need a model for ethnomusicology pedagogy? In prior discussions, I have already highlighted that ethnomusicology currently lacks a coherent vision about the transmission of ethnomusicological knowledge. Some ethnomusicologists indeed suggested that 'I don't think that there is such a thing as an ideal ethnomusicology education that can fit or suit everyone' (Hae-kyung Um, Belfast, 18 November 2003), or 'ethnomusicology education … is regarded as too exotic' (Rüdiger Schumacher, Köln, 22 July 2004).[2] John Baily even commented that 'I don't believe in music education …. The way in which we do music education can tend to be elitist and singles out those who we regard as being gifted' (John Baily, Goldsmiths, 13 February 2004). Such statements indicate the lack of agreement about ethnomusicology pedagogy. Without a pedagogical model, the transmission of ethnomusicology is indeed highly individualised (Witzleben, 2004:139). Nonetheless, my research has shown that there exist general, common trends in the transmission of ethnomusicology across universities, which seem to be shaped by the ways in which ethnomusicology is being disciplined. A model for ethnomusicology pedagogy is thus useful, as it may help ethnomusicologists and music scholars, old and new alike, to get a sense of direction in their teaching of ethnomusicology.

Towards a Model for Ethnomusicology Pedagogy

As suggested earlier, ethnomusicology pedagogy can develop in students an appreciation of universal musicality and an understanding of music as both sonic and social expression: 'It's a more liberal education; it's not just about music. It's about the whole of life, and it's about ethics, and it's about survival of humankind, and music is quite central to that' (Caroline Bithell, University of Manchester, 12 November 2008). A model for ethnomusicology pedagogy may thereby be informed by both ethnomusicological and educational concepts. The model presented here does this by amalgamating the educational concern with effective musical learning (see also Swanwick, 1979:43) through active musical participation during listening, performing and constructing ethnomusicology, and the ethnomusicological concern with an approach towards understanding musics not just as an object in itself but also in the context of human life (Figure E.1).

A few points are noteworthy of mentioning. Firstly, whilst the proposed model resonates closely with Swanwick's 'Comprehensive Model of Musical Experience' (1979:55), which focuses on music as sonic expression and regards skill acquisition and literature studies tangential to musical learning, the study of music as social experience forms a significant portion in the transmission of ethnomusicology. Literature studies, original discovery, skill acquisition during listening and performing, among others, are also central to the transmission of

---

[2]   Musikethnologie … als Forschungsgebiet …. Da wird man einfach sagen, das ist zu exotisch (Rüdiger Schumacher, Köln, 22 July 2004).

ethnomusicology. Secondly, the model is circular in shape, thereby denoting an inclusive and holistic (rather than hierarchical) approach to the transmission of ethnomusicology. The differing activities utilised by ethnomusicologists thereby depend on the educational objective, namely to develop in students insights into music as social experience (music in and as culture) or to enhance understandings of music as sonic experience (music as sound). Throughout the book, I have shown that learning about musical meaning, performance ethnography, the writing of ethnography and ethnographic film making (and to some extent transcription) led students to understand and appreciate the role music plays in people's lives. These activities are represented in the left-hand sphere of the circle. Meanwhile, musical analysis, participation in occasional workshops and 'learning to perform' in preparation of a final performance, and musical transcription (and, if it occurred, musical composition) led students to learn about music's sonic structures. These activities are represented in the right-hand sphere of the circle.

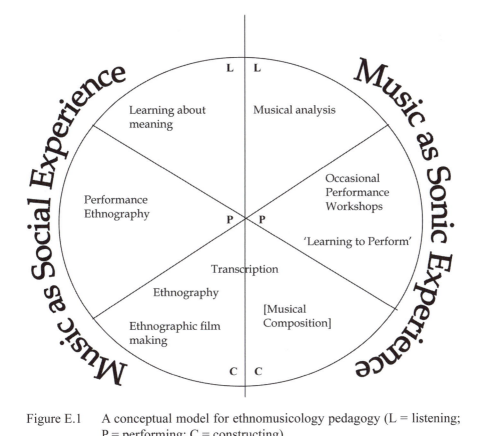

Figure E.1   A conceptual model for ethnomusicology pedagogy (L = listening; P = performing; C = constructing)

Thirdly, the model focuses predominantly on world musics as a subject matter, rather than singling out the transmission of concepts and theories about ethnomusicology. However, this is not to say that the transmission of ethnomusicology as a discipline is not important in ethnomusicology pedagogy. This subject matter is understood as being integral to the model, specifically at undergraduate levels of study. As shown in Chapter 1, world music and ethnomusicology are frequently transmitted separately with a clear distinction made between world musics at entrance level and studies in ethnomusicology at more advanced, postgraduate level. It is questionable whether the ordering of learning in a linear fashion is the best method for transmitting ethnomusicology, as some students may prefer and learn better through random experimentation, rather than ordered learning. The model instead allows ethnomusicologists to transmit theories and concepts as and when relevant to students. For example, ethnomusicological discourse by prominent writers may be used as sample ethnographies when discussing a fieldwork project, a possibility already illustrated in Chapter 11. This integration of subject matters would challenge the notion of progression from simple to more complex studies and division of subject matters into linearly transmitted chunks. Well-integrated theoretical discussions that are informed by current ethnomusicological discourse may also challenge the dangers of reinforcing in students ideas about exoticism, difference and otherness by presenting a web of knowledge to be explored openly and holistically. Hartmut Möller, principal at the Hochschule für Musik und Theater Rostock agrees and promotes a music education that 'realises that there are differing aesthetics. Yet instead of merging these, each exists by itself. The value, the experience that these are equal! ... Integrated by mixing musics .... Deconstructing hierarchies .... Opening up' (Hartmut Möller, Rostock, 25 November 2003).[3] The proposed model embeds such concerns by building on meaning, experience and expression. The model is thus more thoroughly ethnomusicological and points towards new directions in the transmission of ethnomusicology at universities.

New Directions in Ethnomusicology Pedagogy

What is the current state of ethnomusicology education at European universities, and what directions could it take? As described throughout the book, ethnomusicologists often adapted their teaching strategies and curriculum content to suit Western formal education. For example, Chapter 4 has shown how ethnomusicologists appropriated world musics in formal classes, during which

---

[3]   Es ist wichtig zu merken, dass es unterschiedliche Ästhetiken gibt. Aber die nicht auf einen Nenner bringen, [sondern] jede besteht zu ihrer Zeit! Der Wert, die Erfahrung, dass das gleichwertig ist! In dem, was man wissenschaftlich tut, oder in Vorlesungen lehrt, integrieren, Pop und Klassik mixen .... Hierarchien abbauen .... Ich denke auch, dass ... die klassische Kultur ... sich eben öffnet (Hartmut Möller, Rostock, 25 November 2003).

musical and extramusical signs came to bear meaning to students that contributed to their constructing of authenticity and essentialism. Meanwhile, Chapters 6 and 7 have illustrated the conservative orientation and mimetic concern of the first two types of performing ethnomusicology (see further Averill, 2004:100). Whilst some sort of canon may be reinscribed here, mimesis can also generate misconceptions and misunderstandings about specific music cultures in students. Chapter 8 pointed towards problems surrounding essentialism during students' constructing of binary oppositions, and Chapter 10 similarly highlighted the dangers of reinforcing ethnocentric perceptions during musical transcription projects. The transmission of ethnomusicology thus appears at times not ethnomusicological enough, as it tended to reinforce students' ideas of orientalism and exoticism, difference and otherness.

What are the consequences of such a transmission for students' values and perspectives? This question is particularly pertinent for ethnomusicology pedagogy that discards essentialisms and challenges the binary oppositions between past and present, self and other. Such an education may better focus on the processes and space of encounter in which students have cultural and individual experiences. Such an education also involves students in discourse about cultural representation and ownership, authenticity and ethnocentrism (see also Averill, 2004). Ethnomusicology pedagogy should accommodate the development of genuine understandings of both cultural difference and commonality of all musics. This may lead students to recognise that musicality is universal, that all people are inherently musical. Such an education is no longer just cumulative but transformative (see also Doll, 1989) and promotes learning that focuses on meaning, value and perspectives – and humanity (Walser, 2001:219–20). Ethnomusicology pedagogy thus necessitates an inclusive and non-elitist curriculum that accommodates students' transformations and changes in attitude and perspective towards self and others. While such concerns pose significant challenges within the context of institutionalised music education, ethnomusicologists may nonetheless take into consideration some key issues and approaches so as to promote cultural, social and musical inclusion and eclecticism.

Transmitting World Musics as Social and Sonic Experience

One approach is to blend the analysis of music as culture and musical sound, which allows us to take into consideration the ways in which different musics generate and reflect meaning. This is already commonly employed by ethnomusicologists, leading their students to respect musical variety and originality as products of the complexity of cultural traditions. This is not to say that students must enjoy all musics they hear, as musical taste is, as discussed in Chapter 3, shaped by sociocultural factors. Yet it is particularly the cultural aspects – the study of music as social experience – that can lead students towards democratised attitudes towards world musics and their makers, an issue introduced in Chapters 5 and 12. The emphasis on music as social experience thus seems particularly pertinent for ethnomusicology pedagogy. Ethnomusicologists agreed that music education should focus on music as a cultural construct, enabling students to see that their own tastes and preferences are reflectors of their constructed identities. Once students have grasped this, true openness and intellectual development can occur. This view reflects the discussions in Chapters 3 and 5, as ethnomusicologists often transmitted to students a concern with meaning in the listener rather than with scores or composers. Some students even enjoyed the musics they encountered and found personal meaning in them. Even other students expressed more democratic notions and broadened perspectives towards all sorts of differences, as ethnomusicologists exposed students to the human realities that exist in the world and engaged their emergent sense of tolerance and compassion. Meanwhile, Chapter 9 has shown that performing ethnomusicology in the form of performance ethnography was particularly useful for leading students, through social and musical interactions, towards an understanding of the meanings and values people and cultures hold about and place on their music. This was also true for ethnographic research projects and ethnographic filmmaking discussed in Chapters 11 and 12, during which students were encouraged to understand musics not as autonomous, but as relevant to cultural, social and political contexts in which they are embedded, while drawing conclusions about music as a reflector and generator of social meaning. Composing ethnography and ethnographic filmmaking also led students towards presenting multiple approaches and emic perspectives. The key focus here was on constructing local stories of understanding, rather than grand narratives, in order to capture the lived experience of people.

Listening to world musics as sonic experience, by comparison, also meant for ethnomusicologists to acknowledge musical recordings as cultural texts and representations of music cultures. Musical recordings generated in students' different musical experiences in the university classroom. For example, the use of recordings of local and global world musics challenged students' preconception that people in non-Western cultures pass on their music orally. Students were often completely unaware of the common practice of copying and learning from sound recordings that characterises today's musical learning around the globe. Careful listening to musical recordings also enhanced the development of aural skills. Listening in private without external interference also generated opportunities for reflection so as to make more intelligent judgements about music's sonorities and gain richer understandings of people's musicality. Yet whilst across universities the focus on in-depth sonic analysis of music was rare, there may be a stronger emphasis on engaging students even further in deeper-level listening.

Learning Ethnomusicology by Doing

Ethnomusicologists often argue that it does not really matter what musics are being transmitted; what matters is how students learn about and experience world musics (Koskoff, 1999:559). This is at the heart of the model for ethnomusicology pedagogy. The model presented here promotes ethnomusicologists' desire for 'learning by *doing!*' (Jonathan Stock, Sheffield, 10 November 2003) and emphasises the experiential portion of the learning process. Rather than a mere concern with curriculum coverage, the model promotes change and transformation in response to students' own self-reflexivity. Its focus is on values, purposes and beliefs in encouraging new thinking (see also McGettrick, 2005:14). This already often occurred in students' learning as listeners, performers and creators of texts, which demonstrates that effective knowledge construction is already well-integrated in the transmission of ethnomusicology. Yet listening, performing and constructing were rarely transmitted integrally or holistically. There was one noteworthy exception at the University of York where Neil Sorrell combined lectures and independent study on Indonesian *gamelan* with the activities of listening, transcribing and performing. This in-depth exposure benefited students more than sampling many different musical examples. Such an integral approach may indeed see stronger emphasis in the transmission of ethnomusicology across universities.

Meanwhile, transmitting ethnomusicology by doing also enables students to use more informal ways of learning, a strategy already well-established by popular musicians (Green, 2002). Informal learning involves high levels of learner autonomy, peer-directed learning, group learning and choice. The social aspect is particularly important, as informal learning can create musical situations that are shared and integrative, non-static and non-formalised (see also Blacking, 1973:107). Emergent friendships and shared musical taste can generate a deep sense of personal satisfaction and group solidarity. At universities, there were indeed some instances, such as occasional workshops, when informal music making became socially important to students and generated enjoyable and satisfying experiences. Yet ethnomusicologists often tended to adopt more formal educational approaches during students' listening, performing or constructing of ethnomusicology. Yet instead, ethnomusicologists may place stronger emphasis on students' informal learning by being more inactive and allowing students more autonomy in their learning. This would also mean for ethnomusicologists to participate in students' learning in a sharing relationship (Doll, 1989:252). David Hughes, for example, explained that 'our students often have a lot of world experience ... and that's very good for the student cohort because they really learn a lot from each other .... And of course, there are times when they know a lot more about the music than we do, which isn't surprising really .... We really benefit from having that diversity of students .... It's a challenge, but it's a good challenge!' (David Hughes, SOAS, 11 November 2003).

Yet what might such a transmission of ethnomusicology look like? With an emphasis on learning by doing in the transmission of ethnomusicology, curriculum examples may include courses that transmit a cultural emphasis in students' listening encounters; an emphasis on performance as a research technique in ethnomusicology; study more generally the activities surrounding the conduct of ethnography; that aim at the construction of conceptual transcriptions. Whilst the above curriculum examples would fit into the left sphere of the circle, thematic approaches concerned with the cultural study of world musics would be equally suitable to enhance students' understanding of music as social experience. Alternatively, considering a historical course, such as 'The History of African Musics' would complement the fact that historical studies are still often rare in ethnomusicology, which may perhaps be more concise than a survey course on the world musics from around the globe.

Meanwhile, reflecting the right sphere of the circle with its emphasis on music as sonic experience, a basic course on musical analysis may be included in year 1, which would allow students to catch the 'spirit' of the music and could blend informal with more formal learning approaches. At a more advanced level, students' listening may be more focused during a transcription project, necessitating skills and knowledge at a deeper level of musical understanding. In year 3 or beyond, students may even embark on composition projects, while writing and imitating music either in the style of recorded examples, or experimenting and creating new and hybrid forms by using recorded performances as models for new and exciting compositions. Yet composition is still rarely employed by ethnomusicologists and deserves a more central position in the transmission of ethnomusicology.

Composing World Musics: Breaking Tradition or Sparking Creativity?

Musical composition is integral to the model for ethnomusicology pedagogy, even though there is currently no formal framework for transmitting the composition of world musics. Yet many ethnomusicologists may agree that composition is a more creative musical activity (see also Blacking, 1973:99; Hughes, 2004:261), as it would involve students in deep-level listening and absorbing musical form and structure, and then synthesising what they hear and play. Musical composition thus takes on a further, deeper dimension at a cognitive level through the need for intellectual internalisation of sonic structures. Yet David Hughes also warns about the problems associated with world music composition at university, which can arise during formal assessment. Composition means students' individuality as learners, yet their musical interpretation may not resonate with the ethnomusicologist's musical concepts and preferences. Another problem may also emerge from the fact that – depending on the music culture concerned – it may be undesirable for students to extend a musical tradition by means of composition or improvisation. Imitating or even 'faking' a musical tradition brings about ethical concerns, as creativity in non-Western cultures may differ significantly to the kind of freedom expected or desired in Western improvisation (Hughes, 2004:266). Some ethnomusicologists, notably Mantle Hood, even felt no right to compose in the musical style of another culture (Trimillos, 2004a:286). Meanwhile, ethnomusicologists have only limited time available to facilitate students in reaching a stage of real musical creativity (Hughes, 2004:261). The limited exposure to world musics that currently exists at preparatory level would also not sufficiently prepare students for composition and improvisation. The proposed modules on mentioned above would thus be useful in creating a solid foundation for a subsequent module on world music composition.

Nonetheless, some attempts to engage students in composition exist. David Hughes at SOAS used a tripartite, progressive approach that involves students in composing in the style of the culture, repertoire or era; composing in advanced style by preserving the tradition but slightly expanding it; and freely composing, allowing hybrid and syncretic music creation (Hughes, 2004). Yet any composition activity undertaken by students should take into consideration the aforementioned problems so as to promote a kind of appropriate creativity that accommodates educational requirements whilst respecting the musical tradition (Hood, in Trimillos, 2004a:286; Hughes, 2004:281). Proponents of composition like Hood and Hughes feel more comfortable in working within the parameters of the musical genre concerned and, whilst staying close to the source or original, pay tribute to its originators. They may perhaps feel better equipped to understand the creator's intended syntax or even the intended meaning, which also represents the (to ethnomusicology emblematic) emic perspective. Yet other ethnomusicologists, notably Gage Averill (2004:109) also advocate the need to challenge and expand non-Western musical traditions and to compose new expressions in the form of hybrid and syncretic musical styles. This means for students to find their own meanings in the music whilst exploring new sonorities, new ensembles and new musical combinations. This also means to invent new ways of presentation, which could spill out into open spaces and natural environments, as concert halls and formal stages may not be the most suitable environments. In short, freer musical composition may reflect students' own unique circumstances and heritage and the aesthetics of more contemporary music making.

Transmitting World Musics: Authentic but Unreal?

Ethnomusicologists often study and examine the musics of particular geographical areas, and usually centre on those styles that are being regarded as traditional or part of the region's art music tradition. The transmission of ethnomusicology pivoted at times similarly around traditional musics not from the West, as ethnomusicologists may have been trained in 'the so-called old school of ethnomusicology .... Many people see ethnomusicologists as the type of people who are "museum-culture" people' (Neil Sorrell, York, 6 May 2006) (see also Solís, 2004b:11). This was particularly problematic in transmitting to students an authentic musical other, as discussed in Chapter 4. The appropriation of traditional musics not from the West into formal education brings significant ethical implications and generated heavy criticisms about ethnomusicology (see, for example, Solís, 2004b:17). This has led to intensive debates amongst ethnomusicologists in their desire to challenge outdated ethnomusicological discourse and its transmission at universities. For example, many ethnomusicologists have questioned the term 'world music' and regard it to be a culturally constructed genre. They also often accept practices of mixing, syncretic hybridisation, blending, fusion, creolisation and collaboration as it occurs on a global level. Rüdiger Schumacher recognised the importance of globalising developments for ethnomusicology:

> Many of my colleagues still regard music-ethnology, well …, it is about traditional music …, ethnic cultures in the extra-European area …. If we really limit it to that, then we demolish ourselves …. I don't want to say that this doesn't exist anymore, that it dies out, I don't believe that. Yet it doesn't suffice just to focus on this in order to understand human musical behaviour worldwide. It is necessary, also to include processes of change under consideration of so-called popular music. And, in my opinion, music-ethnology, because it applies to a great extent methods of cultural anthropology, and holds less than historical musicology on to a work-oriented aesthetic, is better suited, or actually ideally suited also to take on this area. (Rüdiger Schumacher, Köln, 22 July 2004)[4]

Many ethnomusicologists today acknowledge and include musics that reflect fragmentation, pluralism and multiplicity. The model presented here similarly acknowledges the consequences of globalisation and also includes commercial popular musics and the populist values people express while making, marketing and consuming 'their' music. The model thus questions the mutual exclusivity of elitist and populist values whilst regarding technology as essential in the production and essence of music. This inclusive view can enhance open-mindedness and tolerance in students by focusing on questions surrounding postmodernism and postcoloniality whilst acknowledging that cultures now flow on a global level with a complexity that has led to the emergence of new musical syncretisms and hybridity. Transmitting more popular styles also provides students with more real and relevant musical experiences, as students today 'usually all want pop music really …. That's their first choice!' (David Hughes, SOAS, 11 November 2003) As discussed in Chapter 3, traditional world

---

[4]   Viele meiner Kollegen verstehen ja unter Musikethnologie nach wie vor, so, ja, es geht also um im wesentlichen traditionelle Musik, um im wesentlichen, ja, ethnische Kulturen im außereuropäischen Raum, und ich sagte, wenn wir das tatsächlich darauf begrenzen, dann schaffen wir uns selbst ab, weil ich will nicht sagen, dass es so etwas nicht mehr gibt, dass so etwas ausstirbt, das glaub ich nicht, aber es reicht nicht aus, sich nur allein damit zu beschäftigen, um musikalische Verhaltensweisen der Menschen weltweit verstehen zu können. Da ist es notwendig, eben Veränderungsprozesse auch unter Einbeziehung sogenannter Populärmusik die mit einzubeziehen. Und da ist meines Erachtens die Musikethnologie, weil sie eben zu einem großen Teil Methoden der Kulturanthropologie verwendet, und weniger als die Historische Musikwissenschaft an einer werkorientierten Ästhetik festhält, besser geeignet, oder eigentlich ideal geeignet, diesen Bereich mit zu übernehmen (Rüdiger Schumacher, Köln, 22 July 2004).

musics sounded strange and ominous, or in some way 'other'. Yet the newer syncretic and hybrid styles sound already familiar, as they often blend traditional and Euro-American musical characteristics. Students can thus instantly relate to these musics, and lengthy cultural explanation is less necessary to instil musical appreciation in them. The transmission of popularised musical styles could also involve bringing analytical possibilities from different musical disciplines together. From popular music studies, students can learn to examine the political, industrial, organisational and discursive dimensions of world music, emphasising how these dimensions condition musical representations. From ethnomusicology, students can learn to study the ways in which musical representations are embedded in wider sociocultural processes with particular reference to the changing contours of collective cultural identities. From musicology, students can learn to analyse the music and text itself in order to understand the complexities of musical authorship and agency. Rüdiger Schumacher also proposes to utilise the methods and approaches from cultural studies:

> I think to us, the methods of cultural studies would be a good starting point ... as a complementary possibility, a further method to be included into a holistic conceptualisation about ethnomusicology .... I have a very wide understanding of ethnomusicology .... There are also other new methods in the analysis of popular musics, indeed according to the specific characteristics of a 'work'. Why not? And then it would of course be very interesting to find out in how far one could utilise these analytical methods in certain circumstances ... also for the traditional subject matter of ethnomusicology, i.e. the production mechanisms in a rural environment. (Rüdiger Schumacher, Köln, 22 July 2004)[5]

The transmission of popularised world musics may begin with Western pop star collaborations. Andrew Killick (2000), for instance, proposed the use of familiar musical content, such as the collaboration between the Beatles and Ravi Shankar that may lead students to become more interested in learning about Indian *raga* performance and the sounds of the *sitar*, *tabla* and drone. Such an approach would

---

[5]   Das läuft langsam an, ne Umorientierung. Da sind, glaub ich die Methode der cultural studies für uns ein guter Ansatzpunkt, also ne gute Informationsquelle .... Ich wage zu bezweifeln, dass wir jetzt allein diese Methode der cultural studies übernehmen, aber wir sollten sie als eine weitere Möglichkeit, eine weitere Methode auch in die Gesamttheoriebildung der Musikethnologie übernehmen. Also ich hab diesbezüglich ein sehr weites Verständnis von der Musikethnologie .... Es gibt ja aber auch andere neue Methoden in der Analyse von Populärmusik, durchaus unter dem spezifischen Charakter eines Werks. Weshalb nicht? Und dann wäre es natürlich sehr interessant, festzustellen wie weit man unter Umständen diese Untersuchungsmethoden ... nicht auch für das traditionelle Untersuchungsfeld der Musikethnologie fruchtbar machen könnte, d.h. auch die Produktionssmechanismen in einem dörflichen Umfeld (Rüdiger Schumacher, Köln, 22 July 2004).

enable students to find common points between their own and 'other' musics, and to overcome cultural boundaries and (with it) preconceived ideas and expectations (see Philpott, 2001 for similar claims). Besides listening to more popularised forms of world musics, students may also study these newer musics during performance, transcription and ethnographic writing and filmmaking. The latter may also involve students in virtual spaces with the Internet as the field for investigation and discovery. The idea is to provide students with multiple access points to more unknown musics by starting with the familiar and preferred. Focusing on musics that reflect innovation may challenge the fixed, bounded and essentialist concept of authenticity that students often negotiated and reconstructed in their encounters with world musics. Transmission of such styles may also lead students away from eurocentric musical perceptions, as hybrid world musics could be approached not only as the other of Western culture, but equally as the other of non-Western cultures, effectively creating a music education that is not dominated or centred in the West. A model for ethnomusicology pedagogy that acknowledged notions of hybridity and globalisation through people's mediation between the local and the global would truly be a music education in touch with the twenty-first century.

A Final Note

The model for ethnomusicology pedagogy presented here emphasises students' active involvement in experiential learning within a culturally and musically inclusive and non-elitist environment. Challenging ethnocentric concepts by valuing multiple perspectives is deeply embedded at every stage in the transmission of ethnomusicology. Ethnomusicology pedagogy should enhance students' inclusive and democratic view of all people and their musics. It should celebrate eclecticism and multiplicity and promote a globally, contemporary and democratically informed sense of all musics. Such a music education also facilitates students in reflecting on their own personal lives while showing open-mindedness, compassion and care for others. Yet this is not to suggest that students should discard their own cultural roots. Instead, the emphasis is on students' gentle transformation in attitude and perspectives towards self and others. Such ethnomusicology pedagogy may thus address the long-term aspirations of democratic societies in preparing students to improve the quality of life for others and for full participation in the world at large. The purpose of such an education is not the selfish acquisition of knowledge but the learning that better serves society. If students grasped the basic human values of inclusion, equality and world peace, such ethnomusicology pedagogy would indeed be more thoroughly ethnomusicological for the benefit of all members in society.

Bibliography

Abraham, Otto and Erich M. Von Hornbostel, 'Suggested Methods for the Transcription of Exotic Music', *Ethnomusicology*, 38/3 (1994): 435–56.

Adderley, Cecil, Mary Kennedy and William Berz, '"A Home away from Home": The World of the High School Music Classroom', *Journal of Research in Music Education*, 51/3 (2003): 190–205.

Addo, Akosua Obuo, 'A Multimedia Analysis of Selected Ghanaian Children's Play Songs', *Bulletin of the Council for Research in Music Education*, 129/ Summer (1996): 1–22.

Allsup, Randall Everett, 'Imagining Possibilities in a Global World: Music, Learning and Rapid Change', *Music Education Research*, 6/2 (2004): 179–90.

Alves, William, *Music of the Peoples of the World* (Belmont: Wadsworth, 2006).

Asselineau, Michel, Eugéne Bérel and Trân Quang Haï, *Music of the World* (Courley: Éditions J. M. Fuzeau, 1994).

Aubert, Laurent (translated by Carla Ribeiro), *The Music of the Other: New Challenges for Ethnomusicology in a Global Age* (Aldershot: Ashgate, 2007).

Auner, Joseph, 'Series Editor's Foreword: Studies in Contemporary Music and Culture', in Judy Lockhead and Joseph Auner (eds), *Postmodern Music, Postmodern Thought* (London: Routledge, 2002), pp. i–xi.

Averill, Gage, '"Where's 'One'?": Musical Encounters of the Ensemble Kind', in Ted Solís (ed.), *Performing Ethnomusicology: Teaching and Representation in World Music Ensembles* (Berkeley: University of California Press, 2004), pp. 93–111.

Baily, John, 'Music Censorship in Afghanistan before and after the Taliban', in Marie Korpe (ed.), *Shoot the Singer! Music Censorship Today* (London: Zed Books, 2004), pp. 19–28.

——, 'Learning to Perform as a Research Technique in Ethnomusicology', *British Journal of Ethnomusicology*, 10/2 (2001): 85–98.

——, 'Filmmaking as Musical Ethnography', *The World of Music*, 3/31 (1989): 3–20.

Bakan, Michael, *World Music: Traditions and Transformations* (Boston: McGraw Hill, 2007).

—— (ed.), *World Music Series*, 5 Volumes (Santa Barbara: ABC CLIO, 2004).

Ball, Mike and Greg Smith, 'Technologies of Realism? Ethnographic Uses of Photography and Film', in Paul Atkinson *et al.* (ed.), *Handbook of Ethnography* (London: Sage, 2001), pp. 302–19.

Bamberger, Jeanne and Evan Ziporyn, 'Getting it Wrong', *The World of Music*, 34/3 (1992): 22–56.

Bannister, Roland, 'Difficult but Sensitive: Participant Observation Research in Music Education', *British Journal of Music Education,* 9 (1992): 131–41.

Barber-Kersovan, Alenka, 'Music as a Parallel Power Structure', in Marie Korpe (ed.), *Shoot the Singer! Music Censorship Today* (London: Zed Books, 2004), pp. 6–10.

Barfield, Thomas (ed.), *The Dictionary of Anthropology* (Oxford: Blackwell Publishers, 1997).

Barnes, Jonathan M., 'Creativity and Composition in Music', in Chris Philpott and Charles Plummeridge (eds), *Issues in Music Teaching* (London: Routledge, 2001), pp. 92–104.

Barz, Gregory F. and Timothy J. Cooley (eds), *Shadows in the Field: New Perspectives for Fieldwork in Ethnomusicology*, 2nd edn. (New York: Oxford University Press, 2008).

——, *Shadows in the Field: New Perspectives for Fieldwork in Ethnomusicology* (New York: Oxford University Press, 1997).

Baumann, Max Peter (ed.), *World Music, Musics of the World (Intercultural Music Studies 3)* (Wilhelmshaven: Florian Noetzel Verlag, 1992).

——, *Music in the Dialogue of Cultures: Traditional Music and Cultural Policy (Intercultural Music Studies 2)* (Wilhelmshaven: Florian Noetzel Verlag, 1991).

——, 'Film and Video in Ethnomusicology', *The World of Music*, 3/31 (1989).

Baumann, Max Peter, Artur Simon and Ulrich Wegner (eds), *European Studies in Ethnomusicology: Historical Developments and Recent Trends (Intercultural Music Studies 4)* (Wilhelmshaven: Florian Noetzel Verlag, 1992).

Becker, Judith, 'Anthropological Perspectives on Music and Emotion', in Patrik N. Juslin and John A. Sloboda (eds), *Music and Emotion: Theory and Research* (Oxford: Oxford University Press, 2001), pp. 135–60.

Beere, Jackie, Maggie Swindells, Derek Wise, Charles Desforges, Usha Goswami, David Wood, David Hargreaves, Matthew Horne and Hannah Lownsbrough (eds), *About Learning: Report of the Learning Working Group* (London: DEMOS, 2005).

Bergeron, Katherine, 'Prologue: Disciplining Music', in Katherine Bergeron and Philip V. Bohlman (eds), *Disciplining Music: Musicology and Its Canons* (Chicago: University of Chicago Press, 1992), pp. 1–9.

—— and Philip V. Bohlman (eds), *Disciplining Music: Musicology and Its Canons* (Chicago: University of Chicago Press, 1992).

Berliner, Paul F., *Thinking In Jazz: The Infinite Art Of Improvisation* (Chicago: University of Chicago Press, 1994).

——, *The Soul of Mbira: Music and Traditions of the Shona People of Zimbabwe* (Chicago: The University of Chicago Press, 1981).

Blacking, John, *A Commonsense View of All Music: Reflections on Percy Grainger's Contribution to Ethnomusicology and Music Education* (Cambridge: Cambridge University Press, 1987)

——, *How Musical is Man?* (Seattle: University of Washington Press, 1973).

Blum, Stephen, Philip V. Bohlman and Daniel M. Neuman (eds), *Ethnomusicology and Modern Music History* (Urbana: University of Illinois Press, 1991).

Bohlman, Philip V., *World Music: A Very Short Introduction* (Oxford: Oxford University Press, 2002).

——, 'Epilogue: Musics and Canons', in Katherine Bergeron and Philip V. Bohlman (eds), *Disciplining Music: Musicology and Its Canons* (Chicago: University of Chicago Press, 1992b), pp. 197–210.

——, 'Ethnomusicology's Challenge to the Canon; the Canon's Challenge to Ethnomusicology', in Katherine Bergeron and Philip V. Bohlman (eds), *Disciplining Music: Musicology and its Canons* (Chicago: University of Chicago Press, 1992a), pp. 116–36.

——, 'Of Yekkes and Chamber Music in Israel: The Ethnomusicological Dimensions of Modern Music History', in Stephen Blum, Philip V. Bohlman and Daniel M. Neuman (eds), *Ethnomusicology and Modern Music History* (Urbana: University of Illinois Press, 1991), pp. 254–67.

Born, Georgina and David Hesmondhalgh, 'Introduction: On Difference, Representation, and Appropriation in Music', in Georgina Born and David Hesmondhalgh (eds), *Western Music and Its Others: Difference, Representation, and Appropriation in Music* (Berkeley: University of California Press, 2000b), pp. 1–58.

——, *Western Music and Its Others: Difference, Representation, and Appropriation in Music* (Berkeley: University of California Press, 2000a).

Bourdieu, Pierre, 'The Forms of Capital', in John C. Richardson (ed.), *Handbook of Theory and Research for the Sociology of Education* (New York: Greenwood Press, 1986), pp. 241–58.

——, *Distinction: A Social Critique of the Judgement of Taste* (Cambridge: Harvard University Press, 1984).

Bowen, José A., 'Finding the Music in Musicology: Performance History and Musical Works', in Nicholas Cook and Mark Everist (eds), *Rethinking Music* (Oxford: Oxford University Press, 1999), pp. 424–51.

Boyce-Tillman, June, 'A Framework for Intercultural Dialogue in Music', in Malcolm Floyd (ed.), *World Musics in Education* (Aldershot: Ashgate, 1996), pp. 43–94.

Brand, Manny, 'Collectivistic Versus Individualistic Cultures: A Comparison of American, Australian and Chinese Music Education Students' Self-Esteem', *Music Education Research*, 6/1 (2004): 57–64.

Brittin, Ruth V., 'Listeners' Preference for Music of Other Cultures: Comparing Response Modes', *Journal of Research in Music Education*, 44/4 (1996): 328–40.

Budd, Malcolm, *Music and the Emotions: The Philosophical Theories* (London: Routledge, 1992).

Byron, Reginald (ed.), *Music, Culture, and Experience: Selected Papers of John Blacking* (Chicago: University of Chicago Press, 1995).

Cameron, Francis, 'The Teaching of Ethnomusicology in United Kingdom Universities', in Max Peter Baumann, Artur Simon and Ulrich Wegner (eds), *European Studies in Ethnomusicology: Historical Developments and Recent Trends (Intercultural Music Studies 4)* (Wilhelmshaven: Florian Noetzel Verlag, 1992), pp. 26–41.

Campbell, Patricia Shehan, *Teaching Music Globally: Experiencing Music, Expressing Culture* (New York: Oxford University Press, 2004).

——, 'Unsafe Suppositions? Cutting Across Cultures on Questions of Music's Transmission (Conference Keynote)', *Music Education Research*, 3/2 (2001): 215–226.

——, *Music in Cultural Context: Eight Views on World Music Education* (Reston, Virginia: Music Educators National Conference, 1996).

——, *Lessons from the World: A Cross-Cultural Guide to Music Teaching and Learning* (New York: MacMillan Publishing Company, 1991).

——, 'Orality, Literacy and Music's Creative Potential: A Comparative Approach', *Council for Research in Music Education*, 101 (1989): 30–40.

Champoux, Joseph E., 'Film as a Teaching Resource', *Journal of Management Inquiry*, 8/2 (1999): 240–51.

Chernoff, John Miller, *African Rhythm and African Sensibility: Aesthetics and Social Action in African Musical Idioms* (Chicago: University of Chicago Press, 1979).

Chrispo, Caleb Okumu, 'Music Video as a Constituency for Research in Contemporary African Music', *Bulletin of the Council for Research in Music Education*, 153/4/Spring and Summer (2002): 114–18.

Christopherson, Larry L., 'Video Tape as a Tool in Music Education and Music Research', *Institute of African Studies Research Review,* (http://archive.lib.msu.edu/DMC/African%20Journals/pdfs/-Institue%20of%20African%20Studies%20Research%20Review/1972v8n3/asrv008003006.pdf, 1972) (accessed 15 January 2009).

Claxton, G., *Learning Is Learnable (And We Ought To Teach It)* (UK, The National Commission for Education Report 'Ten Years On', Edited by Sir John Cassell, http://www.guyclaxton.com/-documents/New/Learning%20Is%20Learnable.pdf, 2004) (accessed 21 March 2007).

Clayton, Martin, Trevor Herbert and Richard Middleton (eds), *The Cultural Study of Music: A Critical Introduction* (New York: Routledge, 2003).

Cohen, Judah M., 'Music Institutions and the Transmission of Tradition', *Ethnomusicology*, 53/2 (2009): 308–25.

Cohen, Sara, *Rock Culture in Liverpool: Popular Music in the Making* (Oxford: Oxford University Press, 1991).

Cook, Nicholas, 'Music as Performance', in Martin Clayton, Trevor Herbert and Richard Middleton (eds), *The Cultural Study of Music: a Critical Introduction* (London: Routledge, 2003), pp. 204–14.

——, 'Analysing Performance and Performing Analysis', in Nicholas Cook and Mark Everist (eds), *Rethinking Music* (Oxford: Oxford University Press, 1999), pp. 239–61.

——, *Music: A Very Short Introduction* (Oxford: Oxford University Press, 1998).

—— and Nicola Dibben, 'Musicological Approaches to Emotion', in Patrik N. Juslin and John A. Sloboda (eds), *Music and Emotion: Theory and Research* (Oxford: Oxford University Press, 2001), pp. 45–70.

—— and Mark Everist (eds), *Rethinking Music* (Oxford: Oxford University Press, 1999).

Cooley, Timothy J., 'Casting Shadows in the Field: An Introduction', in Gregory F. Barz and Timothy J. Cooley (eds), *Shadows in the Field: New Perspectives for Fieldwork in Ethnomusicology* (New York: Oxford University Press, 1997), pp. 3–19.

Cottrell, Stephen, *Professional Music-Making in London: Ethnography and Experience* (Aldershot: Ashgate, 2004).

Davies, Kristina Nelson, 'The Qur'ān Recited', in Virginia Danielson, Scott Marcus and Dwight Reynolds (eds), *The Garland Encyclopedia of World Music; Volume 6: The Middle East* (London: Routledge, 2002), pp. 157–63.

Davies, Stephen, *Themes in the Philosophy of Music* (Oxford: Oxford University Press, 2003).

Dewey, John, *Democracy and Education* (Mineola, New York: Dover Publications, 2004).

DfES, *The Future of Higher Education* (Norwich, Crown, http://www.dfes.gov.uk/hegateway/strategy/-hestrategy/%5C/pdfs/DfES–HigherEducation.pdf, 2003) (accessed 21 March 2007).

Dibben, Nicola, 'The Socio-Cultural and Learning Experiences of Music Students in a British University', *British Journal of Music Education*, 23/1 (2006): 91–116.

——, *Music and Social Class: Implications of Widening Participation in Higher Education for Student Experience of Teaching and Learning in Music* (Lancaster: PALATINE, 2004).

Dionyssiou, Zoe, 'The Effects of Schooling on the Teaching of Greek Traditional Music', *Music Education Research*, 2/2 (2000): 141–63.

Doll, William E., 'Foundations for a Post-Modern Curriculum', *Journal of Curriculum Studies*, 21/3 (1989): 243–53.

Dunbar-Hall, Peter, 'Designing a Teaching Model for Popular Music', in Gary Spruce (ed.), *Aspects of Teaching Secondary Music* (London: Routledge, 2002), pp. 173–81.

——, 'Concept or Context? Teaching and Learning Balinese Gamelan and the Universalist-Pluralist Debate', *Music Education Research*, 2/2 (2000): 127–39.

Durrant, Colin, 'Cultural Exchanges: Contrasts and Perceptions of Young Musicians', *British Journal of Music Education*, 20/1 (2003): 73–82.

Edwards, Kay L., 'Multicultural Music Instruction in the Elementary School: What Can Be Achieved?', *Bulletin of the Council for Research in Music Education*, 138/Fall (1998): 62–82.

Eisner, Elliot W., 'Qualitative Research in Music Education: Past, Present, Perils, Promise', *Bulletin of the Council for Research in Music Education*, 130/Fall (1996): 8–16.

Ellingson, Ter, 'Notation', in Helen Myers (ed.), *Ethnomusicology: An Introduction* (New York: Macmillan, 1992b), pp. 153–61.

—— 'Transcription', in Helen Myers (ed.), *Ethnomusicology: An Introduction* (New York: Macmillan, 1992a), pp. 110–49.

Elliott, David J., 'Key Concepts in Multicultural Music Education', *International Journal of Music Education*, 13/1 (1989): 11–18.

——, *Music Matters: A New Philosophy of Music Education* (New York: Oxford University Press, 1995).

——, 'Finding a Place for Music in the Curriculum', *British Journal of Music Education*, 3/2 (1986): 135–51.

Erlmann, Veit, 'Hybridity and Globalization (Intercultural Exchange, Acculturation)', in John Shepherd, David Horn, Dave Laing, Paul Oliver and Peter Wicke (eds), *Continuum Encyclopedia of Popular Music of the World, Volume I: Media, Industry and Society* (London: Continuum, 2003), pp. 241–6.

Everist, Mark, 'Reception Theories, Canonic Discourses, and Musical Value', in Nicholas Cook and Mark Everist (eds), *Rethinking Music* (Oxford: Oxford University Press, 1999), pp. 378–402.

Fabian, Johannes, *Im Tropenfieber. Wissenschaft und Wahn in der Erforschung Zentralafrikas* (München: C. H. Beck Verlag, 2002).

Fargion, Janet Topp, *A Manual for Documentation, Fieldwork, and Preservation for Ethnomusicologists*, 2nd edn. (Bloomington, Ind.: Society for Ethnomusicology, 2001).

Farrell, Gerry, 'Thinking, Saying, Playing: Children Learning the Tabla', *Bulletin of the Council for Research in Music Education*, 133/Summer (1997): 14–19.

——, 'Music Cognition and Culture: A Perspective on Indian Music in the Context of Music Education', *Bulletin of the Council for Research in Music Education*, 119/Winter (1992): 165–9.

——, 'Teaching Indian Music in the West: Problems, Approaches and Possibilities', *British Journal of Music Education*, 3/3 (1986): 267–78.

Farrell, Gerry, Graham Welch and Jayeeta Bhowmick, 'South Asian Music and Music Education in Britain', *Bulletin of the Council for Research in Music Education*, 147/Winter (2000): 51–60.

Fautley, Martin, 'O Fortuna: Creativity in English Music Education considered from a Post-Modernist Perspective', *Music Education Research*, 6/3 (2004): 343–8.

Feay-Shaw, Sheila, 'Multicultural Perspectives on Research in Music Education', *Bulletin of the Council for Research in Music Education*, 145/Summer (2000): 15–26.

Feld, Steven, 'Anxiety and Celebration: Mapping the Discourses of "World Music"', *Changing Sounds: New Directions and Configurations in Popular Music* (Conference proceedings, IASPM 1999, Sydney: University of Technology, 2000), pp. 9–14.

——, 'From Schizophrenia to Schismogenesis: On the Discourses and Commodification Practices of "World Music" and "World Beat"', in Charles Keil and Steven Feld, *Music Grooves*, (Chicago: Chicago University Press, 1994), pp. 257–89.

Finnegan, Ruth, 'Music, Experience, and the Anthropology of Emotion', in Martin Clayton, Trevor Herbert and Richard Middleton (eds), *The Cultural Study of Music: a Critical Introduction* (London: Routledge, 2003), pp. 181–92.

Fletcher, Peter, *World Musics in Context: A Comprehensive Survey of the World's Major Musical Cultures* (Oxford: Oxford University Press, 2004).

Flolu, E. James, 'A Dilemma for Music Education in Ghana', *British Journal of Music Education*, 10 (1993): 111–21.

Floyd, Malcolm, 'Relevance and Transformation: Roles for World Musics', in Gary Spruce (ed.), *Teaching Music in Secondary Schools* (London: Routledge, 2002), pp. 181–92.

——, *Composing the Music of Africa: Composition, Interpretation and Realisation* (Aldershot: Ashgate, 1999).

——, 'World Musics in Higher Education', in Malcolm Floyd (ed.), *World Musics in Education* (Aldershot: Ashgate, 1996c), pp. 250–79.

——, 'Introduction', in Malcolm Floyd (ed.), *World Musics in Education* (Aldershot: Ashgate, 1996b), pp. 1–3.

——, *World Musics in Education* (Aldershot: Ashgate, 1996a).

Frith, Simon, 'The Discourse of World Music', in Georgina Born and David Hesmondhalgh (eds), *Western Music and Its Others: Difference, Representation, and Appropriation in Music* (Berkeley: University of California Press, 2000), pp. 305–22.

Fung, C. Victor, '"Musicians and Nonmusicians" Preferences for World Musics: Relation to Musical Characteristics and Familiarity', *Journal of Research in Music Education*, 44/1 (1996): 60–83.

——, '"Undergraduate Nonmusic Majors" World Music Preference and Multicultural Attitudes', *Journal of Research in Music Education*, 42/1 (1994): 45–57.

Gammon, Vic, 'National Curricula and the Ethnic in Music', *Critical Musicology, A Transdisciplinary Online Journal* (http://www.leeds.ac.uk/music/info/critmus/articles/1999/01/01.html, 1999): 1–15.

Gebesmair, Andreas and Andreas Smudits, *Global Repertoires: Popular Music within and beyond the Transnational Music Industry* (Aldershot: Ashgate, 2001).

Geertz, Clifford, *The Interpretation of Cultures* (New York: Basic Books, 1973).

Geringer, John M. 'Effects of Music with Video on Responses of Nonmusic Majors: Exploratory Study', *Journal of Research in Music Education*, 44/3 (1996): 240–51.

Goody, Esther N., 'Traditional States: Responses to Hierarchy and Differentiation', in E. N. Goody (ed.), *Parenthood and Social Reproduction: Fostering and Occupational Roles in West Africa* (Cambridge University Press: Cambridge, 1982), pp. 110–42.

Green, Lucy, *Music, Informal Learning and the School: A New Classroom Pedagogy* (Aldershot: Ashgate, 2008).

——, 'Music Education, Cultural Capital, and Social Group Identity', in Martin Clayton, Trevor Herbert and Richard Middleton (eds), *The Cultural Study of Music: a Critical Introduction* (London: Routledge, 2003), pp. 263–73.

——, *How Popular Musicians Learn: A Way Ahead for Music Education* (Aldershot: Ashgate, 2002).

——, 'Research in the Sociology of Music Education: Some Introductory Concepts', *Music Education Research*, 1/2 (1999): 159–169.

Gregory, Andrew H., 'The Roles of Music in Society: The Ethnomusicological Perspective', in David J. Hargreaves and Adrian C. North (eds), *The Social Psychology of Music* (Oxford: Oxford University Press, 1997), pp. 123–40.

Guilbault, Jocelyne, 'World music', in Simon Frith, Will Straw and John Street (eds), *The Cambridge Companion to Rock and Pop* (Cambridge: Cambridge University Press, 2001), pp. 176–93.

Hargreaves, David J. and Nigel A. Marshall, 'Developing Identities in Music Education', *Music Education Research,* 5/3 (2003): 263–74.

Harnish, David, '"No, Not 'Bali Hai'!": Challenges of Adaptation and Orientalism in Performing and Teaching Balinese Gamelan', in Ted Solís (ed.), *Performing Ethnomusicology: Teaching and Representation in World Music Ensembles* (Berkeley: University of California Press, 2004), pp. 126–37.

Hood, Ki Mantle, 'Ethnomusicology's Bronze Age in Y2K', *Ethnomusicology,* 44/3 (2000): 365–75.

——, *The Ethnomusicologist* (New York: McGraw-Hill, 1971).

——, 'The Challenge of Bi-Musicality', *Ethnomusicology*, 4/2 (1960): 55–9.

Hoskyns, Janet, 'Music Education: A European perspective', in Gary Spruce (ed.), *Teaching Music in Secondary Schools* (London: Routledge, 2002), pp. 51–62.

Hughes, David, '"When Can We Improvise?": The Place of Creativity in Academic World Music Performance', in Ted Solís (ed.), *Performing Ethnomusicology: Teaching and Representation in World Music Ensembles* (Berkeley: University of California Press, 2004), pp. 261–82.

Johnson, Sherry, 'Authenticity: Who Needs It?', *British Journal of Music Education*, 17/3 (2000): 277–86.

Juslin, Patrik N. and John A. Sloboda (eds), *Music and Emotion: Theory and Research* (Oxford: Oxford University Press, 2001).

Karppinen, Päivi, 'Meaningful Learning with Digital and Online Videos: Theoretical Perspectives', *AACE Journal*, 13/3 (2005): 233–50.

Keil, Charles, 'Participatory Discrepancies and the Power of Music', in Charles Keil and Steven Feld (eds), *Music Grooves* (Chicago: University of Chicago Press, 1994b), pp. 96–108.

——, 'Motion and Feeling Through Music', in Charles Keil and Steven Feld (eds), *Music Grooves* (Chicago: University of Chicago Press, 1994a), pp. 53–76.

—— and Steven Feld (eds), *Music Grooves* (Chicago: University of Chicago Press, 1994).

Killick, Andrew, *What Should They Know of England?: Cross-Cultural Comparison in World Music Teaching and Research* (Paper presented at 46th annual meeting of the Society for Ethnomusicology, Southfield, Michigan, 2001).

——, *Getting Non-Majors involved in the World Music Classroom* (Paper presented at the Conference 'The Community as Classroom', University of Hawai'I at Manoa, 2000).

Kingsbury, Henry, *Music, Talent, & Performance: A Conservatory Cultural System* (Philadelphia: Temple University Press, 1988).

Kisliuk, Michelle, '(Un)Doing Fieldwork: Sharing Songs, Sharing Lives', in Gregory F. Barz and Timothy J. Cooley (eds), *Shadows in the Field: New Perspectives for Fieldwork in Ethnomusicology* (New York: Oxford University Press, 1997), pp. 23–44.

Kisliuk, Michelle and Kelly Gross, 'What's the "It" That We Learn to Perform?: Teaching BaAka Music and Dance', in Ted Solís (ed.), *Performing Ethnomusicology: Teaching and Representation in World Music Ensembles* (Berkeley: University of California Press, 2004), pp. 249–60.

Klinger, Rita, 'From Glockenspiel to Mbira: An Ethnography of Multicultural Practice in Music Education', *Bulletin of the Council for Research in Music Education*, 129/Summer (1996): 29–36.

Koskoff, Ellen, 'What Do We Want to Teach When We Teach Music? One Apology, Two Short Trips, Three Ethical Dilemmas, and Eighty-two Questions', in Nicholas Cook and Mark Everist (eds), *Rethinking Music* (Oxford: Oxford University Press, 1999), pp. 545–59.

Kramer, Jonathan D., 'The Nature and Origins of Musical Postmodernism', in Judy Lockhead and Joseph Auner (eds), *Postmodern Music, Postmodern Thought* (London: Routledge, 2002), pp. 13–23.

Krüger, Simone, *Ethnography in the Performing Arts: A Student Guide* (University of Lancaster: PALATINE, The HEA Subject Centre for Dance, Drama and Music, 2008).

——, *Experiencing Ethnomusicology: Student Experiences of the Transmission of Ethnomusicology at Universities in the UK and Germany* (Unpublished thesis, Sheffield: University of Sheffield, 2007).

Kunst, Jaap, *Ethnomusicology* (The Hague: Martinus Nijhoff, 1959).

Kwami, Robert, 'A Framework for Teaching West African Musics in Schools and Colleges', *British Journal of Music Education*, 12 (1995): 225–45.

——, 'A West African Folktale in the Classroom', *British Journal of Music Education*, 3/1 (1986): 5–18.

Kwami, Robert Mawuena, 'Music Education in and for a Pluralist Society', in Chris Philpott and Charles Plummeridge (eds), *Issues in Music Teaching* (London: Routledge, 2001), pp. 142–55.

Lamont, Alexandra, 'Music Psychology and the Secondary Music Teacher', in Gary Spruce (ed.), *Teaching Music in Secondary Schools* (London: Routledge, 2002), pp. 63–79.

Lange, Barbara Rose, 'Hypermedia and Ethnomusicology', *Ethnomusicology*, 45/1 (2001): 132–49.

LeBlanc, Albert, Young Chang Jin, Lelouda Stamou and Jan McCrary, 'Effect of Age, Country, and Gender on Music Listening Preferences', *Bulletin of the Council for Research in Music Education*, 141/1 (1999): 72–76.

LeCompte, Margaret D. and Jean J. Schensul, *Analyzing and Interpreting Ethnographic Data*, vol. 5 (London: AltaMira Press, 1999b).

——, *Designing and Conducting Ethnographic Research*, vol. 1 (London: AltaMira Press, 1999a).

Leonard, Marion and Robert Strachan, 'Taste', in John Shepherd, David Horn, Dave Laing, Paul Oliver and Peter Wicke (eds), *Continuum Encyclopedia of Popular Music of the World, Volume I: Media, Industry and Society* (London: Continuum, 2003b), pp. 373–4.

——, 'Authenticity', in John Shepherd, David Horn, Dave Laing, Paul Oliver and Peter Wicke (eds), *Continuum Encyclopedia of Popular Music of the World, Volume I: Media, Industry and Society* (London: Continuum, 2003a), pp. 164–6.

Leonard, Marion and Robert Strachan with Lucy Green and Claire Levy, 'Popular Music Education', in John Shepherd, David Horn, Dave Laing, Paul Oliver and Peter Wicke (eds), *Continuum Encyclopedia of Popular Music of the World, Volume I: Media, Industry and Society* (London: Continuum, 2003), pp. 308–12.

Lewis, George, H., 'Who Do You Love?: The Dimensions of Musical Taste', in James Lull (ed.), *Popular Music and Communication* (London: Sage Publications, 1992), pp. 134–51.

Locke, David, 'The African Ensemble in America: Contradictions and Possibilities', in Ted Solís (ed.), *Performing Ethnomusicology: Teaching and Representation in World Music Ensembles* (Berkeley: University of California Press, 2004), pp. 168–88.

——, 'Africa/Ewe, Mande, Dagbamba, Shona, BaAka', in Jeff Todd Titon (ed.), *Worlds of Music: An Introduction to the Music of the World's Peoples*, 4th edn. (Belmont: Wadsworth, 2002), pp. 87–149.

Lockhead, Judy, 'Introduction', in Judy Lockhead and Joseph Auner (eds), *Postmodern Music, Postmodern Thought* (London: Routledge, 2002), pp. 1–11.

Lundquist, Barbara and C. K. Szego (with Bruno Nettl, Ramon Santos and Einar Salbu) (eds), *Musics of the World's Cultures: A Source Book for Music Educators* (Australia: CIRCME/ISME, 1998).

Mansfield, Janet, 'Differencing Music Education', *British Journal of Music Education*, 19/2 (2002): 189–202.

Manuel, Peter, *Popular Musics of the Non-Western World: An Introductory Survey* (New York: Oxford University Press, 1988).

Marcus, Scott, 'Creating a Community, Negotiating Among Communities: Performing Middle Eastern Music for a Diverse Middle Eastern and American Public', in Ted Solís (ed.), *Performing Ethnomusicology: Teaching and Representation in World Music Ensembles* (Berkeley: University of California Press, 2004), pp. 202–12.

Marcus, Scott, Ted Solís and Ali Jihad Racy, '"Can't Help but Speak, Can't Help but Play": Dual Discourse in Arab Music Pedagogy', in Ted Solís (ed.), *Performing Ethnomusicology: Teaching and Representation in World Music Ensembles* (Berkeley: University of California Press, 2004), pp. 155–67.

Mark, Michael L. (ed.), *Music Education: Source Readings from Ancient Greece to Today* (New York: Routledge, 2002).

Marre, Jeremy and Hannah Charlton, *Beats of the Heart: Popular Music of the World* (London: Pluto Press, 1985).

Martin, Peter J., *Sounds and Society: Themes in the Sociology of Music* (Manchester: Manchester University Press, 1995).

Martin, Philip W., 'Key Aspects of Teaching and Learning in Arts, Humanities and Social Sciences', in Heather Fry, Steve Ketteridge and Stephanie Marshall (eds), *A Handbook for Teaching and Learning in Higher Education: Enhancing Academic Practice* (London: Kogan Page, 2003), pp. 301–23.

Marx, Shirley, 'A Zimbabwean Mbira: A Tradition in African Music and its Potential for Music Education', *British Journal of Music Education*, 7/1 (1990): 25–42.

Massey, Ian, 'Getting in Tune: Education, Diversity and Music', in Malcolm Floyd (ed.), *World Musics in Education* (Aldershot: Ashgate, 1996), pp. 7–23.

May, Elizabeth (ed.), *Musics of Many Cultures: An Introduction* (Berkeley: University of California Press, 1980).

McClary, Susan, *Feminine Endings: Music, Gender, and Sexuality* (Minnesota: University of Minnesota Press, 1991).

McGettrick, Bart, *Towards a Framework of Professional Teaching Standards: A Response to the Consultative Document "Towards a Framework for Professional Teaching Standards"* (ESCalate, Education Centre of the Higher Education Academy, 2005).

Merriam, Alan P., 'Definitions of "Comparative Musicology" and "Ethnomusicology": An Historical–Theoretical Perspective', in Shelemay (publ. 1992), Kay Kaufman (ed.), *Ethnomusicology: History, Definitions, and Scope* (New York: Garland Publishing, 1977), pp. 235–50.

——, 'The Bala Musician', in Warren L. d'Azevedo (ed.), *The Traditional Artist in African Societies* (Indiana University Press: Bloomington, 1973), pp. 250–81.

——, *The Anthropology of Music* (Illinois: Northwestern University Press, 1964).

Meyer, Leonard B., *Emotion and Meaning in Music* (Chicago: University of Chicago Press, 1956).

Miller, Terry E. and Andrew Shahriari, *World Music: A Global Journey* (New York: Routledge, 2006).

Mills, Janet, 'Conservatoire Students' Perceptions of the Characteristics of Effective Instrumental and Vocal Tuition', *Bulletin of the Council for Research in Music Education*, 153/4 (2002): 78–82.

Minks, Amanda, 'From Children's Song to Expressive Practices: Old and New Directions in the Ethnomusicological Study of Children', *Ethnomusicology*, 46/3 (2002): 379–408.

Miralis, Yiannis Christos, *Multicultural-World Music Education and Music Teacher Education at the Big Ten Schools: Identified Problems and Suggestions* (Unpublished thesis, UMI Microform 3053780, ProQuest Information and Learning Company: Michigan State University, 2002).

Monaghan, John and Peter Just, *Social & Cultural Anthropology: A Very Short Introduction* (Oxford: Oxford University Press, 2000).

Monson, Ingrid, *Saying Something: Jazz Improvisation and Interaction* (Chicago: University of Chicago Press, 1996).

Montero Diaz, Rita Fiorella, *Sound Transformation: Michael Ormiston – Film Guide* (Unpublished material, Goldsmiths College London: 2008b).

——, 'Sound Transformations: Michael Ormiston', DVD (Goldsmiths College London: 2008a).

Morgan, Robert P., 'Rethinking Musical Culture: Canonic Reformulations in a Post-Tonal Age', in Katherine Bergeron and Philip V. Bohlman (eds), *Disciplining Music: Musicology and Its Canons* (Chicago: University of Chicago Press, 1992), pp. 44–63.

Myers, Helen (ed.), *Ethnomusicology: An Introduction* (New York: W. W. Norton, 1992c).

——, 'Field Technology', in Helen Myers (ed.), *Ethnomusicology: An Introduction* (New York: Macmillan, 1992b), pp. 50–85.

——, 'Fieldwork', in Helen Myers (ed.), *Ethnomusicology: An Introduction* (New York: Macmillan, 1992a), pp. 21–44.

Natvig, Mary (ed.), *Teaching Music History* (Aldershot: Ashgate, 2002).

Nercessian, Andy, *Postmodernism and Globalization in Ethnomusicology: An Epistemological Problem* (Lanham: The Scarecrow Press, 2002).

Netsky, Hankus, 'Klez Goes to College', in Ted Solís (ed.), *Performing Ethnomusicology: Teaching and Representation in World Music Ensembles* (Berkeley: University of California Press, 2004), pp. 189–201.

Nettl, Bruno, *The Study of Ethnomusicology: Thirty-one Issues and Concepts* (Urbana: University of Illinois Press, 2005).

——, 'The Institutionalization of Musicology: Perspectives of a North American Ethnomusicologist', in Nicholas Cook and Mark Everist (eds), *Rethinking Music* (Oxford: Oxford University Press, 1999), pp. 287–310.

——, *Heartland Excursions: Ethnomusicological Reflections on Schools of Music* (Urbana: University of Illinois Press, 1995).

——, 'Heartland Excursions: Exercises in Musical Ethnography', *World of Music*, 34/1 (1992b): 8–34.

——, 'Mozart and the Ethnomusicological Study of Western Culture: An Essay in Four Movements', in Katherine Bergeron and Philip V. Bohlman (eds), *Disciplining Music: Musicology and Its Canons* (Chicago: University of Chicago Press, 1992a), pp. 137–55.

——, *The Western Impact on World Music: Change, Adaptation, and Survival* (New York: Schirmer, 1985).

——, *The Study of Ethnomusicology: Twenty-nine Issues and Concepts* (Urbana: University of Illinois Press, 1983).

——, 'Ethnomusicology: Definitions, Directions, and Problems', in Elizabeth May (ed.), *Musics of Many Cultures: An Introduction* (Berkeley: University of California Press, 1980), pp. 1–9.

Nettl, Bruno and Philip V. Bohlman (eds), *Comparative Musicology and Anthropology of Music: Essays on the History of Ethnomusicology* (Chicago: The University of Chicago Press, 1991).

Nettl, Bruno, Charles Capwell, Philip V. Bohlman, Isabel K. F. Wong and Thomas Turino, *Excursions in World Music* (New Jersey: Pearson/Prentice–Hall, 1992).

Nettl, Bruno, Ruth M. Stone, James Porter and Timothy Rice (eds), *The Garland Encyclopedia of World Music*, 10 Volume Set (London: Routledge, 1999).

Neuman, Daniel M., 'Becoming a Musician', in Daniel M. Neuman (ed.), *The Life of Music in North India: The Organisation of an Artistic Tradition* (Detroit: Wayne State University Press [repr. 1990 Chicago: University of Chicago Press], 1980), pp. 30–58.

Nidel, Richard, *World Music: The Basics* (New York: Routledge, 2005).

Nketia, J. H. Kwabena, 'The Musician in Akan society', in Warren L. d'Azevedo (ed.), *The Traditional Artist in African Societies* (Bloomington: Indiana University Press, 1973), pp. 79–100.

Norman, Katherine, 'Music Faculty Perceptions of Multicultural Music Education', *Bulletin of the Council for Research in Music Education,* 139/Winter (1999): 37–50.

North, Adrian C. and David J. Hargreaves, 'Music and Adolescent Identity', *Music Education Research,* 1/1 (1999): 75–92.

Oehrle, Elizabeth, 'Intercultural Education through Music: Towards a Culture of Tolerance', *British Journal of Music Education,* 13 (1996): 95–100.

Oesch, Hans with Peter Ackermann, Ching–Wen Lin and Heinz Zimmermann, *Außereuropäische Musik. Teil 1: Der chinesische Kulturbereich. Der indische Kulturbereich* (Laaber: Laaber Verlag, 1992a).

Oesch, Hans with Max Haas and Hans-Peter Haller, *Außereuropäische Musik. Teil 2: Der indonesische Kulturbereich. Der arabisch-persische Kulturbereich. Der alt-amerikanische Kulturbereich. Schriftlose Kulturen. Materialien* (Laaber: Laaber Verlag, 1992b).

Okafor, Richard C., 'Music in Nigerian Education', *Bulletin of the Council for Research in Music Education,* 108/Spring (1991): 59–68.

Philpott, Chris, 'Three Curriculum Issues in Music Education', in Chris Philpott (ed.), *Learning to Teach Music in the Secondary School* (London: Routledge, 2001), pp. 238–56.

Philpott, Chris and Charles Plummeridge (eds), *Issues in Music Teaching* (London: Routledge, 2001).

Pitts, Stephanie E., *Valuing Musical Participation* (Aldershot: Ashgate, 2005).

——, 'Lessons in Learning: Learning, Teaching and Motivation at a Music Summer School', *Music Education Research,* 6/1 (2004): 81–94.

——, 'What do Students Learn when we Teach Music? An Investigation of the "Hidden" Curriculum in a University Music Department', *Arts & Humanities in Higher Education,* 2/3 (2003): 281–92.

——, 'Finding the Future in the Past: Historical Perspectives on Music Education', in Gary Spruce (ed.), *Teaching Music in Secondary Schools* (London: Routledge, 2002), pp. 25–35.

——, 'Whose Aesthetics? Public, Professional and Pupil Perceptions of Music Education', *Research Studies in Music Education,* 17/1 (2001): 54–60.

——, *A Century of Change in Music Education: Historical Perspectives on Contemporary Practice in British Secondary School Music* (Aldershot: Ashgate, 2000b).

——, 'Reasons to Teach Music: Establishing a Place in the Contemporary Curriculum', *British Journal of Music Education,* 17/1 (2000a): 33–42.

Poole, Adrian, 'South Asian Music Education in Essex: an Ethnography of Bhangra', *British Journal of Music Education,* 21/1 (2004): 7–24.

Post, Jennifer C. (ed.), *Ethnomusicology: A Contemporary Reader* (New York: Routledge, 2006).

Post, Jennifer, Mary Russell Bucknum and Laurel Sercome, *A Manual for Documentation, Fieldwork, and Preservation* (Bloomington: Society for Ethnomusicology, 1994).

Prosser, Michael, *Research and the Scholarship of Learning and Teaching: Pedagogic Research and its Exemplification in Practice* (Edge Hill University, Lancashire: Keynote speech, 6 June 2006).

Prosser, Michael and Keith Trigwell, *Understanding Learning and Teaching: The Experience in Higher Education* (Buckingham: SRHE and Open University Press, 1999).

Quesada, Milagros Agostini and Terese M. Volk, 'World Musics and Music Education: A Review of Research, 1973–1993', *Bulletin of the Council for Research in Music Education*, 131/Winter (1997): 44–66.

Radocy, Rudolf E., 'Qualitative Research in Music Education: Why the Fuss?', *Bulletin of the Council for Research in Music Education*, 122/Fall (1994): 94–103.

Ramnarine, Tina K., 'Beyond the Academy' in Henry Stobart (ed.), *The New (Ethno)Musicologies* (Lanham, Maryland: Scarecrow Press, 2008), pp. 83–94.

Randel, Don Michael, 'The Canons in the Musicological Toolbox', in Katherine Bergeron and Philip V. Bohlman (eds), *Disciplining Music: Musicology and Its Canons* (Chicago: University of Chicago Press, 1992), pp. 10–22.

Rasmussen, Anne K., 'Bilateral Negotiations in Bimusicality: Insiders, Outsiders, and the "Real Version" in Middle Eastern Music Performance', in Ted Solís (ed.), *Performing Ethnomusicology: Teaching and Representation in World Music Ensembles* (Berkeley: University of California Press, 2004), pp. 215–28.

Reck, David, *Music of the Whole Earth* (New York: Da Capo Press, 1977).

Reily, Suzel Ana (ed.), *The Musical Human: Rethinking John Blacking's Ethnomusicology in the Twenty-First Century* (Aldershot: Ashgate, 2006).

Reimer, Bennett (ed.), *World Musics and Music Education: Facing the Issues* (Reston: MENC – The National Association for Music Education, 2002).

Reyes Schramm, Adelaida, 'Ethnic Music, the Urban Area, and Ethnomusicology', first published 1979, reproduced in Shelemay, Kay Kaufman (ed.), *Ethnomusicology: History, Definitions, and Scope* (New York: Garland Publishing, 1992), pp. 297–316.

Rice, Timothy, 'Toward a Mediation of Field Methods and Field Experience', in Gregory Barz and Timothy J. Cooley (eds), *Shadows in the Field: New Perspectives for Fieldwork in Ethnomusicology* (New York: Oxford University Press, 1997), pp. 101–21.

——, 'Understanding and Producing the Variability of Oral Tradition: Learning from a Bulgarian Bagpiper', *The Journal of American Folklore*, 108/429 (1995): 266–76.

——, *May It Fill Your Soul: Experiencing Bulgarian Music* (Chicago: University of Chicago Press, 1994).

——, 'Towards the Remodelling of Ethnomusicology', *Ethnomusicology*, 31/3 (1987): 469–88.

Roulston, Kathy, 'Introducing Ethnomethodological Analysis to the Field of Music Education', *Music Education Research*, 3/2 (2001): 119–42.

Russell, Philip A., 'Musical Tastes and Society', in David J. Hargreaves and Adrian C. North (eds), *The Social Psychology of Music* (Oxford: Oxford University Press, 1997), pp. 141–58.

Sanger, Annette and James Kippen, 'Applied Ethnomusicology: The Use of Balinese Gamelan in Recreational and Educational Music Therapy', *British Journal of Music Education,* 4/1 (1987): 5–16.

Schensul, Jean J. and Margaret D. LeCompte (eds), *Ethnographer's Toolkit* (London: AltaMira Press, 1999).

Schensul, Jean J., Margaret D. LeCompte, Bonnie K. Nastasi and Stephen P. Borgatti, *Enhanced Ethnographic Methods: Audiovisual Techniques, Focused Group Interviews, and Elicitation Techniques* (London: AltaMira Press, 1999).

Schensul, Stephen L., Jean J. Schensul and Margaret D. LeCompte, *Essential Ethographic Methods: Observations, Interviews, and Questionnaires* (London: AltaMira Press, 1999).

Scott, Derek B. (ed.), *Music, Culture, and Society* (Oxford: Oxford University Press, 2000).

Seeger, Anthony, 'An Ethnomusicological View. Catching Up with the Rest of the World: Music Education and Musical Experience', in Bennett Reimer (ed.), *World Musics and Music Education: Facing the Issues* (Reston: MENC [The National Association for Music Education], 2002), pp. 103–16.

——, *Why Suyá Sing: A Musical Anthropology of An Amazonian People* (Cambridge: Cambridge University Press [repr. 2004 Urbana: University of Illinois Press], 1987).

Shahriari, Andrew, *What Works? Analyzing Approaches to Teaching World Music* (Conference paper presented in Atlanta, Georgia: The Society for Ethnomusicology 50th Annual Conference, 2005).

Shehan, Patricia K., 'Towards Tolerance and Taste: Preferences for World Musics', *British Journal for Music Education,* 3/2 (1986): 153–63.

Shelemay, Kay Kaufman, *Teaching and Research: A Virtual Ethnography of Actual Practice* (AMS Presidential Forum: Unpublished paper, presented on 14 November 2003).

——, *Soundscapes: Exploring Music in a Changing World* (New York: Norton, 2001).

——, *Ethnomusicology: History, Definitions, and Scope* (New York: Garland Publishing, 1992).

Shepherd, John, 'Music and Social Categories', in Martin Clayton, Trevor Herbert and Richard Middleton (eds), *The Cultural Study of Music: a Critical Introduction* (London: Routledge, 2003), pp. 69–79.

Skelton, Kevin D., 'Should We Study Music And/Or As Culture?', *Music Education Research,* 6/2 (2004): 169–77.

Slobin, Mark, 'The Destiny of "Diaspora" in Ethnomusicology', in Martin Clayton, Trevor Herbert and Richard Middleton (eds), *The Cultural Study of Music: a Critical Introduction* (London: Routledge, 2003), pp. 284–96.

Small, Christopher, 'Musicking – The Meanings of Performing and Listening. A Lecture', *Music Education Research*, 1/1 (1999): 9–21.

——, *Musicking: The Meanings of Performing and Listening* (Hanover: Wesleyan University Press, 1998).

——, *Music, Society, Education* (Hanover: Wesleyan University Press, 1977).

Solie, Ruth A. (ed.), *Musicology and Difference: Gender and Sexuality in Music Scholarship* (Berkeley: University of California Press, 1993).

Solís, Ted, 'Community of Comfort: Negotiating a World of "Latin Marimba"', in Ted Solís (ed.), *Performing Ethnomusicology: Teaching and Representation in World Music Ensembles* (Berkeley: University of California Press, 2004c), pp. 229–48.

——, 'Introduction. Teaching What Cannot Be Taught: An Optimistic Overview', in Ted Solís (ed.), *Performing Ethnomusicology: Teaching and Representation in World Music Ensembles* (Berkeley: University of California Press, 2004b), pp. 1–19.

——, *Performing Ethnomusicology: Teaching and Representation in World Music Ensembles* (Berkeley: University of California Press, 2004a).

Spruce, Gary (ed.), *Teaching Music* (London: Routledge, 1996).

Stanbridge, Alan, 'Postmodernism', in John Shepherd, David Horn, Dave Laing, Paul Oliver and Peter Wicke (eds), *Continuum Encyclopedia of Popular Music of the World, Volume I: Media, Industry and Society* (London: Continuum, 2003), pp. 106–11.

Stock, Jonathan P. J., 'Patricia Shehan Campbell (2004), Teaching Music Globally: Experiencing Music, Expressing Culture', *Music Education Research*, 8/1 (2006): 139–41.

——, 'Documenting the Musical Event: Observation, Participation, Representation', in Eric Clarke and Nicholas Cook (eds), *Empirical Musicology: Aims, Methods, Prospects* (Oxford: Oxford University Press, 2004), pp. 15–34.

——, *What is Ethnomusicology? A Potted Definition* (http://www.shef.ac.uk/music/staff/js/EthLink.html, 2003d) (accessed 16 May 2006).

——, 'Music Education: Perspectives from Current Ethnomusicology', *British Journal of Music Education*, 20/2 (2003c): 135–45.

——, 'Ethnomusicological Research in an Urban Setting', in Jonathan P. J. Stock (ed.), *Huju Traditional Opera in Modern Shanghai* (Oxford: Oxford University Press, 2003b), pp. 205–27.

——, *Huju Traditional Opera in Modern Shanghai* (Oxford: Oxford University Press, 2003a).

——, 'Concepts of World Music and their Integration within Western Secondary Music Education', in Gary Spruce (ed.), *Aspects of Teaching Secondary Music* (London: Routledge, 2002b), pp. 182–96.

——, 'Learning *Huju* in Shanghai, 1900–1950: Apprenticeship and the Acquisition of Expertise in a Chinese Local Operatic Tradition', *Asian Music*, 33/2 (2002a): 1–42.

——, 'Concepts of World Music and their Integration within Western Secondary Music Education', in Gary Spruce (ed.), *Teaching Music* (London: Routledge, 1996b), pp. 152–67.

——, *Musical Creativity in Twentieth-Century China: Abing, His Music, and Its Changing Meanings* (New York: University of Rochester Press, 1996a).

——, 'A Case for World Music', *British Journal of Music Education*, 8/1 (1991): 101–18.

——, 'New Musicologies, Old Musicologies: Ethnomusicology and the Study of Western Music', *Current Musicology*, 62 (1989): 40–68.

Stock, Jonathan with Ruth Lenihan, Robert Provine, Katy Grainger, Simon Steptoe, Laura Doggett, Harriet Gaywood, Paul Hayday, Marzanna Paplawska, Helen Roome, Ellen Scott, David Price and Catherine Bancroft (eds), *World Sound Matters: An Anthology of Music from Around the World* (London: Schott, 1996).

Stokes, Martin, 'Globalisation and the Politics of World Music', in Martin Clayton, Trevor Herbert and Richard Middleton (eds), *The Cultural Study of Music: a Critical Introduction* (London: Routledge, 2003b), pp. 297–308.

——, 'Identity', in John Shepherd, David Horn, Dave Laing, Paul Oliver and Peter Wicke (eds), *Continuum Encyclopedia of Popular Music of the World, Volume I: Media, Industry and Society* (London: Continuum, 2003a), pp. 246–9.

——, 'Introduction: Ethnicity, Identity and Music', in Martin Stokes (ed.), *Ethnicity, Identity and Music: The Musical Construction of Place* (New York: Berg Publishers, 1994), pp. 1–27.

Sudnow, David, *Ways of the Hand: The Organisation of Improvised Conduct* (Harvard University Press: Cambridge, MA, 1978).

Sumarsam, 'Opportunity and Interaction: The Gamelan from Java to Wesleyan', in Ted Solís (ed.), *Performing Ethnomusicology: Teaching and Representation in World Music Ensembles* (Berkeley: University of California Press, 2004), pp. 69–92.

Swanwick, Keith, 'Music Education and Ethnomusicology', *British Journal of Ethnomusicology*, 11/2 (2002): 137–44.

——, *Teaching Music Musically* (London: Routledge, 1999).

——, *A Basis for Music Education* (Windsor: NFER/Nelson, 1979).

Tagg, Philip, 'Reading Sounds', *Re Records Quarterly*, 3/2 (1990): 4–11.

Tame, David, *The Secret Power of Music: The Transformation of Self and Society* (Rochester: Destiny Books, 1984).

Taylor, Timothy D., 'Music and Musical Practices in Postmodernity', in Judy Lockhead and Joseph Auner (eds), *Postmodern Music, Postmodern Thought* (London: Routledge, 2002), pp. 93–118.

Tenzer, Michael (ed.), *Analytical Studies in World Music* (Oxford: Oxford University Press, 2006).

Thornton, Sarah, *Club Cultures: Music, Media and Subcultural Capital* (Cambridge: Polity Press, 1995).

Tillman, Joakim, 'Postmodernism and Art Music in the German Debate', in Judy Lockhead and Joseph Auner (eds), *Postmodern Music, Postmodern Thought* (London: Routledge, 2002), pp. 75–91.

Titon, Jeff Todd, 'Knowing Fieldwork', in Gregory Barz and Timothy J. Cooley (eds), *Shadows in the Field: New Perspectives for Fieldwork in Ethnomusicology*, 2nd edn. (New York: Oxford University Press, 2008), pp. 25–41.

——, 'Textual Analysis or Thick Description?', in Martin Clayton, Trevor Herbert and Richard Middleton (eds), *The Cultural Study of Music: a Critical Introduction* (London: Routledge, 2003), pp. 171–80.

——, *Worlds of Music: An Introduction to the Music of the World's Peoples*, 4th edn. (Belmont: Wadsworth, 2002).

——, 'Knowing Fieldwork', in Gregory F. Barz and Timothy J. Cooley (eds), *Shadows in the Field: New Perspectives for Fieldwork in Ethnomusicology* (New York: Oxford University Press, 1997), pp. 87–100.

Toynbee, Jason, 'Music, Culture, and Creativity', in Martin Clayton, Trevor Herbert and Richard Middleton (eds), *The Cultural Study of Music: a Critical Introduction* (London: Routledge, 2003), pp. 102–12.

Trimillos, Ricardo D., 'Subject, Object, and the Ethnomusicology Ensemble: The Ethnomusicological "We" and "Them"', in Ted Solís (ed.), *Performing Ethnomusicology: Teaching and Representation in World Music Ensembles* (Berkeley: University of California Press, 2004b), pp. 23–52.

——, 'Some Closing Thoughts from the First Voice (Interview with Mantle Hood)', in Ted Solís (ed.), *Performing Ethnomusicology: Teaching and Representation in World Music Ensembles* (Berkeley: University of California Press, 2004a), pp. 283–8.

Turino, Thomas, 'The Music of Sub-Saharan Africa', in Bruno Nettl, Charles Capwell, Philip V. Bohlman, Isabel K. F. Wong and Thomas Turino (eds), *Excursions in World* Music, 4th edn. New Jersey: Pearson Prentice Hall, 2004), pp. 171–200.

——, *Moving Away From Silence: Music of the Peruvian Altiplano and the Experience of Urban Migration* (Chicago: University of Chicago Press, 1993).

Van Leeuwen, Theo, *Speech, Music, Sound* (London: Macmillan, 1999).

Van Maanen, John, *Tales of the Field: On Writing Ethnography* (Chicago: University of Chicago Press, 1988).

Veblen, Kari K., 'Truth, Perceptions, and Cultural Constructs in Ethnographic Research: Music Teaching and Learning in Ireland', *Bulletin of the Council for Research in Music Education*, 129/Summer (1996): 38–52.

Vetter, Roger, 'A Square Peg in a Round Hole: Teaching Javanese Gamelan in the Ensemble Paradigm of the Academy', in Ted Solís (ed.), *Performing Ethnomusicology: Teaching and Representation in World Music Ensembles* (Berkeley: University of California Press, 2004), pp. 115–25.

Volk, Terese M., *Music, Education, and Multiculturalism: Foundations and Principles* (New York: Oxford University Press, 1998).

———, 'Folk Musics and Increasing Diversity in American Music Education: 1900–1916', *Journal of Research in Music Education*, 42/4 (1994): 285–305.

———, 'The History and Development of Multicultural Music Education as Evidenced in the "Music Educators Journal", 1967–1992', *Journal of Research in Music Education*, 41/2 (1993): 137–55.

Wachsmann, Klaus P., 'Negritude in Music', *Composer*, 19/1 (1966): 12–15.

Wade, Bonnie C., *Thinking Musically: Experiencing Music, Expressing Culture* (New York: Oxford University Press, 2004).

Wade, Bonnie C. and Patricia Shehan Campbell (eds), *Global Music Series*, 14 volumes (New York: Oxford University Press, 2003).

Wagner, L. and Ramsden, P., *Higher Education Academy, Strategic Plan 2005–2010* (York, Higher Education Academy, 2005).

Walser, Robert Young, *Musical Difference and Cultural Identity: An African Musical Tradition in English Classrooms* (Unpublished thesis, The British Library, British Thesis Service: SOAS, London, 2001).

Weber, William, 'The History of Musical Canon', in Nicholas Cook and Mark Everist (eds), *Rethinking Music* (Oxford: Oxford University Press, 1999), pp. 336–55.

Webster, Peter, 'Creativity as Creative Thinking', in Gary Spruce (ed.), *Teaching Music* (London: Routledge, 1996), pp. 87–97.

Wiggins, Trevor, 'The World of Music in Education', *British Journal of Music Education*, 13/1 (1996): 21–9.

Witzleben, Lawrence J., 'Cultural Interactions in an Asian Context: Chinese and Javanese Ensembles in Hong Kong', in Ted Solís (ed.), *Performing Ethnomusicology: Teaching and Representation in World Music Ensembles* (Berkeley: University of California Press, 2004), pp. 138–51.

Woodford, Paul G., 'Preface', *International Journal of Community Music*, 2/1 (2005b): 1–3.

———, *Democracy and Music Education: Liberalism, Ethics, and the Politics of Practice* (Bloomington: Indiana University Press, 2005a).

Wright, Ruth, 'A Holistic Approach to Music Education', *British Journal of Music Education,* 15/1 (1998): 71–84.

Zaretti, Joan L., *Multicultural Music Education: An Ethnography of Processes in Teaching and Learning* (Unpublished thesis, Michigan: UMI Dissertation Services, Indiana University, 1998).

Zillmann, Dolf and Su-lin Gan, 'Musical Taste in Adolescence', in David J. Hargreaves and Adrian C. North (eds), *The Social Psychology of Music* (Oxford: Oxford University Press, 1997), pp. 161–87.

Index